Hispanic Baroque Ekphrasis
Góngora, Camargo, Sor Juana

LEGENDA

LEGENDA is the Modern Humanities Research Association's book imprint for new research in the Humanities. Founded in 1995 by Malcolm Bowie and others within the University of Oxford, Legenda has always been a collaborative publishing enterprise, directly governed by scholars. The Modern Humanities Research Association (MHRA) joined this collaboration in 1998, became half-owner in 2004, in partnership with Maney Publishing and then Routledge, and has since 2016 been sole owner. Titles range from medieval texts to contemporary cinema and form a widely comparative view of the modern humanities, including works on Arabic, Catalan, English, French, German, Greek, Italian, Portuguese, Russian, Spanish, and Yiddish literature. Editorial boards and committees of more than 60 leading academic specialists work in collaboration with bodies such as the Society for French Studies, the British Comparative Literature Association and the Association of Hispanists of Great Britain & Ireland.

The MHRA encourages and promotes advanced study and research in the field of the modern humanities, especially modern European languages and literature, including English, and also cinema. It aims to break down the barriers between scholars working in different disciplines and to maintain the unity of humanistic scholarship. The Association fulfils this purpose through the publication of journals, bibliographies, monographs, critical editions, and the MHRA Style Guide, and by making grants in support of research. Membership is open to all who work in the Humanities, whether independent or in a University post, and the participation of younger colleagues entering the field is especially welcomed.

ALSO PUBLISHED BY THE ASSOCIATION

Critical Texts
Tudor and Stuart Translations • *New Translations* • *European Translations*
MHRA Library of Medieval Welsh Literature

MHRA Bibliographies
Publications of the Modern Humanities Research Association

The Annual Bibliography of English Language & Literature
Austrian Studies
Modern Language Review
Portuguese Studies
The Slavonic and East European Review
Working Papers in the Humanities
The Yearbook of English Studies

www.mhra.org.uk
www.legendabooks.com

STUDIES IN HISPANIC AND LUSOPHONE CULTURES

Studies in Hispanic and Lusophone Cultures are selected and edited by the Association of Hispanists of Great Britain & Ireland. The series seeks to publish the best new research in all areas of the literature, thought, history, culture, film, and languages of Spain, Spanish America, and the Portuguese-speaking world.

The Association of Hispanists of Great Britain & Ireland is a professional association which represents a very diverse discipline, in terms of both geographical coverage and objects of study. Its website showcases new work by members, and publicises jobs, conferences and grants in the field.

www.legendabooks.com/series/shlc

STUDIES IN HISPANIC AND LUSOPHONE CULTURES

Hispanic Baroque Ekphrasis

Góngora, Camargo, Sor Juana

Luis Castellví Laukamp

Studies in Hispanic and Lusophone Cultures 38
Modern Humanities Research Association
2020

Published by Legenda
an imprint of the Modern Humanities Research Association
Salisbury House, Station Road, Cambridge CB1 2LA

ISBN 978-1-78188-815-5

First published 2020

Copy-Editor: Dr Ellen Jones

CONTENTS

To my parents and my brother

ACKNOWLEDGEMENTS

I wrote my first essay on Góngora in 2011, when I was working as a lawyer in Barcelona. I attached it to my application for the MPhil in European Literature and Culture at the University of Cambridge (2012–2013). That essay later became the germ of the doctoral project (2013–2017) upon which this monograph is based. Such a change in career path would not have been possible without the ongoing support of my supervisor, Rodrigo Cacho. During the last eight years, I have learned more from him than from any other, about literature, but also about history, art, and particularly about reading and writing. If it were not for Rodrigo, I would not be anywhere near where I am today. I would like to thank him for constantly encouraging me to do my best. Moreover, I am grateful to Jeremy Robbins and Caroline Egan for their input at the PhD viva. The generosity of Rosemary Clark and Anna Kathryn Kendrick, who proofread the doctoral thesis and the resulting book manuscript respectively, is beyond measure.

Many other scholars have put their expertise at my disposal. I am much obliged to them for their insightful feedback and contributions in shaping my thinking. In particular, I would like to thank Mercedes Blanco, Brad Epps, Louise Haywood, Dominic Keown, Elizabeth Drayson, Robert Folger, Adam Lifshey, Jesús Ponce Cárdenas and David Jiménez Torres for conversations and criticism. I extend my thanks to Coral Neale, the former and legendary departmental secretary at Cambridge, and to the dedicated staff of all the libraries I have scoured over the years.

In fact, I undertook much of the research for this book at the Kluge Center of the Library of Congress (Washington, D.C.), where I spent the academic year 2015–2016. I would like to thank the Arts and Humanities Research Council (AHRC) for the International Placement Scheme award that made this possible. Through further funding and support from the AHRC, the Cambridge Home and EU Scholarship Scheme (CHESS), the Department of Spanish and Portuguese at Cambridge and Christ's College, I was able to complete my PhD within the required time period. While doing so, I published the article 'Ekphrasis Meets Teichoscopy: The Panoramic Landscape in Góngora's *Soledad Primera*', *Hispanic Research Journal*, 17.6 (2016), 473–88. More recently, I also published the article 'Sor Juana's Diglossia: The Pyramids of *Primero sueño*', *Bulletin of Spanish Studies*, 96.8 (2019), 1195–1219. These pieces are based on Chapters 1 and 6 of the present monograph, though in a different form. I thank the editors and peer-reviewers of *HRJ* and *BSS* for their advice and encouragement.

As a postdoctoral researcher, I benefited greatly from the generosity of the John Carter Brown Library (2017), the Newberry Library (2017), the Modern Humanities Research Association (MHRA) (2017–2018) and the Humboldt Foundation

(2018–2019), which granted me the time and resources necessary to improve the PhD manuscript for publication. I am very grateful to each of these programmes and institutions. I also thank Emilie Bergmann for reading the book manuscript and providing invaluable feedback, as well as my editor Graham Nelson for guiding this book to completion. I would like to highlight that the illustrations in the hardback edition of this book were printed in colour thanks to a subsidy from the Humboldt Foundation.

Most importantly, I give thanks to my family: my parents and grandmothers, for their financial support, shipments of Spanish ham and relentless faith in my project; and my brother, who visits me everywhere I go in my academic life. Sadly, I cannot mention everyone here who helped along the way. However, I want to add that I could not have completed this monograph without my wonderful Christ's College friends: Peter Lunga, Jonasz Słomka, Heewon Park, Niko Amin-Wetzel, Guia Carrara and Cédric Faure. As Erasmus would say: '*Novos parans amicos ne obliviscere veterum*' [When you make new friends, do not forget the old ones].

L.C.L., Manchester, January 2020

LIST OF ILLUSTRATIONS

A NOTE ON TRANSLATIONS

This book targets a broad international and multilingual community beyond the field of Hispanic studies. For this reason, I have included translations of all primary and secondary materials in languages other than English. I have used published renderings where available (with occasional minor adjustments noted when relevant), particularly with Góngora and Sor Juana. In this respect, Chapters 1–2 and 5–6 are indebted to the following texts in translation:

GÓNGORA, LUIS DE. 2012. *The Solitudes*, trans. by Edith Grossman (New York: Penguin). All English quotations of Góngora's *Soledades* follow this edition.

MORE, ANNA (ed.). 2016. *Sor Juana Inés de La Cruz. Selected Works*, trans. by Edith Grossman (New York/London: W. W. Norton & Company). All English quotations of Sor Juana's *Primero sueño,* the *Respuesta a Sor Filotea de la Cruz*, the *loa* to *El divino Narciso* and the *romance* 51 follow this edition. These texts were rendered into English by Edith Grossman, except for the *romance* 51, which was translated by Isabel Gómez. I have also used Grossman's rendering of Manuel Fernández de Santa Cruz's *Carta de Sor Filotea de la Cruz*.

Whenever I reproduce published translations, I credit the source following each extract. Any renderings not otherwise identified are my own.

Camargo's *San Ignacio* has never been translated into English in its entirety. Only a few fragments have been published as prose translations in previous scholarly works. Chapters 3–4 offer a sample of Camargo's poetic voice in English. This would not have been possible without the collaboration of Prue Shaw, with whom I spent several afternoons discussing Camargo's octaves line by line. She also improved my translation of Bernardo de Balbuena's lines for the Epilogue, and of various challenging texts such as Góngora's attributed *Carta en respuesta*. Several other English translations were proofread by Victoria Lafarga.

Finally, I would like to thank Heewon Park for her help with the Latin translations, particularly of Horace, Athanasius Kircher and early biographers of Saint Ignatius of Loyola such as Maffei and Orlandini.

INTRODUCTION

Analyses of early modern Latin American literature have often led to over-generalisations that portray it either as a prolongation of the peninsular Spanish tradition, or as a reaction against Spanish imperialism. On the one hand, critics such as Téllez (2012: 10) have argued that Creoles (i.e. white Spaniards born in the Americas) emphasised their identification with Hispanic culture in order to reaffirm their allegiance to Spanishness. For this reason, they faithfully mirrored the styles and trends previously developed in the Iberian peninsula, particularly during the Baroque period (Lockhart and Schwartz 1983: 161–62). In the words of Colombí-Monguió (1985: 120–21), 'todos ellos, sea en la península o en las Indias, participaban de idéntica concepción del arte poético' [all these authors, whether in the Iberian peninsula or in the Indies, shared the same notion of poetry]. Thus, early modern Latin American literature would be a mere reflection of its Spanish counterpart. This thesis is particularly popular among peninsular Spanish scholars, who tend to conceptualise Spanish America only as Hispanic (Gentic and LaRubia-Prado 2017: 7).

On the other hand, many researchers have read this corpus as evidence of the emergence of a separate Spanish American Creole identity, slowly but steadily detached from that of Spain. By coining the term 'contraconquista' [counter-conquest], Lezama Lima (2001: 80) inspired numerous works that developed this idea. The so-called *Barroco de Indias* [Baroque of the Indies] would entail an implicit rebellion against Spain; Creoles indeed deployed the Spanish Baroque style, but in an anti-imperialist way (Sabat de Rivers 1992: 17–48). Moraña's (1988: 234) conceptualisation of the 'fenómeno de retorno' [critical awakening] can be linked to Lezama Lima's theory: from her perspective, Creoles produced a literature that seemed to mimic that of early modern Spain, but in reality challenged the Spanish hegemonic discourse.[1]

Although both theories make valid points, neither of them is sufficient to account for this corpus in all its complexity. This is particularly true for the study of Gongorism, the *nuevo estilo* [new style] developed by the Spanish author Luis de Góngora that transformed Baroque poetics not only in the Iberian peninsula but also in the Spanish Americas. Carilla (1946: 231) read this phenomenon as a sign of continuity: 'la poesía de la colonia [...] fue gongorista porque la de España lo fue en muchos ingenios' [colonial Latin American poetry was Gongorist because so was

---

1   I refer to Braun and Pérez Magallón (2016: 10) for more bibliography on the Baroque of the Indies as a 'cultural weapon' against colonisation.

that of peninsular Spain].[2] Conversely, Torres (1995: 30) interpreted it as a cultural-political rebellion in literary form: 'ese gongorismo indiano es el proyecto cultural que madurará hacia el proyecto político de las guerras de Independencia' [Latin American Gongorism is the cultural project that will evolve towards the political project of the wars of independence].

In recent years, scholars such as Mayo (2014) have revised these binary oppositions and analysed viceregal Latin American literature in a more nuanced way. Taking her approach as a starting point, this monograph will examine the influence of the *Soledades* (c. 1613) by Luis de Góngora (Spain, 1561–1627) on two of the greatest works that his followers produced in the 'New World': *San Ignacio* (1666) by Hernando Domínguez Camargo (Viceroyalty of Peru, 1606–1659) and *Primero sueño* (1692) by Sor Juana Inés de la Cruz (Viceroyalty of New Spain, 1651–1695). From this, I seek to broaden the scholarly understanding of poetic influence, practices of imitation and transmission of culture between early modern Spain and Latin America. These findings will, in turn, allow me to give due prominence to Creole works within a more inclusive and less hierarchical canon of Spanish Golden Age and viceregal Latin American literatures (Martínez-Osorio 2016: 132).

In fact, one of the advantages of transatlantic studies — as conceptualised by Ortega (2003, 2012) — is their flexibility: they require neither a canon nor a pre-established theoretical framework. Rather, they are an open exploration. The Hispanic Baroque cannot be understood without its transatlantic dimension, which made it one of the first global cultural phenomena (Braun and Pérez Magallón 2016: 2; and Suárez 2007: 37). In this sense, Camargo and Sor Juana wrote from the Americas in Spanish and their poems were published in Madrid. Both authors produced globalised works that have often been read as national texts despite being unconfinable within any seventeenth-century nation (Spain), or proto-nation (Colombia, Mexico). Thus, the study of their oeuvres entails much more than filling in gaps of traditional national literary histories. What Baroque Spanish literature is and can be, as well as what Latin American literature is and can be, immediately needs redefinition when poets such as Camargo and Sor Juana are examined. This also holds true for national entities (e.g. Spain and its American possessions) and for constructs such as Creolism.

When reading the *San Ignacio* and *Primero sueño*, one gains the impression that Góngora was as present in Latin America as in Spain. However, the big picture is more complex than that. The intricacy of Latin American Gongorism and its multiple implications, from the ideological to the visual, should not be underestimated. Based on the premises of the Church and/or the Court, viceregal writers such as Camargo and Sor Juana followed expansive creative agendas. Within the framework provided by the *nuevo estilo*, these poets developed alternative ideological mechanisms and imageries. Moreover, by modelling themselves on

---

2   Unlike Carilla and many other scholars, I will not use the adjective 'colonial' but 'viceregal', meaning 'relating to a Viceroyalty'. During the period of Habsburg rule, Spanish American territories were kingdoms of the Crown of Castile (Elliott 2007: 9). Klor de Alva (1992) and Adorno (1993: 143–44) explain the inappropriateness of 'colonial' terminology for this context.

FIG. I.I. Unknown creator, *Mass of Saint Gregory* (1539), Musée des Amériques – Auch, France. This featherwork is based on a print produced by the German printmaker Israhel van Meckenem c. 1490.

Góngora, Camargo and Sor Juana decentred Gongorism from Europe. In fact, other Western templates had undergone a similar fate after the conquest of the Aztecs by the Spanish. An example from the visual arts will illustrate this point.

Twenty-two years before the birth of Góngora, the recently established Viceroyalty of New Spain produced a work of art that is rare and of rich aesthetic value: the *Mass of Saint Gregory* (1539) (Figure I.1), a feather mosaic that represents Christ as a Man of Sorrows appearing to Pope Gregory I while he was saying Mass.

This work of art shares common ground with the *San Ignacio* and *Primero sueño*. Indeed, as I will explain in more detail below, both the mosaic and the poems (i) were crafted in the Americas; (ii) follow European models; (iii) target not only their immediate audience but also that of Europe; (iv) would have been short-lived, had they not been sent to Europe; (v) deploy a technique (featherwork) or style (Gongorism) appreciated on both sides of the Atlantic; (vi) resort to (pictorial or verbal) images for spiritual purposes; (vii) add American motifs to their European base; and (viii) make use of mnemonic techniques.

Let us start with the first four features. The *Mass of Saint Gregory*, created by indigenous artists in post-conquest Mexico City, reproduces a European printed image with the medium of featherwork. Copying from print models was a common practice in the 'New World'. Indeed, viceregal painters were often commissioned to produce paintings after prints from their patrons. In the words of Hyman (2017: 104): 'invention was in fact bound, paradoxical though it may seem, to the very act of copying'. Moreover, as evidenced by the inscription of the frame, the mosaic was created under the patronage of the governor Diego Huanitzin; its addressee was none other than the Pope Paul III. Although the *Mass of Saint Gregory* is unlikely to have reached him personally, the mosaic was sent to Europe, where it has been preserved to the present day (Mundy 2015: 103–13).

The parallels with Camargo and Sor Juana are numerous. These Creole poets spent their whole lives in the Americas, where they produced works that emulate European models. In a 1691 letter to Sor Juana, Manuel Fernández de Santa Cruz (the Bishop of Puebla) affirmed that her *Carta atenagórica* [*Letter Worthy of Athena*] had been published in order to 'manifestar a la Europa [...] que la América no solo es rica de minas de plata y oro, sino mucho más de aventajados ingenios' [show Europe [...] that the Americas are not only rich in silver and gold mines, but also and to a greater extent in wit] (Soriano 2014: 191). The same simile appears in the foreword to Camargo's *San Ignacio* (Torres Quintero 1960: 35). Both texts take pride in showing to Europe what the 'New World' could achieve. One could thus earn transatlantic prestige, as happened with Sor Juana. Moreover, although manuscripts are not as ephemeral as feathers, many viceregal works that remained unpublished are no longer extant.[3] Getting them into print (especially in Europe) increased

---

3   Vollendorf and Wray (2013: 106) examine the literary rivalry between Creoles and peninsular Spanish writers. The case of Sor Juana's friend Carlos de Sigüenza y Góngora (1645–1700) is paradigmatic. Most of his prolific output is now lost because he could not afford to publish it (Leonard 1929: 90–91).

their chances of circulation and ultimately of survival. This is what happened with Camargo's and Sor Juana's oeuvres.

As for features (v) to (viii), featherwork was the most highly regarded art form in pre-Hispanic and early post-conquest New Spain. Judging from the Spanish chronicles, the conquistadores and missionaries also appreciated it.[4] In terms of content, the *Mass of Saint Gregory* adds an 'exotic' element (pineapples) to the Western setting, and delivers a representation of Christ with gushing blood that is orthodox by European standards for the subject. Furthermore, the message of acceptance of the Catholic faith is clear. So is the use of the visual arts for religious purposes, and the display of mnemonic aids around the central Eucharistic image to remind viewers of the episodes of the Passion (Pierce and others 2004: 94–102).

For their part, by resorting to Gongorism, Camargo and Sor Juana set their works in a Hispanic Baroque global network, where that style was a synonym of prestige, high culture and good practice. This was especially the case in the Americas, where the *nuevo estilo* did not meet the opposition it encountered in Spain. These viceregal poets understood the overwhelming visual power of Gongorism and deployed it for spiritual purposes. This goal is more explicit in the *San Ignacio* than in *Primero sueño* but both poems equally are influenced by the ethos of the Counter-Reformation. They also combined an orthodox content with different forms of heterodoxy: either secular (Camargo) or esoteric (Sor Juana) imagery. Moreover, Camargo included in his poem a few allusions to the 'New World' as topoi of decorative exoticism. Sor Juana filled part of her oeuvre — *Primero sueño*, *Neptuno alegórico* [*Allegorical Neptune*], the *villancicos* [carols] and some *romances* [ballads] — with bicultural motifs (Aztec/Spanish) and showed a certain interest in Nahuatl language and culture. Finally, as early modern writers learned the mnemonic technique known as the art of memory in rhetoric courses, its impact on the aesthetic imagination of Camargo and especially Sor Juana was considerable.

Given its own composite, accumulative nature, the Baroque permitted a blending of varied components. From a Eurocentric perspective, Spain transmitted culture to the Americas, but only as an inalienable good that remained Hispanic despite its displacement. Were this the case, the above-mentioned comparison of mines and wit would be asymmetric, as 'New World' gold/silver was simply taken without keeping any original American identity (Hyman 2017: 117).[5] In fact, Góngora provided a prestigious template according to which Creoles began to represent the world in ways that incorporated local elements and increasingly deviated from metropolitan assumptions (Beverley 2008: 143). Indeed, Creoles engaged in the project of creating another Europe, outside of Europe. This entailed the reconstitution — and not just the prolongation — of European literature, which in the 'New World'

4 Acosta (1590: 285): 'Algunos indios, buenos maestros, retratan con perfección de pluma lo que ven de pincel, que ninguna ventaja les hacen los pintores de España' [Some Indians, good artists, portray with the perfection of feathers what they see in canvases; Spanish painters cannot outdo them in anything].

5 Sor Juana's *romance* 37 makes this point clear (Méndez Plancarte 1994a: 103): 'Europa mejor lo diga, | pues ha tanto que, insaciable, | de sus abundantes venas | desangra los minerales' [Europe knows this well, | as, for such a long time, | it has bled insatiably | the gold-bearing veins of the Americas].

was influenced by native American and Afro-descendant cultures. The resulting partial negation of the Spanish model was the outcome of a complicated process, which combined indirectness with exaggeration. Camargo's and Sor Juana's strategy consisted of embracing Góngora with such hybrid convolutedness, that their yeses to the *Soledades* might be turned, to some extent, into noes. To borrow a phrase popularised by Bhabha (2004: 127), that form of difference, which is 'mimicry', enabled viceregal literature to become 'almost the same but not quite'. This was not a case of submissive but of differential *imitatio* (Luiselli 2017: 178). The deliberate representation of (apparent) sameness called into question the original.[6]

Obviously, none of these arguments, which draw on postcolonial theory, can be found in the early studies of Spanish American Gongorism: the pioneering article by Schons (1939), and the books by Carilla (1946) and Buxó (1960). In fact, Schons (1939: 33) reached the following conclusion: 'All in all, then, the imitation of Góngora in Mexico was limited to externals and never came to be an integral part of Mexican thought or art'. For his part, Buxó (1960: 10) defended the opposite thesis: 'Desde ese momento [1640] Góngora regirá, incansablemente, la poesía novohispana' [From that moment onwards [1640] Góngora will rule, unceasingly, the poetry of New Spain]. Carilla also believed in Góngora's dominance, not only in this Viceroyalty, but also in the rest of Spanish America. Indeed, after including dozens of poets, he concluded his monograph by affirming that the long life of Gongorism had no equivalent in Spanish American literature from the seventeenth to the twentieth century (Carilla 1946: 235).

In his *Discurso sobre el estilo de don Luis de Góngora* [*Discourse on Góngora's Style*], Martín Vázquez Siruela, a seventeenth-century scholar, famously said: '¿Quién escribe hoy que no sea besando las huellas de Góngora, o quién ha escrito verso en España, después que esta antorcha se encendió, que no haya sido mirando a su luz?' [Who writes today without following in Góngora's footsteps, or who has written poetry in Spain, after this torch was lit, without being led by its light?].[7] These lines are often quoted. However, the assessment is an exaggeration, particularly if applied to the Americas. Does Carilla mention enough significant examples of Góngora's influence? By 'significant', I mean examples more substantial than a scattered output over the centuries (a sonnet here, a cento there) by this or that Creole writer that he had uncovered. Having considered the works he hails as the most representative of Latin American Gongorism, the answer is a definite 'no'. In fact, when I explored viceregal epics included in Carilla's monograph, such as Pedro de Oña's *El Vasauro* [*The Golden Goblet*] (1635), Antonio de Oviedo y Herrera's *Santa Rosa de Lima* [*Saint Rose of Lima*] (1711), Francisco Ruiz de León's *Hernandía* [*Hernandiad*] (1755), and various shorter poems by the eighteen-century Jesuit Juan Bautista Aguirre, I realised that all of them (except for Aguirre) were more indebted to Ercilla than to Góngora.[8]

---

6   This paragraph follows Echeverría's conceptualisation of the Baroque (1996: 81–82 and 87) and Martínez's (2016: 143) approach to mimicry.

7   Cerdan and Vitse (1995: 93). Saiko Yoshida edited this particular text.

8   I read the first two in Oña (1941) and Oviedo y Herrera (1867). Espinosa Pólit and Zaldumbide (1960) edited Bautista Aguirre's poetry.

Thus, the books by Buxó and Carilla have two limitations. Firstly, they work as anthologies that offer a panoramic overview but not as in-depth studies of any author. Secondly, they include too many poets (especially Carilla), some of them with minimal Gongorist features.[9] A more recent monograph has refined the findings of these early scholars. Tenorio (2013) offers a sustained, extended analysis of Mexican Gongorist poetry. This critic chooses her texts (overall) more carefully, reads them in the light of Gracián's theory of wit, and makes insightful distinctions between different forms of Gongorism. Nevertheless, Tenorio still devotes sections of her book to authors such as Bernardo de Balbuena, Matías de Bocanegra and Francisco Ruiz de León, whose Gongorism is either non-existent or sporadic, as she herself admits. Unlike Buxó (1960: 23), who limited his scope to the seventeenth century, Tenorio stretches her findings to the early nineteenth century, i.e. to reminiscences of Gongorism.

Therefore, her monograph suffers from the same two limitations as those of her predecessors, although to a lesser extent. Due to the sheer number of writers in her corpus, Tenorio cannot always elaborate on each. Despite this shortcoming, the monograph is an important contribution that suggests avenues for further research. See, for instance, how she characterises Gongorism as a language of images and conceits: 'Góngora mostró cómo, por medio de una serie de procedimientos estilísticos, elaborar imágenes y conceptos, para con ellos potenciar al máximo la capacidad denotativa de la lengua' [Through a series of stylistic procedures, Góngora showed how to elaborate images and conceits in order to maximize the denotative capacity of language] (Tenorio 2013: 172). Hence, she argues, the relevance of descriptions in the *Soledades* and *Primero sueño*.

In fact, the relationship between Gongorism on both sides of the Atlantic and the visual arts was persistently missing in scholarship, particularly with regard to ekphraseis or poetic descriptions. Mayers (2012) produced the first ambitious attempt to fill this gap. She only included four authors in her corpus: Góngora and three viceregal writers who undeniably imitated him — Hernando Domínguez Camargo, Juan de Espinosa Medrano and Sor Juana. Mayer's measured choice has greatly influenced mine: as the Baroque ideal goes, less is more. However, our respective approaches are different. Mayers reads these works through the lens of political control, performances of power and Creole identity. She also relates the motif of ekphrasis to visions of empire. Partly to avoid overlaps, I have not dealt with these topics in the same detail as she does.

I decided to organise the corpus around Góngora and two viceregal poets, who would fulfil three requirements. They had to be (i) profoundly influenced by the *Soledades*, particularly by its descriptions; (ii) insufficiently studied from the viewpoint of ekphrastic writing; and (iii) great authors in their own right, who deserved more than a footnote in anthologies of Gongorism. Having closely

---

9   The same criticisms apply to later works such as the book by Sánchez Robayna (2018: 99–100) that mentions Gregório de Matos (1636–1696) and Manuel Botelho de Oliveira (1636–1711) as exponents of Brazilian Gongorism. Matos (1990) occasionally imitated the early Góngora, but never his *Soledades* (Carreira 2018). The influence of the Cordovan poet in Botelho de Oliveira (2005) is even less significant.

read the above-mentioned works (*San Ignacio* and *Primero sueño*) alongside several others,[10] I reached the following conclusion: Camargo and Sor Juana were the major Baroque followers of Góngora in Spanish America. They wrote their most ambitious poems in emulation of the *Soledades*, and they developed many of the themes, tropes and techniques of their model.[11] Naturally, occasional references to other works by Góngora — particularly the *Polifemo*, which was also very influential in the Americas (Holloway 2017: 191) — will be made when appropriate. However, the first third of this monograph will focus on the *Soledades* because it constituted the most ambitious and challenging template in the eyes of Camargo and Sor Juana. Their clarity of vision and aestheticised sense of the world is due in great part to this poem.

Moreover, the fact that scholarship on Camargo remains scarce was an added incentive. As for Sor Juana, the towering figure of viceregal literature, she has been the object of countless philological studies. Numerous works also analyse her as a Mexican icon and as a precursor of feminism.[12] However, *Primero sueño*'s affinity with the visual arts, which cannot be explained without Gongorism, has not yet been sufficiently studied. In recent years, the relationship between painting and poetry in the Spanish Golden Age that critics such as Orozco (1947), Pabst (1966) and Bergmann (1979) studied early on has undergone a revival in academic interest. This is a welcome trend, as an understanding of the links between the 'sister arts' is indispensable to explain Baroque Spanish culture.

The Habsburg kings were art lovers and collectors. Their taste shaped that of the nobility, to the extent that an appreciation of paintings became a sign of aristocratic refinement (Sánchez Jiménez 2011: 25). It is therefore not surprising that writers such as Góngora, Lope, Quevedo and Calderón were interested in art. The bond between painting and poetry left a noticeable imprint on the Hispanic world. Early modern theorists were eager to provide painting, historically considered a mechanical manual task, with the dignity of a liberal art with rights equivalent to poetry. Thus, they developed discourses based on classics such as Aristotle's *Poetics* (1448a and 1460b) and Horace's *Ars poetica*, which contains the famously misread '*ut pictura poesis*' [painting is like poetry] (lines 361–62). Neither Aristotle nor Horace identified both arts as the Renaissance and Baroque critics did; they merely suggested analogies (Rensselaer 1940: 196–203). However, given that Greco-Latin

---

10   For instance, Rodrigo de Carvajal y Robles' *Poema heroico del asalto y conquista de Antequera* [*Epic Poem on the Assault and Conquest of Antequera*] (1627) and *Fiestas de Lima por el nacimiento del príncipe Baltasar Carlos* [*Celebrations in Lima for the Birth of Prince Baltasar Carlos*] (1631) —Carvajal y Robles (1950, 2000) in the bibliography to this book — and Diego Sáenz Ovecuri's *Thomasíada* [*Thomasiad*] (1667). Both viceregal poets praise Góngora but criticise Gongorism, a style that neither of them follows.

11   Sabat de Rivers (1997: 10): 'No es solo con el *Polifemo* que este poema establece coordenadas, pues lo hace todavía más con las *Soledades*' [Camargo's *San Ignacio* does not only have common ground with the *Polifemo*, but also and to a greater extent with the *Soledades*]. According to Méndez Plancarte (1994a: xxxiv), *Primero sueño* constitutes 'la más auténtica emulación, en su aristocracia formal, del Góngora de las *Soledades*' [the most authentic emulation, in its formal aristocracy, of Góngora's *Soledades*].

12   I refer to the bibliography in Pérez-Amador (2015) and Bergmann and Schlau (2017).

antiquity left a considerable corpus of writings on poetry and rhetoric but little on artworks, critical theory concerning the visual arts was based on these two texts (Ford 1997: 1). As can be inferred from Carducho's *Diálogos de la pintura* [*Dialogues of Painting*] and Pacheco's *Arte de la pintura* [*Art of Painting*], published respectively in 1633 and 1649, the main reason why the two arts were deemed to be engaged in almost identical pursuits was that imitation of reality constituted a key driving force behind the production of both painters and poets.[13]

Artists emulate the world with lines and colours as writers do with words. Like Spain, seventeenth-century Spanish America produced a rich body of ekphraseis or poetic descriptions. In this respect, the Greek ideal of *enargeia* (*evidentia*, in Latin rhetoric), in which vivid descriptions bring the subject matter before the readers' eyes, was at the heart of Greco-Latin discourses on ekphrasis. Depictions of any kind of persons, places, objects or even actions would be deemed an ekphrasis if they appealed to the mind's eye of listeners/readers. In other words, the subject of ekphrasis was irrelevant for the definition; an ekphrasis was distinguished by its effect on the audience (Webb 1999: 8–13, and 2009: 61–70).

In the introduction to *Imagines*, Philostratus the Elder (2014: 5) explains that he wrote descriptions of works of art so that 'by this means the young may learn to interpret paintings'. Ekphrasis can also be linked to the rhetorical technique of *amplificatio*, and even to mnemonic techniques of visualisation. According to Webb (2009: 19), students of ancient rhetoric were encouraged to engage actively with ekphrastic texts by thinking themselves into the scenes and feeling as if they were present.

Interestingly, major Counter-Reformation saints had a similar approach to vision and imagination. Teresa of Ávila (2011: 305) claims the Holy Spirit instructed her to start praying by imagining a Holy Week 'paso', i.e. a float with sculptures representing the Passion of Christ. Moreover, visualisation of a religious setting is a key preamble to prayer in Ignatius' *Ejercicios espirituales* [*Spiritual Exercises*] (2013: 164), as we shall explore in Chapter 3 when examining ekphrasis and the Jesuit *composición de lugar* [mental representation of the place].

Before going any further, I should make a terminological clarification. Nowadays, there is no scholarly consensus on the meaning of ekphrasis; rather, it is an umbrella term deployed to designate a variety of concepts concerned with interactions between the verbal and the visual (Koopman 2018: 2). Indeed, modern criticism has used the word ekphrasis with multiple meanings. On the one hand, Heffernan (1991: 299) and especially Spitzer (1955: 207) have proposed restrictive definitions: 'the verbal representation of graphic representation' and 'the poetic description of a pictorial or sculptural work of art' respectively. In Heffernan's view, ekphrasis represents representation itself, the shield of Achilles, with its multiple engravings, being the classic example (*Iliad*, XVIII. 478–608).

On the other hand, these scholars exclude a good deal of what other authors (all

13   Carducho (1865: 144) affirmed that between these two arts there is great 'semejanza, unión e intención' [similarity, union and intention]. According to Pacheco (1956: I. 84), 'la poesía también, a su modo, imita con palabras, aunque no como el pintor con líneas, y colores' [poetry also, in its own way, imitates by using words, although not like the painter, who deploys lines and colours].

the ancient and many modern) would also deem ekphrasis — namely pictorialism, i.e. poetry that deploys 'artistic' techniques in its descriptions, irrespective of the nature of the objects portrayed. Krieger (1992: 266), for instance, defines ekphrasis as any sort of poetry that 'takes on the "still" elements of plastic form which we normally attribute to the spatial arts'. According to Padrón (2004: 95), ekphrasis is 'the verbal depiction of space or of an object in space'. These expansive definitions include texts that refer neither to paintings nor to sculptures, but that are still evocative of a visual experience of art (Mayers 2012: 2).

For the purposes of this monograph, which concerns itself broadly with Gongorist descriptions and Spanish American poetry, all of these definitions are useful. However, I will use 'ekphrasis' as an umbrella term with the general sense of a poetic description, which aims at a vivid evocation in the mind's eye of the reader. I propose this definition for three reasons. Firstly, its broadness/flexibility is more in keeping with the original meaning of the Greek word than Heffernan's or Spitzer's contributions. Secondly, it acknowledges the fact that, in ancient rhetoric, *enargeia* or vividness is the quality 'which makes an ekphrasis an ekphrasis' (Webb 2009: 128). Thirdly, it can subsume a whole range of related concepts — including definitions by scholars who have preceded me.

A third of the corpus is devoted to ekphrasis in the restrictive sense promoted by Heffernan and Spitzer: the poetic representation of a sculptural (Chapter 3) or a pictorial (Chapter 5) representation, a crucifix by Camargo and a canvas by Sor Juana respectively. These ekphraseis do not portray artefacts that exist or have ever existed, as the subject matter is purely fictive. Therefore, contemporary listeners/readers had to exercise their imagination to visualise the description. To this end, they would have resorted to their knowledge of art (Koopman 2018: 262). For this reason, I will compare the texts examined with early modern paintings, sculptures and occasionally with buildings.

Inspired by the examples of ancient rhetoric, which often include architecture (e.g. the Alexandrian acropolis) within the notion of ekphrasis (Webb 2009: 81 and 174), I felt the need to expand Spitzer's definition slightly in the last essay (Chapter 6). Architecture appears in art history books for a reason — namely, because it belongs to the visual arts. In fact, there is a wealth of scholarship on the topos *ut architectura poesis* [architecture is like poetry].[14] In this respect, Sor Juana's portrayal of the pyramids in *Primero sueño* can be read as an 'architectural ekphrasis', to borrow the expression from Hollander (1995: 56).

As for Góngora, this poet had a superb descriptive talent and thus excelled in providing pictorial visions of food, artefacts, animals, nature and human activities such as fishing and hunting, which are both intensely material and full of multivalent symbolism. His *Soledades* tests the limits of the most restrictive notions of ekphrasis. The passages that I study — a landscape and a seascape (Chapters 1 and 2) — allude to no work of art in particular, but can still produce an effect in the mind's eye comparable to that of a painting. Note the assessment of Francisco Fernández de Córdoba (the Abbot of Rute), a friend of Góngora (Artigas 1925: 406): 'La poesía

14   I refer to the bibliography in Palme (1959) and Webb (2000).

en general es pintura que habla, y si alguna en particular lo es, lo es esta: pues en ella ([...] como en un lienzo de Flandes) se ven industriosa, y hermosísimamente pintados mil géneros de ejercicios rústicos, cacerías, chozas, montes, valles, prados, bosques, mares, esteros, ríos, arroyos, animales terrestres, acuáticos y aéreos' [Generally, poetry is painting that speaks. This is particularly true of this poem: for in it ([...] as in a Flemish painting) we see, industriously and beautifully painted, a thousand kinds of rustic tasks, hunting, huts, mountains, valleys, meadows, forests, seas, estuaries, rivers, streams, land, aquatic and flying animals].[15]

Indeed, this poem deploys a highly artificial language in order to represent nature as art (Cacho 2007: 446). For this reason, Béhar (2009: 24) resorts to ekphrasis as a tool of literary criticism with which to study it. Likewise, Mayers (2012: 12) uses this term to approach Camargo's Gongorist still lifes, which are — together with a religious rapture and a pagan funeral procession — the subject of Chapter 4. From my perspective, Krieger's notion of ekphrasis allows for the inclusion of descriptions that are more pictorial for their style and effect than for their subject matter.[16] Gongorism is not only a way of understanding language but also a way of seeing the world as if it were a work of art. Due to its aesthetically appealing representations of landscapes/seascapes (i.e. of space), this worldview is particularly noticeable in the *Soledades*, which Padrón (2004: 236–37, and 2007: 366) includes within the uncharted land of Hispanic cartographic literature.

Far from being ornaments, or marginal rhetorical tropes, ekphraseis can fulfil key functions within longer narratives. For instance, they are frequently the best scenario to witness the dissonance or fissures of a work, given the 'many figures of difference that energize the dialectic of the imagetext' (Mitchell 1994: 181). Following this insight, Mayers (2012: 7) examines how ekphraseis in Spanish American poetry 'embody ideological struggles between classes, genders, and political factions'. The descriptions of the corpus I have chosen also herald ideological tensions, although not of the same kind. Benjamin (1977: 177) identified 'the synthesis which is reached in allegorical writing as a result of the conflict between theological and artistic intentions'. Kluge (2014) deploys the term diglossia to mean this doublespeak, which she exemplifies with the Baroque moralisation of pagan literature. My work argues that this conflict was not exclusive to Spain. In fact, diglossia is often more conspicuous in viceregal Latin American literature than in peninsular texts. Two growing Creole realisations will help explain why this happened.

The first was that their allegiance to Spain was not taken for granted. Indeed, the mistrust towards American-born Spaniards, an entrenched feeling in the viceregal Court and Church, increased towards the late sixteenth century and caused reactions of outrage among Creoles (Lucena 2016: 175–78). As a result, like the *Mass*

---

15   Pineda (2000: 258) broadens the notion of ekphrasis to include descriptions of nature: 'Existe también [...] un tipo especial de écfrasis, en la que lo descrito no es una obra de arte, sino una escena natural, real o no, generalmente un paisaje, que se presente como si de una pintura se tratase' [There is also a [...] special type of ekphrasis, in which what is described is not a work of art, but a nature scene, real or not, usually a landscape, which is presented as if it were a painting].

16   Given that *descriptio* in Latin is the closest equivalent to ancient ekphrasis (Webb 2009: 9), I will use both terms (i.e. description and ekphrasis) interchangeably to avoid repetition.

of Saint Gregory, viceregal literature tends to embrace empire and/or Christianity almost with the ferocity of the convert, at least in its external forms. We shall see conspicuous examples of this in Camargo's *San Ignacio*, which ends prophesying the universal rule of Catholicism: 'por nuestros hijos ver alcanzaremos, | que abracen de la Cruz los cuatros extremos' [through our offspring we shall see | how the four continents embrace the cross] (book V, canto V, CLXVI.7–8). As for Sor Juana, she served the Church as loyally as she served the State. The nun excelled as a sycophant, assuming authorial roles such as the 'poet of empire' and the 'court advisor' in her vast output of occasional works (Thomas 2012: 109).[17]

The second Creole realisation was that, after the landmarks of the peninsular Spanish Baroque, Europeans would not be easily impressed by their writings. Viceregal literature does not only reflect anxiety concerning the detrimental effect of 'belatedness' or lack of priority in creation, as Bloom (1973: 61) defines it. It also suffers from anxiety concerning reception, to paraphrase a title from Newlyn (2000). On the one hand, Creoles tended to have exaggerated needs for validation in Spain, where better distribution, broader intellectual circles, and honours and prestige awaited (Kirk 2016: 144). On the other hand, they feared that peninsular readers, biased by prejudice, would not appreciate their works. Note, for instance, Sigüenza y Góngora's characterisation of Europe displaying an arrogant contempt for Creoles.[18] Thus, viceregal poets followed Spanish models (e.g. Ercilla, Góngora) to show that they could master their techniques, while simultaneously diverging from them to offer something different, which would cause readers to wonder anew. The displacement and defamiliarisation of the known explains why their literature often produces an impression of familiar strangeness. This is also the case of the *Mass of Saint Gregory*, which copies a German model with a non-European technique, arguably causing a comparable effect.

Both the *San Ignacio* and *Primero sueño* reveal a profound diglossia. On the one hand, their authors experienced the pressure of hegemonic Baroque culture, broadly understood from an ideological, political and even religious perspective (Maravall 2011). Indeed, Camargo and Sor Juana reflect the *Weltanschauung* of imperial Spain with an emphatic acceptance, which seems an overreaction to peninsular bigotry against Creoles. On the other hand, signs of rebelliousness emerge in these works. In this respect, it is my contention that ekphrasis is a key tool they deploy to vent issues (be they aesthetic or religious) that were at odds with the predominant contemporaneous ideology (Kluge 2014: 241–42). For this reason, an analysis of

17   Hill (2000: 70): 'Regional pride in the seventeenth century did not even approximate the nineteenth century's vindication of Mexicanness: she [i.e. Sor Juana] and Sigüenza y Góngora were perhaps the most ardent defenders of monarchical absolutism in all of colonial New Spain'. Despite their glorification of the Spanish viceregal apparatus, Creole authors are often claimed for Latin American national literatures. Anastácio (2013) criticises similar tendencies in Brazil.
18   Sigüenza y Góngora (1959: 85): 'Piensan en algunas partes de la Europa [...] que los que de padres españoles casualmente nacimos en ellos, o andamos en dos pies por divina dispensación, o que aun valiéndose de microscopios ingleses apenas se descubre en nosotros lo racional' [In some parts of Europe, people have the following opinion about those of us who were born by chance in the Americas: either we walk on two feet by the grace of God, or even using English microscopes one would barely be able to find reason in us].

this motif is fundamental in order to comprehend viceregal literature and, more broadly, the differences between the peninsular and the Creole worldviews. I will illustrate this point with two examples, which will receive further attention in Chapters 3–6.

Throughout the *San Ignacio*, Camargo conformed to the taste and tenets of the Counter-Reformation. However, he also filled his poem with exuberant (often extravagant) Gongorist imagery, superimposed on the hagiography. The outcome is a bizarre, hybrid epic that tells from the 'New World' a sacred story of the 'Old', using European literary traditions, but departing from that content at will for the sake of aesthetics. Indeed, Camargo is so ready to leave the religious subject matter at the slightest occasion that he often seems a precursor of art for art's sake — an approach of which Góngora would have approved. Yet, despite all that, the epic remains an example of Jesuit proselytisation written *ad maiorem Dei gloriam* [to the greater glory of God]. Hence, the presence of diglossia.

Likewise, Sor Juana made use of the ambiguities of ekphrasis. If we set aside her talent, one of the reasons why her texts were so acclaimed in Spain is ideological: she was a successful, 'exotic' product of empire (Grossi 2007: 13–14). The above-mentioned 1691 letter by the Bishop of Puebla, with the simile comparing the nun with the Spanish American mines, carries this imperial overtone (Soriano 2014: 191). Sor Juana took advantage of, but did not always conform to, that portrait. In fact, *Primero sueño* deploys syncretic sources (in her case, the Hermetic esoteric tradition, and Egyptian imagery, partly inspired by Góngora) to diverge from the aesthetic and religious orthodoxy of her time. Indeed, Sor Juana fixes her attention on Egypt, an even more unknown reality for Creoles than Europe, where the ekphrasis comprises simultaneous criticism of and fascination with the pyramids. Thus, diglossia helps to understand the oddity in this poem, which is as striking as that of the *San Ignacio*. Like its epic forerunner, *Primero sueño* accumulates different hermeneutic layers in a typically Baroque fashion, leading to a palimpsest, to borrow Torres' title (1993).

Thus, there is more to these descriptions than a mere evocation of the still moment of art, as Krieger (1992: 266) put it. In fact, Heffernan (1991: 302) pointed out that ekphrasis tends to display a narrative impulse. This is particularly true in the epic genre, where authors not only deploy this motif to summarise the ideological or political content of a poem but also for plot-related reasons. Let us remember again the shield of Achilles, where the fixed figures of plastic art perform successive actions, some of them concerning the Trojan War. From the *Iliad* onwards, poets often complement pictorial stasis with storytelling, thereby loading the ekphrasis with a narrative content that paintings can only imply by connotation. For this reason, seeing ekphrasis as a combination of description and narration is the most fruitful line of enquiry (Koopman 2018: 13).

This narratological component is also noticeable in the present corpus, although it manifests itself in different ways. For example, Góngora shows through a *mise-en-abyme* the setting where the protagonist-pilgrim of the *Soledades* will ramble. This enables him to reinforce the poem's internal consistency, as the nutshell representation of the whole anticipates future events of the plot. Interestingly, the proleptic function of ekphrasis is also present in the *San Ignacio* and in *Primero sueño*. However, unlike Góngora, Camargo does not write brief descriptions that fit into the rest of his poem. Quite the opposite: his long ekphraseis thrust in multiple directions (e.g. banquets, clothes, animals, insects), which are often completely unrelated to the protagonist-saint. Thus, Camargo's 'deliberate incoherence', narratologically speaking, is his way of diverging from Góngora. As for Sor Juana, the nun did not render a servile imitation of the *Soledades* either. Rather than letting readers infer the narrative role of the description, as Góngora did, she revealed openly the connection between her architectural ekphrasis and the plot: the pyramids represent the protagonist-soul of *Primero sueño*. This metaphorical explicitness breaks away (if only for a moment) from the elitist obscurity that dominates the *Soledades* and most of her own poem.

Before setting out the analysis of this viceregal corpus, it is worth examining the main model that Camargo and Sor Juana emulated, with an emphasis on ekphrasis. For this reason, Chapter 1 addresses the reflection of Horace's *ut pictura poesis* in Góngora, focusing on the panoramic landscape admired by the pilgrim from a cliff in the *Soledad primera*, lines 182–211. The first thesis is that this passage delivers a 'pictorial' representation of the scenery. The second thesis is that it also offers an *agudeza paradoja* [paradox conceit] — to use Gracián's terminology — for there is a paradoxical dissonance between the objectives of offering a total vision by placing the protagonist on a high vantage point (epic trope of teichoscopy), and poetically describing the landscape he sees as a dazzling work of art (ekphrasis *lato sensu*). This paradox will be resolved by resorting to Panofsky's notion of *Idea* (1968).

Chapter 2, devoted to the ominous seascape that the pilgrim and an elderly angler observe from a cliff (*Soledad segunda*, lines 388–426), takes these ideas to their logical culmination. My reading offers a narratological, stylistic and symbolic analysis of the passage that also makes use of art theory about the landscape and Gracián's conceptualisation of wit. Góngora deploys teichoscopy to depict another area of the natural world as a work of art: the Atlantic ocean. The poet deploys multiple ekphrastic means that either enrich or complement those used in the *Soledad primera*. By doing so, he composes an *agudeza compuesta* [compound conceit], which encompasses both the intersections of the verbal and the visual, and the liminal zone between vision and imagination. Baroque culture is at home with paradoxes, and so is this structural macro conceit. Moreover, special attention will be given to the 'shipwreck with spectator' motif, an ancient topos, which Góngora reinvigorates by using it to reflect on the 'man against nature' conflict and to criticise the Spanish exploitation of the 'New World'.

Chapters 3 and 4 explore how the desacralisation of aesthetics promoted by the *Soledades* reached even the hagiographic genre in the Americas. Camargo's *San Ignacio*, a viceregal epic about a key Counter-Reformation saint, oscillates between the transcendental content that one would expect in a hagiography, and pictorial descriptions in the manner of Góngora. Chapter 3 examines this diglossia in the ekphrasis of a crucifix (book II, canto IV) that Ignatius had in Manresa, the town where he lived as a hermit in 1522 and wrote his *Ejercicios espirituales*. On the one hand, Camargo follows Counter-Reformation guidelines when depicting the cross. The poet lingers on both Christ's torment and Ignatius' penances displaying an attitude, which is close to what Cioran (1995) would call 'voluptuousness of suffering'. On the other hand, he takes advantage of the fact that he is not describing Christ, but a sculptural representation of Christ, to idealise the icon. The outcome is a Gongorist ekphrasis of a precious work of art, where pain and beauty intermingle, becoming indistinguishable from one another.

Chapter 4 addresses Ignatius' ecstatic rapture in Manresa (book II, canto V). This essay highlights the originality of Camargo's *San Ignacio* when compared to its epic predecessors: the poems about the saint by Luis de Belmonte Bermúdez (1609), Antonio de Escobar y Mendoza (1613) and Pedro de Oña (1639). My main thesis is that, although Camargo's starting point is the Ignatian hagiographies in prose and Escobar's work, the poet deploys Gongorism in order to swerve from this tradition. I also suggest Giambattista Marino's *Adone* (1623) as a possible influence in Camargo's diglossic experimentation. The essay is divided into two sections. Firstly, I examine the rapture *ad intra* (the ecstatic vision in itself), where Camargo displays a cult of *préciosité* typical of Marinism, and a heavily ornamented Gongorist style. Secondly, I analyse the rapture *ad extra* (the setting), as the poet frames the religious episode within two profane descriptions: a rural banquet and a pagan procession. I conclude this section with the obelisk, which Camargo describes before leaving Manresa, as this Gongorist motif is also present in Sor Juana.

Indeed, the word 'obeliscos' appears in line 2 of *Primero sueño*, a philosophical poem that portrays a soul who surveys the universe in search of complete knowledge. This protagonist-soul, which is sharp like an obelisk, tries to represent her vision in a painting. Chapter 5 addresses the resulting cosmographic canvas, linked by the poet with the mirror of the lighthouse of Alexandria (lines 266–301). My main contention is that Sor Juana pushes Gongorist ekphrasis in three directions: (i) the nun represents holistically not only the visible world of things, as Góngora does in the *Soledades*, but also the invisible world of Ideas; (ii) ekphrasis is unequivocally placed within the realm of imagination, as evidenced by the fact that the canvas is painted by human fantasy; and (iii) Sor Juana displays certain ambivalence, which is the result of combining vague Christian allusions with the Hermetic art of memory.

Finally, Chapter 6 offers an analysis of Sor Juana's description of the Memphis pyramids, her best known architectural ekphrasis (lines 340–411), paying attention to its sources. It is my contention that Sor Juana reflects the early modern awareness of its distance to antiquity. I also argue that the nun's address to Egypt constitutes an example of diglossia. Chapter 6 will use Kluge's term (2014) to describe Sor Juana's ambiguous approach to Egypt, comprising both criticism and praise. This dual assessment appears somewhat balanced until the nun uses Homer as a source, who tips the scales in favour of these constructions by revealing their allegoric nature. According to Sor Juana's perception, Homer represented a receptacle of ancient, revered wisdom that predated Greece. In this sense, it is her understanding of this

Greek poet, rather than his writings themselves, that is key to my reading of the pyramids. The conclusion will frame Sor Juana within two poetic/historiographical concepts — Góngora as the Spanish Homer and the *translatio studii* — in order to shed further light on *Primero sueño*.

Sor Juana's bold use of Homer attests to her self-confidence as a poet, possibly nurtured by the high praise she received throughout her career, particularly in Spain. This aplomb is also present in her famous autobiographical *Respuesta a Sor Filotea de la Cruz* [*Reply to Sor Filotea de la Cruz*], which I quote extensively in Chapters 5 and 6. Like many Sor Juana scholars, I tend to read the nun biographically at times. However, I am aware that this tendency is problematic because it can lead to taking literally some of the statements made in her letter without always considering its strategic performance. Moreover, since I present relatively little biographical criticism in the case of Góngora and Camargo, my approach might leave a sense of imbalance.

I acknowledge these shortcomings, but I have followed this path for a reason, namely: although I do not take at face value every page of the *Respuesta* — particularly not the biographical anecdotes (Luciani 1995; Perelmuter 1983) — I find Sor Juana's account of the obstacles she had to overcome as a female writer wholly credible and relevant to the understanding of her work. This is why I resort to this letter with more frequency than to biographical texts about the other two authors examined — which are limited in the case of Camargo. Unlike the nun, they faced no comparable hurdles when it came to writing. In fact, I believe their lives (particularly Góngora's, which was almost uneventful) are less illuminating than that of Sor Juana when it comes to exploring their respective oeuvres.

Sor Juana is indeed an unparalleled figure: arguably the best poet (of either gender) in viceregal Latin America. Nevertheless, as my colleague Caroline Egan once told me, it is important not to make her a Baroque 'monstruo' [freak] by trapping her biographically in the highly rhetorical and performative world of her poetry and prose. Sor Juana's self-fashioning as a child prodigy in the *Respuesta* contributed to her own mythologisation; so did — to a greater extent — the hyperbolic praise from her contemporary readers.[19] No wonder the nun claimed she did not understand their enthusiasm. Her reaction is due to a growing estrangement from her European readership. If we are to believe Sor Juana's *romance* 49, they would have exhibited her like a circus curiosity: 'Qué dieran los saltimbancos | a poder, por agarrarme | y llevarme, como monstruo | por esos andurrïales' [What would the charlatans not give | if they could to grab me | and display me like a monster | in godforsaken places] (Méndez Plancarte 1994a: 147).

---

19   Merrim (1999: 30): 'Should it be so desired, the learned woman would be celebrated as an exception to her sex, as prodigious, as a *rara avis*, as a freak'. In a paratext to Sor Juana's *Segundo volumen de las obras* [*Second Volume of Her Works*] (1692), the friar Pedro del Santísimo Sacramento called her 'monstruo de las mujeres, y prodigio mexicano' [monster of women, and Mexican prodigy]. Perelmuter (2004: 104–07) and Kirk (2016: 130–31) examine the challenges faced by female literary production in patriarchal New Spain.

In this respect, there could be one more common feature between the *Mass of Saint Gregory* and the viceregal corpus explored in this monograph: all of these works were misunderstood in Europe. In their indigenous context, featherworks were asymmetrical gifts offered by leaders to inferiors who could not reciprocate, so that the power imbalance would be clear. Nevertheless, once in Europe, these magnificent mosaics were just seen as evidence of the revenues that the conquest would entail (Mundy 2015: 106). Likewise, we saw earlier how Camargo's and Sor Juana's intellectual output was presented to Europe as consumable commodities comparable to gold or silver. This is unlikely to have been their authorial intent, at least in the case of Sor Juana, as evidenced by her *romance* 51.[20]

Sor Juana received many complimentary texts from Creole and European readers, and she authored four epistolary *romances* in reply to her admirers. All of them share the typical topoi of false modesty. However, her *romance* 51, the only one that she addressed to a group, heaps reproaches upon her Spanish audience. The poem describes Spain as a distant land, where misreaders produce a portrait in which the nun cannot recognise herself (Zamora 1995: 138; and Martínez-San Miguel 2008: 166–76): '¿Tanto pudo la distancia | añadir a mi retrato?' [Could it be that distance embellished | my portrait to such an extent?]. Spanish peninsular admirers have created an image that is a reflection of their own selves. Hence, their exaggerated, self-congratulatory praise: 'La imagen de vuestra idea | es la que habéis alabado' [The image of your own idea | is all that you've been praising]. Sor Juana illustrates her disappointment with a metaphor of strokes and blots of ink: 'Bien así, a la luz de vuestros | panegíricos gallardos, | de mis obscuros borrones | quedan los disformes rasgos' [So it is that, in the light | of your gallant panegyrics, | my obscure blots are left exposed | as paltry deformed traces]. The Baroque chiaroscuro points at the distorting effect of European readings of her oeuvre (Zamora 1995: 139).

The nun tends to use the noun 'borrones' to define her own works, as if they were just unpolished drafts (Glantz 2005: 185). However, the word is polysemic enough to encompass a pictorial meaning, particularly since Sor Juana also used it in the context of drawing.[21] From this viewpoint, the *romance* 51 seems almost a refutation of Horace's *ut pictura poesis* in its literal sense: the greater the distance between onlookers and canvas (i.e. European readership and viceregal poem), the likelier the misinterpretation. Spanish readers appropriate Creoles' achievements as their own, without even being aware of how insufferably self-centred they are. In fact, Sor Juana's lines also reveal scepticism about the ability of language to mean the same across multiple geographies. Her literary output, critically examined through the narrow lens of her gender and place of enunciation, would necessarily be read differently on the other side of the Atlantic. Thus, the nun questions the limits of the Hispanic world as a shared cultural space (Hyman 2017: 120–21).

---

20   Méndez Plancarte (1994a: 158–61). The poem is not dated, although its incompleteness suggests a late composition. I use the English translation by Isabel Gómez (More 2016: 156–59) with minor adjustments.

21   *El divino Narciso* [*The Divine Narcissus*]: 'a ver si dibujan | estos obscuros borrones | la claridad de Sus luces' [let us see | if these blurry smudges of paint | portray the clarity of His lights] (Méndez Plancarte 1994b: 26).

In this sense, Sor Juana's disillusionment is relevant for two reasons. Firstly, because I shall discuss a parallel between Gongorism and the *pintura de borrones*, a pictorial technique 'based on the use of thick brushstrokes' to which she might be alluding here, at the end of Chapter 1.[22] Secondly, and more importantly, because the image testifies that the nun wanted to be read from a 'nonrepressive and nonmanipulative' perspective, as Said (2003: 24) would have put it. While preparing this monograph, I have always had in mind the *romance* 51. Grossi (2007: 15) read this ballad as a call not to trivialise Sor Juana's writings. Indeed, its lesson proves invaluable to early modern Hispanic studies, where viceregal authors are more often read as either sub(versions) of Spain or subversions of empire, rather than as individual creators of un-borrowed visions — which is what they were.

---

22   I borrow the definition from Roe (2016: 283).

PART I

Góngora's *Soledades*:
Ekphrasis Meets Teichoscopy

CHAPTER 1

The Panoramic Landscape
in the *Soledad primera*

Landscape became well established as a genre during the early sixteenth century thanks to painters such as Joachim Patinir (c. 1480–1524), Albrecht Altdorfer (c. 1480–1538) and Herri met de Bles (c. 1510–1550). What had been mere background in earlier paintings ended up swallowing the foreground, to the extent that religious or mythological subjects often dwindled to a pretext (Gombrich 1978: 108). Northern landscapes from Flanders and the Netherlands were admired in Italy, where the genre was developed by the painters Annibale Carracci (1560–1609), Nicolas Poussin (1594–1665) and Claude Lorrain (c. 1600–1682).

In early modern Spain, despite occasional works by Velázquez, landscapes played a secondary role in the output of local painters. Art theorists often snubbed the genre, which they deemed to be inferior. However, these paintings were both commercially successful and highly esteemed.[1] Moreover, the ties between Spain and Flanders, the Netherlands, and Italy enabled importing of landscape paintings into the Iberian peninsula. Knowledge of the genre was also facilitated by print collections, the use of which was extensive among painters (Brown 1991: 5). Thus, there is no doubt that certain Spanish milieus were familiar with the development of landscape art (Huard-Baudry 2012: 145).

Likewise, given that the *locus amoenus* had formed the principal motif of nature descriptions since Greco-Latin antiquity, poetic landscapes were also well known in Spain. These portrayals of the natural world first appeared as background settings in the pastoral works of Theocritus and Virgil. However, they were soon detached from broader contexts and became autonomous rhetorical descriptions (Curtius 1990: 195). Although it is hard to trace a parallel between the development of representations of nature in painting and in poetry (Woods 1978: 19), there is no doubt that landscape descriptions proliferated in the Spanish Golden Age.

In this respect, landscapes are a key feature of the *Soledades* (c. 1613) by Luis de Góngora (1561–1627). The flexible metrical form the poet chose — the *silva* —

---

1   Despite the fact that Butrón (1626: 89ᵛ) is very critical of painters who 'por no alcanzar lo superior del Arte, se abaten a copiar los campos, y sus prados' [rather than reaching the loftiest in Art, limit themselves to copies of fields, and their meadows], Morán and Checa (1985: 241) stress that 'apenas hay coleccionista que no posea varios cuadros de pintura de paisaje' [there is hardly a collector without several landscape paintings].

favoured the proliferation of long, conscious ekphraseis. Blanco (2012a: 129–30) suggests that Góngora's works are highly visual due in part to the incorporation of images from paintings. Although it is hard to ascertain exactly how much the poet knew about the fine arts, he undeniably took a keen interest in them, as evidenced by his ballad *Ilustre ciudad famosa* [*Illustrious Famous City*] (1586), his *décima* [song with ten-line stanzas] *Pintado he visto al Amor* [*I Have Seen Love Painted*] (1607), and his five sonnets about portraits.[2] In addition, Góngora was acquainted with major painters and art theorists of his time such as Velázquez (who even produced a portrait of him), El Greco, Pacheco and Pablo de Céspedes. Moreover, some of his patrons — notably, the Duke of Lerma and the Cardinal Archbishop of Toledo — were prominent art collectors (Huergo 2001: 193). Góngora's interest in art could account for the descriptive talent he displays in the *Soledades*, a poem that underlines its own artificiality by portraying nature as art.

The tension between *naturaleza* [nature] and *artificio* [artfulness], and the emphasis upon the latter, is a defining feature of Baroque culture, as is evidenced in countless early modern works, from Alciato's 1531 emblem IC ('*Ars naturam adiuvans*' [*Art assisting nature*]) to Gracián's *Criticón* (1938: I. 243): 'Es el arte complemento de la naturaleza y un otro segundo ser que por extremo la hermosea y aun pretende excederla en sus obras [...] sin este socorro del artificio, quedara inculta y grosera' [Art complements nature and is a second being that greatly embellishes it and even aims to outdo it in its works [...] without the aid of artfulness, nature would remain rough and crude]. In a literature that exalted authors who could build an artificial cosmos in addition to nature ('Préciase de haber añadido un otro mundo artificial al primero') [He is proud of having added another artful world to the first], it is no coincidence that Góngora's elaborate poetry, with its ambivalent approach to the natural world, would become central (Read 1983: 162–67).

By deploying a language loaded with self-conscious artfulness, Góngora elevated the humble bucolic setting of the *Soledades* to the category of the sublime (Roses 1994: 184). The poem's ekphraseis of nature produced mixed reactions among early readers. On the one hand, Francisco Fernández de Córdoba (the Abbot of Rute), friend and supporter of the poet, and the art theorist Vicente Carducho both praised them for being highly pictorial and rendering the natural world visible and almost tangible to the reader (Artigas 1925: 435; and Carducho 1865: 146). On the other hand, Juan de Jáuregui, Góngora's leading detractor, considered that these descriptions were not worthy of the protagonist's reactions of wonder (Woods 1995: 94).[3] In any case, by defining the pilgrim as an onlooker ('mirón'), Jáuregui involuntarily offered one of the keys to understanding the poem (Joiner Gates 1960: 89 and 96).

---

2   I quote *romance* 22 from Carreño (1982); *décima* 10 from Pezzini (2018); and sonnets 4, 11, 19, 29 and 45 from Ciplijauskaité (1975).

3   'Porque el navegante se asoma a mirar un valle, dice: "Muda la admiración, habla callando". No le queda a Vm. qué decir cuando describa la muerte mísera del Magno Pompeyo o algún espectáculo semejante' (Joiner Gates 1960: 124) [You say: 'Wonder is mute, it speaks by being silent' because the navigator looks at a valley. I wonder what will be left to say when you describe the miserable death of Pompey the Great or a similar spectacle].

Góngora surely had good reasons for choosing such a protagonist. When looking at the surroundings afresh, wanderers create a space for the picturesque that the locals themselves are often incapable of providing. Throughout the poem, seeing and being are presented as the same thing: there is no difference between the 'I' and the 'eye'. The work is not built upon its plot but upon a series of ekphraseis that are linked together by the leading figure of the pilgrim. This was deemed a defect by Jáuregui. However, if today we can read the *Soledades* as a revolutionary experimental *Wunderkammer* of the Baroque, this is because the pilgrim wanders aimlessly around, providing the poet with countless opportunities to digress from the plot and describe an imaginary and verbally sophisticated environment.

In this respect, one of the longest ekphraseis of nature in the *Soledad primera* is that of a river landscape as admired by the pilgrim from a hilltop (lines 182–211). I shall focus on this view because it illustrates better than any other Góngora's use of teichoscopy (etymologically, 'looking out from the wall'), an epic trope which consists of describing a landscape from a high vantage point.[4] I shall argue that the poet employs teichoscopy in order to offer a complete view of an allegoric poetic landscape. My theory is that the vision from above has the purpose of anticipating the route that the pilgrim will follow (namely, a proleptic function), and providing a miniature yet panoramic version of the whole of the *Soledades*, a nutshell expression of its ambition of totality in the depiction of nature (*mise-en-abyme*).

Moreover, I shall explore the ambivalent relationship between teichoscopy and ekphrasis. On the one hand, the vision from a bird's-eye perspective facilitates the depiction of the scenery as a poetic painting in the following five ways: (i) the landscape appears to be surrounded by a 'natural' frame, which is implied by the stillness of the dumbstruck pilgrim; (ii) it is so spectacular that it is admired as if it were a work of art; (iii) it offers highly detailed and stylised scenery, divided into different levels, and limited by a lofty horizon, reminiscent of certain early modern paintings; (iv) it resembles a map, an analogy which strengthens its link with the visual arts; and (v) it enables nature to be appreciated in all its diversity, thus fulfilling the pictorial ideal of *varietà*. On the other hand, I shall argue that there are certain dissonances between teichoscopy and ekphrasis, since Góngora also deploys literary equivalents of three artistic modes (*sfumato*, *estofado* and the illusion of depth) that impede the total vision intended by the epic trope.

Few of the above-mentioned roles and aspects of the passage are immediately apparent on an initial reading. Therefore, the principle of deferred or postponed significance can be of help when trying to come to terms with it. To use Genette's terminology (1980: 76), the ekphrasis is delivered as a seed whose importance will not be discovered until later, retrospectively. This is clearly the case from the viewpoint of narrative discourse, since neither the proleptic nor the *mise-en-abyme* functions can be recognised until the poem has been read in its entirety. Likewise, only after having grasped the influence of various bucolic, epic and pictorial motifs throughout the *Soledades* will one be able to disentangle the complex, paradoxical

---

4   The classic example is *Iliad* III. 146–244, in which Helen of Troy, standing on the walls of the besieged city, describes the Greek heroes she sees on the Trojan plain to king Priam.

interplay between teichoscopy and ekphrasis. These features show that, while interpreting is always an act of creation, this is especially the case when reading the *Soledades*. The poem was designed as an intellectual game that can only be fully understood and enjoyed if one accepts the invitation to embark on a continuous rereading.

Teichoscopy, a Reinforcement of Ekphrasis (I)

After the arrival of the shipwrecked pilgrim in an unknown land, a community of shepherds takes in the protagonist and offers him a frugal meal. Having enjoyed the dinner, and exhausted by the accident-ridden journey, the protagonist goes to sleep. The following morning, a goatherd escorts the guest along a stretch of his route. However, shortly after their departure, the host strays from the path and takes the pilgrim to a hilltop where he will delight in the magnificent view of the surroundings. The passage studied includes lines 182–211 of the *Soledad primera*, which describe the river scenery:[5]

> Agradecido pues el peregrino
> deja el albergue y sale acompañado
> de quien lo lleva donde, levantado,
> distante pocos pasos del camino,
> imperïoso mira la campaña
> un escollo apacible, galería
> que festivo teatro fue algún día
> de cuantos pisan Faunos la montaña.
> Llegó y, a vista tanta
> obedeciendo la dudosa planta,
> inmóvil se quedó sobre un lentisco,
> verde balcón del agradable risco.
> Si mucho poco mapa les despliega,
> mucho es más lo que (nieblas desatando)
> confunde el Sol y la distancia niega.
> Muda la admiración habla callando,
> y ciega un río sigue, que, luciente
> de aquellos montes hijo,
> con torcido discurso, aunque prolijo,
> tiraniza los campos útilmente:
> orladas sus orillas de frutales,
> quiere la Copia que su cuerno sea,
> si al animal armaron de Amaltea
> diáfanos cristales;
> engazando edificios en su plata,
> de muros se corona,
> rocas abraza, islas aprisiona,
> de la alta gruta donde se desata
> hasta los jaspes líquidos, adonde
> su orgullo pierde y su memoria esconde.

5   All quotations from the poem follow the edition by Jammes (2001) and the English translation by Edith Grossman (Góngora 2012: 18–21).

[And so, filled with gratitude, the pilgrim
leaves the refuge and goes out accompanied
by one who leads him to the place where, lofty,
distant but a few paces from the path,
imperious, gazing at the countryside,
rises a ridge, peaceable gallery
that long ago a rollicking theatre was
for every faun that once dwelled on the mountain.
There he arrived, and his hesitant foot,
obedient to the sight of that expanse,
remained unmoving on a mastic tree,
green balcony to the pleasant crest of reef.
If this small map unfolds so much to them,
much more, clouds of mist lifting, lies beyond,
confounded by sun and by distance denied.
Wonder is mute, it speaks by being silent,
and, blind, it follows a river, that — shining
child of those precipices —
in convoluted discourse, and digressive,
benevolent it tyrannizes the fields;
with its banks ornamented by fruit trees,
Copia herself desires it for her horn
– if the creature of Amalthea had been armed
with crystal transparency –;
setting edifices in its silver,
crowning itself with walls,
it embraces rocks, imprisons islands,
from the high grotto where it first breaks free
to the opaque jasper waters deep where
pride is lost and memory hides away.]

Though central to key episodes in ancient Greek (*Iliad*), Roman (*Aeneid*, *Thebaid*, *Argonautica*), medieval (*Alexandreis*) and even early modern epic poetry (*Gerusalemme liberata*), teichoscopy is, in a certain sense, at the margins of epic. By often portraying women who watch from afar their beloved at war, the trope tends towards the tragedy or even the elegy (Lovatt 2013: 6). This hybrid potential could have attracted Góngora, since the *Soledades* — like the *Polifemo* — is halfway between genres. However, there are different ways of viewing from above. The perspective of civilians from walls or towers of besieged cities is different from that of the protagonist of the *Soledades*. The pilgrim has neither battles nor armies to observe but simply a landscape. Góngora takes the trope from a tradition that, while recognising the suffering that wars cause, also exalts them as a site where heroes excel in bravery, self-reliance and steadiness. In Greco-Latin epics, teichoscopy serves a number of positive functions. For instance, it may fulfil a choreographic role, as movements of troops are often portrayed as if they were beautiful dances. Teichoscopy may also operate as a poetic 'archive', since the characters seen from above are named and thus their martial deeds preserved for posterity. From an aesthetic and historical viewpoint, teichoscopy is a way of presenting wars as an image of cosmic order.

This *Weltanschauung* is at odds with the *Soledades*, where peace is praised as the most fitting state for human creativity (Blanco 2012b: 71–83). The pilgrim, standing with the goatherd on a hilltop, looks down at a placid, panoramic landscape. The vision from that height (teichoscopy) enables the poet to describe the setting as if it were a poetic painting (ekphrasis) by five different means. The first of them is a parergon: the implied natural frame suggested by the stillness of the protagonist. Ekphraseis tend to begin with a description of an element that frames the landscape. Reality is not framed; art often is. By isolating a scene from its surroundings, the frame focuses the eye of the beholder, turning a landscape into a work of art (Pineda 2000: 259). Frames, like windows, evoke an attitude of contemplation. Thus, it is not a coincidence that windows are one of the most common frames of ekphraseis. From a high viewpoint, the eye can sweep uninterruptedly from left to right in a vast, continuous landscape. A window helps to determine the scope and boundaries of a potentially limitless view. Their ubiquity in landscape art suggests how enduring the tradition of framing is for seeing nature in a clear-cut rectangular section (Andrews 1999: 111–22).

There are no windows in the passage transcribed. However, a much subtler form of frame is provided by the protagonist's own stillness. Indeed, the ekphrasis contains not only an elaborate description of the staffage (i.e. the accessory items of the landscape, such as trees or buildings) but also an exploration of a spectator facing the scene and reacting to it in amazement. The strength of the pilgrim's impression is suggested by the lines 'obedeciendo la dudosa planta, | inmóvil se quedó sobre un lentisco', which indicate that the experience has a physical impact.[6] This point emerges even more strongly a few lines later, when Góngora portrays him as dumbstruck: 'Muda la admiración habla callando, | y ciega un río sigue, que, luciente'. Wonder is expressed in the double oxymoron of silent speech and blind vision (Hunt 1988: 252). Considered as a mere topos of praise regarding the beauty of the landscape, four lines about the pilgrim's static awe would perhaps be excessive, as they postpone the actual description of the scenery. Nevertheless, there might have been a strong reason for such emphasis. Early modern texts advising painters highlighted the convenience of choosing a landscape that could be depicted without its spectators having to turn their heads. Ignoring this rigid restriction would involve awkwardly expanding the focus of the work, misplacing its centre of attention (Andrews 1999: 114). Indeed, when we look at a scene as if it were framed, suddenly the view becomes organised, and form reigns where previously there stood only the 'formlessness' of spatial continuity (Lefebvre 2006b: xv). Thus, the static position of the pilgrim enables him to avoid this risk by naturally framing the landscape within the boundaries of his view. Being invisible but present, the concept of 'frame' is deconstructed by Góngora. Although it is arguably there, a mere turn of head would make its fragile boundaries disappear.

---

6   Serrano de Paz (1673a: 217^v): 'así también los pies, que seguían a los ojos, se quedaron inmóviles, y con el mismo pasmo, dudosos, de que pudiesen admirar cuanto se descubría' [while his feet, which followed his eyes, also remained motionless, with the same astonishment, doubting that they could admire all that was discovered].

Furthermore, the epic trope of teichoscopy is approached pictorially because the poet brings it into the field of the pastoral. Since the eclogues of Garcilaso (a key model for Góngora), Golden Age bucolic poetry tended to stylise and beautify nature, distancing it from its referents in the real world (Friedman 2002: 56). Hence, the attitude of the characters vis-à-vis the landscape. Unlike the heroes of his epic forerunners, who always have a practical purpose when looking from a high vantage point — either to inform themselves about the troops involved in a battle (*Iliad* III. 146–244; *Thebaid* VII. 243–373; *Gerusalemme liberata* III. stanzas 9–40) or to deliver a speech (*Alexandreis* II. 325–71) — the goatherd of the *Soledad primera* takes the pilgrim to the cliff in order to enjoy a good view. This intention marks a difference between the epic and the bucolic genres, given that *otium*, including leisurely activities such as the contemplation of nature, is often the main endeavour of the poetic world of shepherds when they are not lamenting unrequited love (Poggioli 1975: 6). Hospitality is one of the highest pastoral duties, and in the *Soledades* it seems to include not only physical but also immaterial goods, such as the delight that viewing a landscape can inspire. Moreover, the goatherd draws the pilgrim's attention to the heroic past of the ruined fortifications that can be faintly discerned from the hilltop (Padrón 2007: 380). His speech (lines 212–21) casts the scene in a historical/mythic perspective, thereby emphasising the importance of the landscape.

The protagonist makes the most of the occasion. As reflected in the long description, he arguably intends to preserve in his memory the vision of a land to which he shall never return after the pilgrimage. Each element of the landscape seems to be harmoniously placed for his enjoyment, as if it were a tapestry. In this sense, the shores of the river are described as 'orladas' with fruit trees, a word which is often used for elaborate decoration at the edges of fabrics. Nature, the object of admiration, provokes such an extreme reaction that, for a long time, there is neither further action nor dialogue between the pilgrim and the goatherd. Due to its beauty, the scenery is appreciated for its own sake.

The impact of the landscape is the result of teichoscopy, for this trope enables Góngora to arrange the staffage in a highly pictorial manner. This is the third way by which the gaze from above reinforces the ekphrastic components of the landscape. We should bear in mind that the panoramic view from a cliff is a recurrent device in landscape art. For instance, the works of Patinir would offer vast panoramas seen from sheer rocky outcrops. An encyclopaedic profusion of detail, a tendency towards stylisation, and elevated horizons were often their defining features (Sutton 1987: 16). In this respect, Góngora might have been familiar with Patinir's *Landscape with Saint Jerome* (Figure 1.1), for the painting was kept at El Escorial during his lifetime (Huergo 2001: 226–27).

Perhaps emulating the Flemish painter, Góngora describes a bird's-eye view of the landscape whose numerous elements are naturalistic only in isolation, since the overall effect is somewhat stylised. Besides, unlike other passages of the *Soledad primera* (for instance, lines 602–11), the ekphrasis does not include any reference whatsoever to the sky, an aspect which could enable the reader to imagine a broad

FIG. 1.1. Joachim Patinir, *Landscape with Saint Jerome* (1516–1517),
© Museo Nacional del Prado, Madrid.

landscape with a lofty horizon like those of Patinir. In this sense, a recurrent interest of early modern painters was in organising vast portions of land into different levels. In Renaissance and Baroque paintings, the foreground, middle ground and background were often arranged as a series of layers linked together by diagonal lines, usually those of a path or river that would guide the beholder through the different levels of the landscape (Rossholm 1990: 20; Blanco 1996: 271). The painter Pacheco (1956: II. 127), for instance, hinted at how to create a complex interplay of spatial relationships by dividing the canvas into 'tres, o cuatro, distancias, o suelos' [three, or four, distances, or levels].

Góngora shared this fascination with his contemporaries. A river is precisely the element that draws the pilgrim's attention from the foreground to the background of the scene. Hence, the comparison: just as blind people follow sighted guides, so too the 'admiración [...] ciega un río sigue' (Salcedo Coronel 1636: 53^v). The stream enables the poet to divide the landscape into four levels, as suggested by Pacheco: (i) the cliff on which the protagonist and the goatherd stand; (ii) the mountains where the torrent originates; (iii) the plains with rural buildings and fields irrigated by the stream; and (iv) the mouth of the river.

By tracing the river from the mainland to the coast, Góngora anticipates the twofold itinerary that the pilgrim will follow and whose parts were entitled precisely 'La soledad de los campos' [The Solitude of the Fields] and 'La soledad de las riberas' [The Solitude of the Shore], according to an early commentator (Díaz de Rivas 1624: 105^r). The poet emphasises the geographical obstacles that the protagonist will face in his pilgrimage so that the reader can appreciate the geographical dimension of the quest (Serrano de Paz 1673a: 214^v). Furthermore, the meanders of the river ('con torcido discurso, aunque prolijo') subtly announce the winding itinerary of the pilgrim. Thus, the match between teichoscopy and ekphrasis fulfils a proleptic function, preparing the reader for the action to follow. One might have the feeling that something important will occur in this landscape. In fact, all the action of the *Soledades* will take place within its boundaries (Blanco 2012b: 270–71). The landscape is both the scenery and an allusive guide (that is, a chart) of the future events of the entire poem.

Since, when describing the view, Góngora mentions the word 'map' ('Si mucho poco mapa les despliega'), it seems clear that he wanted to trace parallels between the levels of the landscape, paintings and cartography. This is the fourth way in which teichoscopy reinforces the link between the poetic description and the visual arts. Despite our tendency to think of landscapes as art and maps as science, the works of the landscapist and the cartographer were intimately related. In fact, the distinction was not firm in early modernity, as maps were deemed a kind of picture and paintings a fount of knowledge. Moreover, many artists also engaged in map-making. The term *descriptio* was often used to designate charts. Cartographers were referred to as 'world describers'. The same expression could have been applied to landscape artists, as their aim was also to represent, on a surface, a wide range of information about the earth. Cartographers portrayed elements such as mountains, rivers and villages in an artistic manner. Sometimes they even included horizons in their charts (Alpers 1983: 122–28). Thus, maps had a remarkable pictorial aspect. This common ground makes Góngora's comparison plausible (Jammes 2001: I. 238). As visual sources of knowledge, both landscapes and maps enrich our understanding of the world and widen our horizons when showing lands that we do not know (Andrews 1999: 77–82).

These ideas are partially synthesised in the line 'imperïoso mira la campaña' which, though referring to the cliff itself, also captures the masterful view of the beholder who is eager to absorb all the visual information available. The vantage point of the pilgrim is so elevated that the territory seems to become a flat surface. In this sense, the passage contains a latent paradox that almost exceeds the limits of verbal logic. On the one hand, the scenery is described as 'poco mapa' because it can be appreciated at a glance and easily framed within the boundaries of his view. On the other, it also 'mucho [...] les despliega', for it apparently enables the pilgrim to see a vast territory as if it were represented in a map (Blanco 2012b: 272–73).

In Borges' literary forgery *Del rigor en la ciencia* [*On Rigour in Science*] (1989: I. 847), cartographers create 'un Mapa del Imperio, que tenía el tamaño del Imperio y coincidía puntualmente con él' [a Map of the Empire, which was the size of the

Empire and matched it exactly]. Paraphrasing Korzybski's maxim ('The map is not the territory'), Borges seemed to realise that words are not what they name and names are not what they represent. There is a certain vanity in the idea that a chart can fully picture (i.e. understand) the world. Crafting a rigorous map does not imply transcribing all available information in order to replicate reality: such a chart would be as useless as that of Borges' parable. Equally ironically, Góngora blurs the distinction between the map and the territory by defining his poetic landscape as 'poco mapa'. The scenery becomes at once a landscape (literally) and its own map (figuratively), i.e. a 'mapscape'. It is thus no wonder that 'mucho [...] les despliega', for the landscape is more than its representation: the map is the actual real world.[7]

Epics have tried to emulate maps on countless occasions. Let us recall, for instance, the *Libro de Alexandre* (lines 276–94), *Os Lusíadas* (Canto X) of Camões and *La Araucana* (Second part, Canto XXVII) of Ercilla. However, in these examples, literary maps were used to convey the feeling of being monarchs of vast territories. They were the embodiment of discourses on conquest and empire, for charts can provide us with a sense of power, from which there evolves a metaphorical vocabulary of dominion (Andrews 1999: 77). Góngora, poetically speaking, was not interested in political borders. His is a purely physical cartography of a segment of the earth that, paradoxically, cannot be verified anywhere in particular. Its elements being so universal (e.g. cliff, tree, river, fields),[8] the landscape could be interpreted as an attempt to transgress the inevitable partiality of human perception by offering an abbreviated world, which is precisely what a map is (Serrano de Paz 1673a: 220[r]).

In the Baroque period, this cartographic view of the globe goes hand in hand with allegory: the map — the world — is both a vision and guide to a symbolic system (Ciocchini 1960: 55). Thus, Góngora's 'mapscape' could conceivably represent his ambition to account for the vast, almost infinite natural world in the finite form of the *Soledades*. The audience may also read into the trajectory of the river a metaphor for Góngora's poetic endeavour, which originates in the dark grotto of the imagination and pours onto the page, where the literary map becomes a visual spectacle for public delectation (Padrón 2007: 392). Like the waterway ('con torcido discurso, aunque prolijo'), the *Soledades* advances in a roundabout manner, through layers of embedded conceits, clauses, paradoxes and metaphors, which form 'rocas' and 'islas' in the poetic stream — attractive, but bewildering focal points for readers to wrap their minds around (Collins 2002a: 93).[9]

Like the shield of Achilles (*Iliad*, XVIII. 478–608), which covers cities and countryside, peace and war (even including a scaled-down Trojan War), Góngora's

7   This paragraph is indebted to Bosteels' (1998: 145–74) discussion of maps.
8   Interestingly, these elements had already appeared, almost in the same order, in the above-mentioned twelfth-century epic by Walter of Châtillon (2007: 61–62). The reminiscence of pagan gods is also similarly present in both cases, an aspect which reinforces the possibility that the *Alexandreis* could be one of the sources of the passage.
9   An earlier version of the passage compared the islands of the river to the use of parentheses in written discourses, and its meanders to a legal process full of twists and turns. However, Góngora deleted these analogies following the advice of his friend Pedro de Valencia (Alonso 1955: 305–07).

Fig. 1.2. Jan van Eyck, *Portrait of Giovanni (?) Arnolfini and his Wife* (1434),
© The National Gallery, London.

landscape is not just a frame for the action, but also a microcosm of the entire work. In this sense, the ekphrasis can be understood as a self-reflexive embedding of the whole of the poem (*mise-en-abyme*). This device has often been deployed in the visual arts: a picture appearing on a smaller scale within itself. See, for instance, Jan van Eyck's *The Arnolfini Portrait*, where a convex mirror duplicates — from the back — the figures of the couple portrayed. If the *Soledades* is understood as a poetic *Wunderkammer* of rural views, then the panoramic landscape would be the summa that includes them all.[10] Indeed, in subsequent descriptions in the poem, Góngora will always zoom in on elements previously seen by the pilgrim from the cliff.

The aim of exploring natural life in all its exuberance and variety is also highly pictorial, and in fact became a mark of the celebrated Venetian school of painting. In this respect, with his emphasis on the manifold, Góngora seems to align the aesthetics of his work with the artistic ideal of *varietà* (Vitagliano 2013: 22–23). This is the fifth and last reason to explain, from an ekphrastic viewpoint, the need to see the landscape from above: the greater the height of the vantage point, the more expansive and diverse the portion of earth that can be captured.[11] The poet's goal also becomes evident from his tendency towards compilation. In fact, in the *Polifemo* and the *Soledades* alone, Góngora offered a depiction of the earth's life with no fewer than seventy-eight animal and forty plant species. Given Baroque culture's predilection for symbols, such an abundance could indicate a deeper significance beyond mere scenic decoration. In the absence of a clear-cut plot, the process of the enumeration of matter that continues throughout the *Soledades* appears central to its comprehension. If nature is understood as a synonym for the cosmos (i.e. the world order that frames human life), then the contemplation of a landscape may be deemed an attempt to capture the all-encompassing Whole or *Gestalt* in one of its parts (Ritter 1978: 10). The poem could thus be read as an attempt to arrive at a *Totalperspektive*, a complete vision of the world such as that iconically represented by the protagonist on the hilltop (Kluge 2002: 166–69, and 2010: 152).

Nonetheless, although teichoscopy captivates the senses through its potential to capture the infinite in the finite, and through its apparently harmonious reinforce-ment of ekphrasis, there are also tensions between the two poles. Góngora's typically Baroque attitude towards teichoscopy becomes manifest in the obstacles faced by the protagonist. Unlike his Greco-Latin models, and notably unlike his own *Polifemo*,[12] the *Soledades* deliberately raises barriers to a full view of the world (Blanco 2012b: 274). Paradoxically, these are also the consequence of Góngora's

10   Marcaida (2014: 66): 'En un plano simbólico, por tanto, las *Kunst- und Wunderkammern* del Renacimiento podrían ser interpretadas como un intento de recreación del mundo a través de la recopilación y el reordenamiento de sus partes más significativas' [Thus, on a symbolic level, the *Kunst- und Wunderkammern* of the late Renaissance could be interpreted as an attempt to recreate the world through the compilation and rearrangement of its most significant parts].

11   Variety is also crucial to Gracián's conceptualisation of wit (2001: I. 49): 'variedad, gran madre de la belleza' [variety, great mother of beauty].

12   Ponce Cárdenas (2010: 211): 'Polifemo se vincula también a [...] la portentosa capacidad visiva del ojo gigantesco que luce en su frente' [Polyphemus is also linked to [...] the portentous visual capacity of the giant eye on his forehead]. The Cyclops has such good sight that he can even perceive, from Sicily, the shields' engravings of soldiers in Libya (stanza LXI).

ekphrastic approach. The panoramic view will become a relatively unsatisfactory experience, at least from an epistemological viewpoint. This is certainly a limitation, though it can also be cast in a positive light by means of Panofsky's notion of *Idea* (1968). In any case, the polarity between vision and blindness, a feature central not only to the landscape studied but also to the *Soledades* as a whole, shows that Góngora's landscape is neither a superfluous rhetorical exercise nor an addition for the sake of variation. A full understanding of its multi-layered nature is necessary if the poem is to present its deepest meaning consistently.

Ekphrasis, an Obstacle to Teichoscopy?

After the allusion to the map in line 194, and before describing the landscape, Góngora provides the reader with information regarding the limitations of vision: 'mucho es más lo que (nieblas desatando) | confunde el Sol y la distancia niega'. These lines are thought-provoking for two reasons. In the bucolic tradition, pastoral lands are blessed with a pleasant, immutable weather (Poggioli 1975: 6). As the sudden appearance of the fog here shows, this is clearly not the case in the *Soledades*, where atmospheric conditions vary and will even become hostile at some points in the second part. Furthermore, being placed between the reference to the map and the landscape, the lines quash the trope of the scenery being a 'mapscape', i.e. one thing and another at the same time. If the weather is not favourable, people standing on a cliff will not see the entire scenery that a chart reveals. In fact, they might see very little, or perhaps even nothing at all, no matter how high their vantage point may be. The two lines transcribed highlight the presence of three obstacles to teichoscopy: the fog, the sun and distance. In addition, there is a fourth impediment that will become apparent a few lines later: the blinding brightness of the landscape's staffage. In order to understand these features of the *Soledades*, we should take into account that, when crafting many of his ekphraseis, the poet seems to have had in mind not only the main pictorial genres of his time but also various artistic techniques (Buxó 2004b: 33).[13] This might be the case here, since Góngora arguably deploys literary equivalents of three painting modes (*sfumato*, *estofado* and the illusion of depth) in order to portray conditions that obscure vision.

Before analysing the fog, it is worth noting that one of the most uniquely descriptive aspects of the *Soledades* is the effort to represent not just objects but also purely visual phenomena, from the flow of a stream to the silhouette of birds flying in the sky (Blanco 1996: 273). Moreover, when describing nature, Góngora is fond of showing — but not completely — and of hiding — but not in full (Huergo 2001: 227). Thus, it is understandable that he felt attracted by the way mist covers a landscape in the morning, since this visual phenomenon gave him the means to deliver an illusion of partial concealment. Consciously or not, when choosing this feature, Góngora managed to represent his own style symbolically. Indeed, from a linguistic — and even, before his allusions and conceits are understood, intellectual

---

13   Occasionally, this is even made explicit in the text: 'pintadas siempre al fresco' [ever painted al fresco] (*Soledad primera*, line 613) (Góngora 2012: 48–49).

— viewpoint, his is often an aesthetics of bewilderment. On a visual note, fog often makes a landscape more engaging: when contemplating a painting, uncertainty entrances the receptive beholder who appreciates the challenge of trying to decipher what exactly is being represented. In this case, the mist arguably enables the reader to imagine a landscape with a blurred horizon and uncertain forms, an effect which will be emphasised by the sunlight at dawn.

Throughout the *Soledades*, Góngora displays a fascination with how different forms of light behave and reflect off surfaces, a phenomenon that concerned Venetian as well as Flemish oil painters (Vitagliano 2013: 930). This penchant is especially noticeable in the passage studied, in which morning sunbeams generate mist and swathe a river valley in haze (Collins 2002b: 93–94). Furthermore, in the same way that early modern painters strove for the best pictorial representation of reflected lights (Barasch 1978: 63), Góngora enriches the scene by adding sparkling reflections of colours between the sun and the river, which had been previously presented as 'luciente' because it is bathed in sunlight.

In Renaissance art theory, light was particularly revered because it makes the world visible, and thus subject to being enshrined on canvas (Barasch 1978: 16). Paradoxically, but in a rather Baroque manner, Góngora converts light into an actual obstacle to the total vision sought by the pilgrim. The sun, instead of clarifying the atmosphere, makes it even denser and more hazy by fusing together different landscape components ('confunde el Sol'), spreading the fog ('nieblas desatando') and blinding the viewer (Blanco 2012b: 276).[14] According to Padrón (2007: 380), who sees this passage as a challenge to the conjunction of cartography, geographic knowledge and imperialism, the 'glare of the sun in the dissolving mists [...] denies the pilgrim the optical clarity typical of cartography's claims for itself'. The adjective ('ciega') is particularly suggestive in this respect. By combining it with the metonymic 'la admiración' to refer to the amazed onlooker (Woods 1995: 60), Góngora could be pointing to the fact that the pilgrim is almost blinded by the sun and its reflections. Likewise, the impact of sunlight on the mist blurs the contours of the landscape even more for the reader, potentially achieving a result in the mind's eye comparable to that of paintings which are depicted with the *sfumato* technique — that is, the blurring of borders between colours so that tone transitions become almost imperceptible (Hall 1992: 94).[15]

The blinding effect of sunlight is emphasised by the comparison of the components that make up the landscape with precious stones ('jaspes líquidos'), crystals ('diáfanos cristales') and silver ('en su plata'), since these metaphors strengthen the brightness of its colours. As highlighted by Blanco (2012b: 275), Góngora's shining lexicon could be echoing that of Homer (*Iliad*, XIV. 178–86). Even clearer is the influence on him of the Petrarchan tradition, in which a set of terms that belong

---

14   Salcedo Coronel (1636: 53^r) offers a natural explanation of this phenomenon: 'Cuando sale el sol, se levantan de los ríos y lagunas ciertos vapores, y de la tierra asimismo, que confunden mucha parte de ella' [When the sun rises, certain vapors rise up from the rivers, and the lagoons, and from the earth as well, which confuse much of it].

15   The classic example of a hazy landscape produced by *sfumato* is Leonardo da Vinci's *Mona Lisa* (1503–1506). This technique reduces the level of detail in the painting.

to a few lexical families (e.g. precious metals, luxurious textiles, delicate flowers) encloses a whole universe of allusions, the direct reference of which is deliberately omitted (Ponce Cárdenas 2010: 113). Instead of simply enumerating each visible detail that might appear in a realistic painting, Góngora deploys a code of carefully chosen terms exclusively formed by valued objects. However, far from falling into stereotypes, he revises this poetic convention according to his own aesthetic agenda. In this sense, the point of evoking a flow of dazzling images may be threefold.

Firstly, by associating the landscape with these emblematic images, Góngora elevates the allure of nature to an ideal realm. This procedure is similar to that often used by Petrarch and many of his followers, such as Garcilaso, who tended to link their descriptions of female beauty to a higher form of being (Bergmann 1979: 240). In the passage studied, there is a special emphasis on shining elements that, although originally produced by the natural world, are ordered and embellished by human activities ('engazando edificios en su plata'). Thus, by choosing this kind of feature, Góngora seems to be tacitly conceding that man is capable of aesthetically improving a landscape through artfulness.

Secondly, the poet's metaphors of shining (e.g. the word 'plata' for stream) also contribute to bring the ekphrasis closer to the pictorial tradition, for they could be compared, *mutatis mutandis*, to the *estofado* technique that was typical of the Gothic period but still used in early modern Spanish art. This method — usually associated with polychrome sculpture — consisted of layering a gesso base of gold or silver leaf, overlaying it once dried with oil paint, and finally scratching away the paint in the desired pattern to reveal the precious metal underneath (Pacheco 1956: II. 119–24). Similarly, in the *Soledades*, a silvery stream is the element that, by wetting the fields and fruit trees, nourishes the landscape in the same way that the leaf sustains the paint of a canvas after the *estofado* or silver-gilding.

Thirdly, metaphors of sparkling objects may suggest that the protagonist is making connections between features of the scenery and the most valued objects of the Court he left (e.g. precious metals). The pilgrim keeps his thoughts simultaneously fixed on items from two moments in time so that their respective features are finally merged in his mind. In this sense, the river is firstly described as 'diáfanos cristales' and then as 'plata', words which reinforce the effect of artificial luminosity produced by objects from the Court. Its stream goes 'engazando edificios', as if it were threading jewels on a string, and then 'de muros se corona', because the walls it surrounds end up looking like crowns from above.[16] The impression is further emphasised by the semi-precious stones with which the poet identifies the sea ('jaspes líquidos'). It is thus no wonder that the pilgrim is blinded by this myriad of lights and colours from his past and present.

The dazzling effect caused by these landscape components is emphasised by the breadth and reach of the view: distance is the fourth and last element that hinders

16   Salcedo Coronel (1636: 55ᵛ): 'Engazar, decimos, aquel trabar, o ensartar las cuentas con hilos de plata, oro, o alambre [...] Dijo, que se coronaba de muros, porque rodeándolos, quedaban en forma de corona, en medio de sus aguas' [*Engazar*, we say, to mean to thread beads on a string of silver, gold or wire [...] He said that the walls crowned the river because, by being surrounded by it, they take the form of a crown, in the middle of its waters].

the pilgrim's perception. Unlike Flemish landscapes, which would typically depict all details of the canvas, no matter how near or far, with the same miniaturist's accuracy, the scenery cannot be appreciated in its entirety due to the considerable space between the observer and what is observed. In this sense, Góngora shared the early modern fascination with depth, an artistic illusion that painters were better equipped to produce after the Renaissance 'discovery, rediscovery, or invention' of geometric perspective (Jay 1988: 5).[17] Like art, poetry can trigger an illusion of spatial form. Distance is indispensable in landscape descriptions because it allows objects to be consistently grouped in the mind's eye. Not only does Góngora's ekphrasis attain this aesthetic goal, but it also shows an incipient interest in the confusing effects of distance on the eye (Woods 1978: 121). From this viewpoint, the description is more realistic than contemporary Flemish landscapes. Just three words ('la distancia niega') are enough to stress that the magnitude of the space impedes a complete view.

All the obstacles point to the same idea: the actual content of the landscape is uncertain, and this is the reason why it defies adequate description. In the prologue to *Elogio de la sombra* [*In Praise of Shadows*], Borges dismisses the notion of certitude in fiction arguing that it is much more convenient to 'simular pequeñas incertidumbres [...] narrar los hechos [...] como si no los entendiera del todo' [feign small uncertainties [...] narrate the facts [...] as if I did not understand them completely] (1989: I. 975). The same approach can be adopted with landscapes, since painting or describing them requires a certain blindness, a partial refusal to be aware of all the options. An artist will intuit more about what he is representing than he will see, and in the space between sensing and seeing, he will tenaciously pursue an Idea.

In the context of the *Soledades*, the gulf between the view that the protagonist could potentially enjoy and his limited actual perception is paradoxical. Although the land extends widely ('Si mucho poco mapa les despliega'), the sun and its reflections, the fog diffused by it, and the distance hide much more ('mucho es más lo que (nieblas desatando) | confunde el Sol y la distancia niega'). These lines summarise the key contradiction of the passage. On the one hand, teichoscopy reinforces ekphrasis, for it is in great part thanks to the view from above that the landscape can be presented as a work of art. On the other, ekphrasis hinders teichoscopy, since various pictorial features of the scenery constitute obstacles to the *Totalperspektive* that is fundamental to the epic trope.

This paradox can serve to apply Gracián's conceptualisation of wit to the passage studied and to understand the attitude that Góngora expected from his readers. According to Gracián (2001a: I. 79), Góngora was 'en toda especie de agudeza eminente' [versed in all kinds of conceit]. In this respect, the essential type of wit offered by the landscape appears to be an *agudeza paradoja* [paradox conceit]: there is a paradox in being on a hilltop from which one can barely see, but that stimulates

17   All three terms are used depending on how one interprets previous visual knowledge. The other discoveries, perhaps more important, were shading and chiaroscuro, referred to in Garcilaso's description of the tapestries in his third eclogue (Sánchez de las Brozas 1600: 67[r]).

another kind of view. In this sense, Gracián's famous praise of the Cordovan author as an 'águila en los conceptos' [eagle of conceits] could be taken literally (an eagle, by connotation, combines height and sharpness of vision) in order to argue that, in the *Soledades*, the landscape seen from a bird's-eye perspective is a conceit: an end (of clear sensory input) yet a beginning (of a mental process that culminates in a pristine visualisation). The ekphrasis cannot only be read as a mapscape, but also as a mindscape, that is, an inner vision.

Furthermore, Góngora's proclivity to slow things down — often so much that they come to a standstill, as in the lines at hand — may give some hints as to the ideal readership that the poet had in mind. The above-mentioned conceit shows that there is much more to Góngora's work than lingering over the details of nature. Throughout the *Soledades*, and especially here, the poet seems subtly to convey to the reader the adage of *festina lente* [make haste slowly]. Given that halting at the sight of a landscape corresponds to a contemplative pause for the pilgrim himself, the ekphrasis does not entail any break in the narrative but is simply absorbed into it, protracting the rhythm of the poem. In accordance with this pace of narration, Góngora seems to expect his audience to take all the time required and pay complete attention to unravelling the thread of conceits. Their brilliance, variety and abundance are striking. In fact, they arguably bring the reader certain vicarious pleasure by the evocation of living nature. By generating a sense of amazement comparable to that experienced by the pilgrim, wit can potentially enhance the emotional unity between them (Woods 1995: 115–16).[18]

This bond is important because, without it, the passage could be regarded as something of an oddity. Since their beginnings in the paintings of early modern Europe, landscapes have provided artists with a site for personal expression in the exploration of the experimental side of the genre (Rossholm 1990: 69–71). Similarly, Góngora uses nature descriptions for his boldest innovations. The poet progresses as he digresses. What he writes 'off topic' is where the real significance of the poem lies. Although written in the context of psychoanalysis, Phillips' (2006: xi) central contention that 'digression is secular revelation' fits the Baroque poet like a glove. Landscape is crucial in the *Soledades* because it provides the site for the encounter between ekphrasis and teichoscopy. The clash between these two poles will be fertile both within the narrative (for the pilgrim) and outside it (for the reader).

For the pilgrim, low visibility serves as a major stimulant. In fact, the passage is less a description of the landscape than an analysis of his own perceptual and mental activity: the impact of his first impression, the awareness of the obstacles to his view, and finally his inner voyage of discovery. His contemplation contains an entire intra-story, which is what Góngora recounts. Should there be any doubts as to whether the poet was interested in the faithful portrayal of a real landscape or not, these few lines quash them completely. The features the pilgrim glimpses are little more than mere schemata that serve as a springboard for his fantasy. Given the impossibility of enjoying a panoramic view, almost everything contained in the landscape appears to be not in nature but in the pilgrim's imagination

---

18   This paragraph is indebted to Genette (1980: 100–05).

(Guillén 1998: 119–20). Like Góngora's renowned song *Qué de envidiosos montes levantados* [*What Envious Lofty Mountains*] (1600), the *Soledades* describes the process of seeing with the mind's eye as if it consisted of direct visual observation (Woods 1995: 86–87).[19] This fiction contributes significantly to the artistic impression given by the lines, since the pilgrim's fantasy depicts the vision as that of a painter who conceives a work of art before actually executing it (i.e. a *disegno interno* or inner design, in the words of Zuccaro 1768: 8–10).

This approach alters the significance of Góngora's teichoscopy when compared to its epic predecessors. After the intrusion of the obstacles, the *Totalperspektive* traditionally granted by the trope is not possible anymore: to provide a complete vision, teichoscopy must become an act of creative introspection, the opposite of the word's etymological meaning — no longer a looking-out from above, but a looking inside of oneself. As pointed out by Panofsky (1968), who traces the evolution of the concept from Plato to early modern art theorists and Neoplatonic philosophers, the notion of an Idea that appears in the mind's eye of the painter is a constant in art history. Whether it would be present *a priori* in the mind of the artist or brought forth by him *a posteriori* (whether it precedes or is a consequence of experience) has been the subject of several theories. In the *Soledades*, the latter case seems to reflect that of the pilgrim; the sum and selection (that is, the purification) of his former sensory and intellectual experiences could have been transformed into a mental image of an ideal landscape: natural beauty in the highest form possible, including the *artificio* of human intervention.

As if he were following the advice of Pacheco, and given the lack of clear visual input, the pilgrim resorts to the Idea that he had previously developed, creating a microcosm that mirrors — and embellishes, since nature is landscaped/mapped, i.e. rinsed through the sieve of culture — his natural and humanistic macrocosm.[20] This could be the reason for the dazzling, idealised beauty of the landscape portrayed. Language not only describes reality: it alters the way we perceive it. Góngora focuses on the pilgrim's mental process as a challenging improvement on nature, rather than as a futile imitation of it. The elevation of reality above earthly experience can be read as an example of the paradigmatic artistic endeavour to

19   'Grandemente y sin imitación ha logrado esta pintura con las mayores alusiones que pudo formar la Idea de Don Luis' [He has achieved this painting greatly and without imitation, with the greatest allusions that Góngora's Idea could form] (Pellicer 1630: 404). Lines 251–52 of the *Polifemo* are also relevant in this respect: 'ni lo ha visto, si bien pincel süave | lo ha bosquejado ya en su fantasía' [Galatea has not seen Acis, but a soft brush | has already sketched him in her fantasy] (Ponce Cárdenas 2010: 165). I devoted an article — Castellví Laukamp (2015a) — to the pictorial dimension of this poem.

20   Pacheco (1956: I. 250): 'con los preceptos y la buena y hermosa manera viene bien el juicio y elección de las bellísimas obras de Dios y de la Naturaleza [...] Y cuando esto faltare, o no se hallare con la belleza que conviene [...] viene admirablemente el valerse de las hermosas ideas, que tiene adquiridas el valiente artífice [...] De manera que la perfección consiste en pasar de las Ideas a lo natural, y de lo natural a las Ideas' [with precepts and with good and beautiful manner comes the judgment and choice of the wonderful works of God and Nature [...] And when this is lacking, or one does not find the required beauty [...] it is convenient to resort to beautiful ideas, which the brave artist has acquired [...] Thus, perfection consists in going from Ideas to the natural, and from the natural to Ideas].

surpass human boundaries and create a new world of ineffable grace. The ekphrasis strives for aesthetic perfection above and beyond mere truth regarding nature, and thus links the scenery with the highest, purest sphere, the place where the Idea of beauty lies (Panofsky 1968: 48; Bergmann 1979: 72; 240–41).[21]

In these circumstances, the comparison of the landscape with a map may also fulfil an important role in the depiction of the pilgrim's imagination. An educated nobleman and sea traveller, he was presumably versed in cartography, as mapping was a fundamental practice and a common pastime (Blanco 2012b: 338–39; Alpers 1983: 127). The analogy therefore seems fully consistent with the notion of Idea, for a map also offers a quintessential whole formed by the most significant data gathered from previous individual experiences. Indeed, the pilgrim thinks of a map as a summarising abstraction. No matter how reduced the view may be, his imagination complements what is beyond the reach of his eyes, broadening the landscape in his mind as if he were stretching it out on one of his charts. Thus, Góngora's scenery is produced after a demanding intellectual process on the part of the recipient, since visualisation is only achieved when all traces of the landscape that the protagonist glimpses reflexively refer to each other to represent an Idea. In this respect, there might be a link between the creativity of the pilgrim and that expected from the audience, since Góngora's talent in crafting a knot of intellectual hurdles would have to be matched by the readers' skill in unravelling it.

Ut pictura poesis Revisited

An analysis of the main panoramic landscape of the *Soledades* draws veiled implications concerning the challenge posed to the readership, which is no less thought-provoking than that faced by the pilgrim. In an attributed *Carta en respuesta* [*Letter in Response*] (1613), arguably written by Góngora to defend his own aesthetics, the poet describes the mental process entailed by the deciphering of his work (Carreira 1999: 2):

> y si la obscuridad y estilo intricado de Ovidio [...] da causa a que, vacilando el entendimiento en fuerza de discurso, trabajándole [...] alcance lo que así en la lectura superficial de sus versos no pudo entender luego, hase de confesar que tiene utilidad avivar el ingenio, y eso nació de la obscuridad del poeta. Eso mismo hallará vuesa merced en mis *Soledades*, si tiene capacidad para quitar la corteza y descubrir lo misterioso que encubren

> [and if Ovid's obscurity and intricate style [...] provokes the reader's understanding, doubtful given the difficulty of the discourse, by working on it [...] finally reaches what it could not comprehend with a superficial reading of the lines, then one must confess that it serves to sharpen the wit, engendered by the poet's very obscurity. Sir, you will find the same in my *Soledades*, if you are able to remove the kernel and discover the mystery it conceals].

---

21   According to Gracián (2001: I. 54), wit also contributes to attaining this goal: 'No se contenta el ingenio con sola la verdad, como el juicio, sino que aspira a la hermosura' [Wit is not content with only truth, like judgment, but aspires to beauty].

In other words, after an initial stage of confusion, those who have sufficient intellectual capacity and invest enough time and effort will finally discover the poem's significance within the shell. Nevertheless, the implicit lesson is that the meaning(s) of the *Soledades* — whatever they may be, for they are invariably different for each reader — once the difficulties have been overcome, are not as important as the fact that the aesthetic obscurity of the poem will have served to 'avivar el ingenio'. The idea that difficulty sharpens the wit is not exclusive to Góngora and was widespread in the Baroque. However, no author pitched this claim as high as the Cordovan poet allegedly did in this letter (Jones 1963: 1).

In fact, his approach subverts the Horatian balance between *prodesse* and *delectare* (*Ars poetica*, line 333) by fusing the two concepts into one (Morpurgo-Tagliabue 1987: 34). The activity of solving the three levels of difficulty (language, allusions and especially the conceits; Jammes 2001: I. 102–25) offered by the poem becomes a kind of intellectual game, a process of learning that produces pleasure precisely because it is so demanding, an exercise in which readers can discover a consistent form of *utile dulci*. This might be the reason why, in the words of the Neo-Baroque writer Lezama Lima (2001: 49), a self-confessed admirer of Góngora: 'Solo lo difícil es estimulante' [Only that which is difficult is stimulating], for more accessible literature might entertain, or even teach, but not merge both aims while privileging the former as the *Soledades* does. Often in Góngora, once the difficulties of a passage have been surmounted, connections with the rest of the poem, and between its own constituents, become perceptible.[22] From an external viewpoint, the landscape studied anticipates the route that the pilgrim will follow (proleptic function) and presents, in a nutshell, the entire scenery of *Soledades* (*mise-en-abyme*). Internally, the passage betrays an apparent contradiction. Teichoscopy enhances ekphrasis, while ekphrasis obstructs teichoscopy, and yet the pilgrim seems to 'see' something, for otherwise there would be no description at all.

An *agudeza paradoja* [paradox conceit] is the fundamental conceit that underlies the passage. However, in order for the reader to reconcile teichoscopy and ekphrasis, it is necessary to go one step further than Gracián's scheme of wit. Art theory, and more precisely the notion of Idea as explored by Panofsky (1968), provides the means to solve the paradox by inverting the conventional meaning of teichoscopy: from looking-out from above to looking inside of oneself. Given the impossibility of perceiving clearly with his senses, the pilgrim resorts to a previously configured Idea of a landscape. The passage thus constitutes the perfect incarnation of thought serving image (a mind creating a landscape), and of image serving thought (a landscape tutored by an Idea).[23] The Idea is, of course, not this or that particular beauty, but Beauty itself. In this respect, Góngora seems to share with some of his

22   This can be linked to Gracián's analogy between the *agudeza compuesta* [compound conceit] and a constellation (2001a: I. 63): 'Cada piedra de las preciosas, tomada de por sí, pudiera oponerse a estrella, pero muchas juntas en un joyel, parece que pueden emular el firmamento' [Each precious stone, taken on its own, could be compared to a star, but many of them together in a jewellery box appear to be able to emulate the skies].

23   To paraphrase Spitzer (1955: 224–25). The last lines of this paragraph are indebted to Hadot (1993: 20–21).

artistic peers the Neoplatonic belief that the one thing worthy of being fixed in a work of art is not sensible reality, but the beauty of an ideal form.

Therefore, what concerns him most is how to redeem the world of matter, expunge its flaws and bring it closer to that Idea. Góngora's language, deemed inappropriate for the subject-matter of his poem by many of his contemporaries, is consistent in this light. Only an elevated, epic style may seriously attempt a landscape description that not only participates in the Idea of the beautiful, but that also pretends to compete with it on an equal footing. Interestingly, the friar Jerónimo de San José drew a parallel between this manner and that of the late Titian, which is rarely quoted (1651: 127):

> Cansado el Ticiano, del ordinario modo de pintar a lo dulce, y sutil, inventó aquel otro tan extraño, y subido de pintar a golpes de pincel groseros, casi como borrones al descuido, con que alcanzó nueva gloria [...] Lo mismo parece pretendieron en este tiempo nuestro Hortensio, y Góngora [...] subiendo ambos el estilo hasta la celsitud del precipicio en el hablar, y el escribir.

> [Titian, tired of the ordinary way of painting sweetly, and subtly, invented a strange style, elevating the painting with rough brush strokes, almost like careless smudges, with which he attained new glory [...] Nowadays, our Paravicino and Góngora seem to have the same intention [...] both elevate the style to the loftiness of the precipice in speaking and writing]

The friar is referring to the Venetian *pittura a macchia*, a style based on strokes and smudges of paint ('borrones', in Spanish) which, in the words of Carducho (1865: 193), 'de cerca apenas se dan a conocer, si bien apartándose a distancia conveniente, se descubre con agradable vista el arte del que la hizo' [close up they are scarcely comprehensible, but from a convenient distance, one discovers the pleasant sight of the artist's craft]. Titian's *The Penitent Saint Jerome* (Figure 1.3) illustrates this style. Like Góngora's *nuevo estilo*, this pictorial manner was in vogue but controversial in Baroque Spain, as is evidenced by Pacheco's (1956: I. 79) disapproval of the late works of El Greco (Gauna 1998: 68–72).

What is the point of this analogy between the two styles, which has also been suggested by modern scholars?[24] As noted by Cacho (2012a: 111–12), the comparison may enable us to explore the links between painting and poetry by revisiting Horace's famous *ut pictura poesis*, which fits the case perfectly. According to the Latin poet: '*ut pictura, poesis: erit quae, si propius stes, | te capiat magis, et quaedam, si longius abstes*' [painting is just like poetry: some works will captivate you more if you stand closer, and some, if you stand further away] (Horace 1989: 70). The latter case is precisely that of the *pittura a macchia*, which forces onlookers to distance themselves from the canvas in order to appreciate its hidden forms, fill with their imagination the gaps left by the artist, and finally transform the medley of colour into a finished image (Gombrich 2002: 167–69). Thus, the *macchie* enable the

---

24 Huergo (2017: 289): 'la "afinidad artística" entre el Greco y Góngora radica en la forma sin contornos del borrón' [the 'artistic affinity' between El Greco and Góngora lies in the form without defined outlines of the *borrón*]. According to Wölfflin (1950: 14), the Baroque painterly style shows 'the gradual depreciation of line' and produces works that tend 'to look limitless'.

FIG. 1.3. Titian, *The Penitent Saint Jerome* (c. 1575),
© Fundación Colección Thyssen-Bornemisza, Madrid.

beholder to experience something of the thrill of 'creating', which was traditionally the privilege of the artist. What we enjoy is not so much seeing these works as the high level of participation that they entail. It is thus no wonder that a poet such as Quevedo praised the 'manchas distantes' [distant smudges of paint] of Velázquez (line 89 of *El pincel* [*The Paintbrush*] in Cacho 2012b: 201). He possibly perceived the similitude between the mental effort required by the *borrones* and the intellectual exercise demanded by his literary display of wit.

In this sense, the distance provided by teichoscopy between the pilgrim and the landscape could be understood as a metaphor of how one should come to grips with the passage studied in the *Soledades*. The poet merges several traditions in an extraordinarily complex ekphrasis that reflects the encyclopaedic, contradictory spirit — of the person and the time — that made its existence possible.[25] In the same way that a painting covered by *borrones* can only be configured by the onlooker from a distance, Góngora's bewildering landscape is only fully understandable (i.e. seeable) if one separates oneself from a mere close reading of the passage and reflects not only on the artistic motives and techniques that he poetically emulated, but also on the wit that underlies it.

For these reasons, the similarity between the *borrones* and Góngora's work could be taken at a higher level than that of the elevated style. In terms of the polemic regarding the role of *naturaleza* and *artificio*, Góngora's prioritisation of poetics over nature is central to his notion of beauty (Holloway 2013: 29). His lyric predecessors (e.g. Petrarch, Garcilaso) found in the natural world — the epitome of inspiration in their episteme, to use Foucault's terminology (1966: 32–91) — the source from which to extol the beauty of the beloved. Conversely, Góngora subsumed nature into the true centre of his work, which is the poetic discourse (Friedman 2002: 65). From this viewpoint, a highly artificial, self-referential style may also attempt a description of an ideal landscape and succeed in pushing its frontier towards the sphere of the sublime. It is thus no wonder that genres such as the bucolic and the epic appear in a new light with this treatment. Although none of them is exclusive to Góngora, what is unique to him is the elaborate manner in which he merged two of their traditional tropes (i.e. the ekphrastic portrayal of a bucolic landscape and the epic undertone of teichoscopy) to serve the purpose of surpassing nature through art.

---

25   Kluge (2013: 162–67) reached a similar conclusion in her analysis of the *Polifemo*. I also refer to Gracián (2001a: II. 217): 'Vívese con el entendimiento, y tanto se vive cuanto se sabe' [One lives through understanding, and one lives as much as one knows].

CHAPTER 2

The Panoramic Seascape
in the *Soledad segunda*

The arrangement of the *Soledades* in a diptych is based upon a distinction between two genres: the pastoral and the piscatorial (Callejo 1986: 47). Despite its use of the epic trope of teichoscopy, the *Soledad primera* is primarily a bucolic work. It thus belongs to a tradition that often portrays the natural world as a supportive setting.[1] This helps to understand Góngora's Neoplatonic penchant for the ideal landscape, which provides the perfect framework for a pastoral poem starring characters with elemental, down-to-earth lives. Conversely, the *Soledad segunda* is a piscatorial work with more salient epic features. The poet wrote it drawing on the Neo-Latin and Italian tradition that had started with the publication of Sannazaro's *Eclogae piscatoriae* [*Piscatorial Eclogues*] ([1526] 1966). Unlike shepherds, often portrayed as benevolent caretakers of cattle in the pastoral world, poetic anglers tend to behave more aggressively with their environment.

The brutality of the *Soledad segunda* is thus unsurprising. Góngora conceived of it as a poetic break from the placid natural world presented in the first part of the poem (Jones 1963: 3–5). From this viewpoint, the two parts of the *silva* function as inverted mirrors (Cacho 2007: 446). The evolution from the pastoral to the piscatorial has an impact in the work's panoramic descriptions, which in the *Soledad segunda* are focused on turbulent fishing scenes. In this respect, I shall now examine a passage in which violence is especially conspicuous: the seascape beheld by the pilgrim and the elderly angler where the latter's children fish not only tuna, but also dangerous sea creatures (*Soledad segunda*, lines 388–426). This description portrays, at closer range and with much more detail, the 'jaspes líquidos' [jasper waters] (*Soledad primera*, line 210) that the protagonist could barely see from the mainland hilltop.

The seascape is not the peaceful estuary it seemed from afar but the setting of frenetic action with epic undertones. The influence of Homeric teichoscopy is as relevant here as in the previous passage. The elderly angler stands on a cliff from which he observes the ocean. He can no longer participate actively in life and

---

1   Garcilaso's first eclogue encapsulates this idea (Sánchez de las Brozas 1600: 29^r): 'Con mi llorar las piedras enternecen | su natural dureza, y la quebrantan' [With my sobbing the stones soften | their natural hardness, until they shatter].

has become a mere spectator.[2] Thus, he presides over the 'ejercicio piscatorio' [piscatorial exercise] (*Soledad segunda*, line 213) of his daughters and sons like a wise king, choosing for his offspring the most convenient fishing devices (Blanco 2012b: 267). He suffers immensely when he sees both his daughters defying sea creatures and ships being wrecked. Since both spectacles have a double facet (heroic but also tragic), readers of epic would acknowledge in his reaction the mix of wonder with pity and fear that is typical of teichoscopy (Lovatt 2013: 1 and 227).

The connection between the actions observed by the elderly angler and his own emotional response shows how ekphraseis can be linked to broader narratives. Although the description has a certain independence from the adjacent lines, it is closely linked to the whole poem. Indeed, from a narratological perspective, teichoscopy fulfils a proleptic function: the poet delivers yet another panoramic view that announces forthcoming events. Moreover, the trope serves a further purpose. The passage offers both a general reflection of man's place in nature and a specific criticism of the exploitation of resources on the other side of the Atlantic. In this sense, the ekphrasis complements the censure of the Spanish conquest of the Americas delivered in the *Soledad primera* (lines 366–502).

Another link between the two parts of the *Soledades* is the fact that, when depicting the piscatorial scenes, Góngora uses again teichoscopy for the portrayal of nature as a work of art. Indeed, the epic trope enables the poet to 'pictorialise' the ocean in five ways. Three of them were germinal in the panoramic landscape. Indeed, seventeenth-century landscape paintings typically included creatures such as human beings, pagan gods and animals, as nature as such was not deemed an appealing subject. There were reminiscences of these ekphrastic strategies in the landscape, which contained human traces in the form of architecture, an allusion to the Fauni, and a reference to the mythological goat Amalthea (*Soledad primera*, lines 206, 189 and 204 respectively).

The seascape ekphrasis enables Góngora to go one step further, since the ocean seen by the elderly angler and the pilgrim from a cliff: (i) reflects the theory that the beauty of nature is enhanced by human presence, as evidenced by the inclusion of two men and two women fishing on the sea; (ii) alludes to four deities from the Greco-Latin tradition (Aurora, Diana, Thetis and Proteus) who have an important role in the depiction of the scene; and (iii) enables not only nature but also fish and sea creatures to be described when they are caught by the fishermen.

Furthermore, teichoscopy enhances the appreciation of the seascape as a work of art in two new ways, which were non-existent in the panoramic landscape: (iv) by combining the epic trope with the technique known as *scrittura particolareggiata* [writing which is extensive in details about small elements], Góngora brings his ekphrasis closer to the early modern landscapes in which the panoramic gaze goes hand in hand with the most pictorial minuteness; and (v) the allusion to sinking

---

2   Góngora's angler can be compared to the elders who sat upon the Trojan walls to behold the battles because they were too old to fight (*Iliad* III. 146–53). Teichoscopy is also common in the piscatorial tradition. For instance, one finds it in the eclogue IX attributed to Camões (1834: II. 244): 'Eu, vigiando aqui como atalaia' [I, watching here [i.e. from a cliff] as a sentinel].

vessels consolidates the bond with the plastic arts because a shipwreck is *per se* an archetypical seascape motif.

In fact, the shipwrecks also allow a political/existential reading, since they portray Spain's imperial endeavours as menaced by an ominous and proliferating sea. In the *Soledad segunda*, the Atlantic Ocean is so aggressive that nature has provided land with the protection of 'walls' in form of cliffs.[3] From that safe haven, the angler and the pilgrim (who vicariously 'sees' the violent scenes by hearing his host's story) respectively observed in the past and imagine in the present the shipwreck of the vessels and the dangerous fishing. In this passage, Góngora deploys the ancient topos of the shipwreck with spectator, which Lucretius and Horace had used as the basis for philosophical reflections.

Thus, taking the work of Blumenberg (1995) as a starting point, an analysis of how the poet adapted the topos for his own purposes will be indispensable. In particular, I will examine how the duality (angler | pilgrim) between seeing and imagining the shipwrecks, and between being and not being directly concerned about them, is echoed from the viewpoint of *conceptismo* with an *agudeza paradoja* [paradox conceit]. On the one hand, the coast is a place of memory for the angler. As reflected in the narration, his main interest is not the aesthetics of the setting but his children. Thus, to him the sea is just a mere background. On the other hand, the coast is a springboard for the pilgrim's imagination, which will represent the scenes he is being told. Feeling detached from past events, which interest him less than the beauty of nature, he can arguably see a seascape where his host sees just a sea.[4]

Therefore, the setting is not the same to each beholder. To the pilgrim, it is neither a neutral backdrop, nor a mere poetic postcard to be admired — far from it. The seascape is almost a character in its own right, with a role to play in the development of themes through its allegorising presence.[5] This role is so prominent because the ocean, seething with wild creatures, defends itself through them against the angler's daughters. Since the beasts appear demonised as intemperately savage, I shall argue that they enable Góngora to explore poetically the notion of monstrosity (and, therefore, of evil), which he contrasts with the thus far peaceful estuary at which the pilgrim had arrived earlier. In the *Soledad segunda*, the Neoplatonic Idea of the beautiful no longer appears in a pristine manner. However, its might is reinforced once the fisherwomen defeat their nemeses.

---

3   Salcedo Coronel (1636: 250ᵛ): 'Llama muros a las rocas, porque defendían la isla de los asaltos del mar' [He calls the rocks ramparts, because they defended the island from the assaults of the sea].
4   Proust (1981: II. 556) expressed a similar idea in his novel *In Search of Lost Time*: 'in the conversations which they held on the subject I sought only a poetic pleasure. Without being conscious of it themselves, they procured me this pleasure as might a couple of farmers or sailors speaking of the soil or the tides, realities too little detached from their own lives for them to be capable of enjoying the beauty which personally I undertook to extract from them'.
5   These lines are indebted to Elliot and Purdy's (2006: 286–87) analysis of cinematic landscapes.

Teichoscopy, a Reinforcement of Ekphrasis (II)

The *Soledad segunda* begins in a transitional space evocative of the Neo-Latin and Italian piscatorial tradition: an estuary where the tide meets the river that zigzagged through the previous landscape. The pilgrim crosses it and finds harbour in another hybrid place, a land with the form of a turtle which, depending on the tide, becomes either an isle or a peninsula. There he is hosted by an elderly angler, father of two sons and six daughters, who escorts him on a tour of the land. When they return from the walk, the young women set the table under the shade of six poplars and serve him varied and abundant fish. Having expressed his gratitude for their hospitality, the pilgrim listens to the following speech of his host (lines 388–426):[6]

> «Días ha muchos, oh mancebo — dijo
> el pescador anciano –,
> que en el uno cedí y el otro hermano
> el duro remo, el cáñamo prolijo;
> muchos ha dulces días
> que cisnes me recuerdan a la hora
> que, huyendo la Aurora
> las canas de Titón, halla las mías
> (a pesar de mi edad) no en la alta cumbre
> de aquel morro difícil (cuyas rocas
> tarde o nunca pisaron cabras pocas,
> y milano venció con pesadumbre),
> sino desotro escollo al mar pendiente,
> de donde ese teatro de Fortuna
> descubro, ese voraz, ese profundo
> campo ya de sepulcros, que, sediento,
> cuanto en vasos de abeto Nuevo Mundo
> (tributos digo américos) se bebe
> en túmulos de espuma paga breve.
> Bárbaro observador (mas diligente)
> de las inciertas formas de la Luna,
> a cada conjunción su pesquería,
> y a cada pesquería su instrumento,
> más o menos nudoso, atribuído,
> mis hijos dos en un batel despido,
> que, el mar cribando en redes no comunes,
> vieras intempestivos algún día
> (entre un vulgo nadante, digno apenas
> de escama, cuanto más de nombre) atunes
> vomitar ondas y azotar arenas.
> Tal vez desde los muros destas rocas
> cazar a Tetis veo
> y pescar a Dïana en dos barquillas:
> náuticas venatorias maravillas
> de mis hijas oirás, ambiguo coro

---

6   As mentioned, all quotations from the poem follow the edition by Jammes (2001) and the English translation by Edith Grossman (Góngora 2012: 108–11).

menos de aljaba que de red armado,
de cuyo, si no alado,
arpón vibrante supo mal Proteo
en globos de agua redimir sus focas.

["It has been a while, my boy,"
the ancient fisherman said,
"since I handed over to both my sons
the harsh oars and lengthy hemp;
for many sweet days now swans
waken me at the hour that
Aura, fleeing white hair of Tithonus,
discovers mine, in spite of my age, awake,
not on the high peak of that toilsome highland
whose rocks few goats ever troad,
goshawks vanquished only with tribulation,
but on that other reef rising from the sea;
there I watch Fortune's theater,
the voracious, the profound
graveyard thirstily drinking
from goblets of fir all that the New World
– I mean the tributes from the Americas –
pays in mausoleums of short-lived spume.
An observer not learned but diligent
of Luna's changeable forms,
to each conjunction a kind of fishing,
to each kind of fishing its own implements
– more knots or fewer — accord,
I bid farewell to my two sons in their boat,
who sieve the sea with uncommon nets;
you should one day see tuna
– among swimming commoners barely worthy
of having scales, much less names –
spewing waves and lashing sands.
And perhaps from the ramparts of these rocks
I can see Thetis hunting
and Diana fishing in two small boats:
about my daughters marvels nautical
and venatic you will hear, a dubious choir:
armed not with quiver or net,
against whose if not winged then vibrant harpoon
Proteus could not defend his herds of seals
even in globes of water.]

The seascape echoes the panoramic landscape of the *Soledad primera* in many ways, opening a dialogue that strengthens the internal consistency of the poem. The pilgrim could hardly perceive the landscape due to the atmospheric conditions, which forced him to imagine it in his mind. Similarly, his fantasy will play a key role before the fishing and shipwrecking stories, which he hears from his host. Moreover, the two poetic scenes are depicted from a ridge: compare the 'escollo apacible' of the *Soledad primera* (line 187) with the 'escollo al mar pendiente' of the *Soledad segunda* (line 400). Given Góngora's tendency to 'pictorialise' nature, teichoscopy will serve again the purpose of presenting the panoramic view as a verbal painting. The first way of doing so is the inclusion of the angler's sons and two of his daughters in the ekphrasis.

Landscapes without human traces are rare in early modern art. Nature as such, without any buildings or people, can only be found in drawings and sketches: it hardly ever appears in finished canvases.[7] Unless it included some sign of human intervention, the natural world was not deemed a compelling topic. However, landscapes — initially deemed a mere setting — were gradually emptied of historical, mythological or biblical subjects. Thus, the space left for human presence became increasingly accessory, until figures ended up being little more than staffage (Andrews 1999: 174). Nonetheless, no matter how overwhelming the panoramic views over mountains, rivers or seas might have been, men and women would not be completely excluded (Rossholm 1990: 4 and 29). Figures were not only included to animate the scene and engage the beholders' attention but also to provide a benchmark for scale. Indeed, the insignificant size of human bodies could serve to emphasise the greatness of nature. Moreover, the myriad activities depicted would illustrate diverse relationships with the environment. All of them conveyed the message that humankind is an integral part of the natural world (Sutton 1987: 7).

Góngora was aware of these artistic ideas, which also have classic literary precedents. Perhaps imitating Philostratus the Elder and/or early modern artists, he delivered ekphraseis in which the beauty of the natural world is not opposed to human presence. Quite the opposite: his characters endow the scene with meaning (Ponce Cárdenas 2014: 381–82). Even in the uninhabited landscape of the *Soledad primera*, the river was 'engazando edificios en su plata', i.e. bypassing buildings that, in light of their location, were likely to be mills, primitive dams and farmers' houses (Pellicer 1630: 405; Serrano de Paz 1673a: 230^r). The belief that human intervention enhances the beauty of nature is more noticeable in the seascape, which, as mentioned, contains four human beings. By describing a view from the distant, high cliff where the elderly angler stands, teichoscopy strengthens the bond between the ekphrasis and seascape art. His offspring will appear in the mind's eye of the pilgrim as far-off, atemporal bodies whose role is primordially plastic. Thus, they can be compared with the anonymous genre figures depicted in landscapes, the identity of which we do not have to know in order to appreciate a painting (Blanco 2012b: 155).

Since Spanish art theorists often spurned landscapes as mere exercises in the imitation of nature, the introduction of human figures was possibly a way of bringing these works closer to genres that were more 'dignified' such as literary, religious or mythological painting. Indeed, the early modern prejudice that landscape art appealed to the eyes, but not to the intellect, could probably be faced

---

7   I refer to Pacheco's (1956: II. 130) advice on landscape painting: 'La primera distancia donde se planta la figura (que es lo primero que se dibuja y lo postrero que se bosqueja y se acaba) por ser la parte superior en grandeza y la más principal con que se concluye' [The foreground where the human figure is placed (the first part that is drawn and the last part that is sketched and finished) because it is the greatest part and the most important one, with which one concludes].

more steadfastly by offering to the beholder something more than nature. This might be the reason why Spanish landscapists such as Juan Bautista Martínez del Mazo (c. 1611–1667) and Benito Manuel Agüero (c. 1629–1668) peopled the natural world not only with anonymous human figures but also with Greco-Latin deities and nymphs (López Torrijos 1990: 43).

By including a reference to the festivals of ancient Rome in honour of Faunus (line 189: 'de cuantos pisan Faunos la montaña'), Góngora had already endowed the landscape of the *Soledad primera* with a mythic component. However, this isolated feature did not have any further impact on either the ekphrasis or the plot. Conversely, the seascape of the *Soledad segunda* resorts to Greco-Latin deities with a prominent role. The passage is preceded by two lines that describe a spectacular sunrise, personified in the goddess Aurora, over the summit of the cliff (lines 394–95). Unlike their brothers, two of the angler's daughters have names, those of the goddesses Diana and Thetis: 'cazar a Tetis veo | y pescar a Dïana en dos barquillas'. Given the distance granted by teichoscopy, for a moment the young women seem to lose their identity.[8] The father focuses all his attention on the majesty they exhibit while fishing, and thus ends up associating them with these dominating deities. Their respective prey are a seal, which the sea-god Proteus is unable to protect (lines 425–44), and an enormous, unidentified sea creature that, judging from the description, could well be an orca (lines 445–511).

Góngora's portrayal of Éfire and Filódoces is completely at odds with the tradition in which the passage is based (Ravasini 2014: 397). Female characters are important in Neo-Latin and Italian piscatorial poetry, either in presence or — more frequently — in absence. However, their role is often limited to being the passive object of an unrequited love.[9] This is also the case in all of Góngora's own fisher *romances* [ballads]. On other occasions, perhaps following models such as the story of Perseus and Andromeda (Ovid's *Metamorphoses*, IV. 663–764), writers portray women as helpless victims who have to be rescued from sea creatures by male heroes: see Antonio Ongaro's *Alceo* (1998), third act, first scene. The wilderness can thus become a site for male protagonists to reassert their hegemony not only over nature but also over their gender subordinates.[10]

This is clearly not the case in the *Soledad segunda*, where the deeds of the godlike daughters overshadow those of their nameless brothers. The phallic implements of the fisherwomen, like the patron's 'jabalina' [lance] in the dedication to the *Soledades* (line 21), violate the bodily integrity of animals, tearing them open and spilling great quantities of blood (Chemris 2008: 69). Conversely, the brothers are unable to net anything other than tuna, abundant but minor when compared to the

---

8   They will recover it shortly thereafter, when the father reveals that their real names are Éfire and Filódoces (*Soledad segunda*, lines 445 and 448).
9   This happens in the piscatorial eclogues II and V by Jacopo Sannazaro (1966); VII and IX by Bernardino Baldi (1992); II, V, VI, VIII, XII and XIV by Berardino Rota (1990); and in the three piscatorial songs (XIII, XIV and XV) in the first volume of Luigi Tansillo's *Il Canzoniere* (1996). All the fisher idylls attributed to Camões (1834: II: eclogues VI, VIII, IX and X) are devoted to the same topic.
10   I borrow this idea from Ingram's (2008: 36) study of gender in environmentalist movies.

FIG. 2.1. Jan Brueghel the Elder, *Allegory of Water* (c. 1575–1625),
© Musée des Beaux-Arts, Lyon. Photograph by Alain Basset.

prey of the fisherwomen. Although these kinds of comparisons must be made with caution, if the harpoons of Éfire and Filódoces that penetrate the flesh of the sea creatures are considered a phallic substitute, then the nets in which the fishermen catch the fish could be equally emblematic of its vaginal counterpart. Góngora inverts the meaning of both fertility symbols, as here they do not create life but cause death.

In this context of protean reversal of gender roles and symbols, the double hypallage with which the poet interchanges the traditional attributes of the goddesses appears as completely natural. They are both amphibious, equal opposites in balance, and indistinctively bring death in land and sea. The fisherwomen will thus be transmuted into all-encompassing deities for the pilgrim as well, who only 'sees' the seascape through his host's narration. In other words, the double hypallage manipulates the nouns 'Tetis' and 'Dïana' so that they are perceived as divine destructive forms, irrespective of their specific mythological identities.[11] Therefore, the seascape offers a complex interaction between (pagan) divine and human beings, illustrating yet another feature of Góngora's ekphraseis that he might have learned from Philostratus the Elder and/or early modern landscapists.

After the inclusion of gods and humans in the passage, the addition of fish and other sea creatures is consistent with the genre. Indeed, the depiction of living animals is part of the tradition of landscape art (Brueghel's *Allegory of Water* — Figure 2.1). The panoramic landscape of the *Soledad primera* contained a reference for the fields' abundance (the mythological goat Amalthea, lines 203–04), not the

11   I paraphrase Chemris' (2008: 25) analysis of the double hypallage in the *Soledad primera*, line 44: 'montes de agua y piélagos de montes' [mountains of water, open seas of mountains] (Góngora 2012: 8–9).

description of an actual real animal. The 'escollo' or ridge of line 187 was a perfect observatory from which to admire the land the pilgrim traversed, the rich fauna of which Góngora described in other passages. Conversely, the second teichoscopy enables readers to appreciate not only the ocean but also some of its inhabitants.

The first fish that Góngora describes are 'un vulgo nadante, digno apenas | de escama, cuanto más de nombre [...]' (*Soledad segunda*, lines 415–16). In other words, he starts precisely with the 'morralla o peces pequeños' [herring or whitebait] (Díaz de Rivas 1624: 262^r), one of the smallest among visible sea creatures. Like the angler's sons, these fish are so insignificant that they do not even have a name. Despite their apparent irrelevance, and the contempt of the narrator's (that is, the angler's) voice, the fact that Góngora mentions these creatures is revealing of his Lucretian attitude towards the natural world. One of the main lessons of *De rerum natura* is that there is no such a thing as a worthless theme. Lucretius proved that 'things have their poetry, not because of what we make them symbols of, but because of their own movement and life' (Santayana 1947: 34). Indeed, the poet's penetrating gaze admires the beauty and infinitude of nature in all forms alike: 'chaque corps, si petit soit-il, contient un monde' [no matter how small, each body contains a world] (Deleuze 1988: 8, 1993: 5).

Nature, represented by bucolic landscapes in the first part of the poem, takes the form of a sea suitable for fishing in the *Soledad segunda*. In fact, Góngora had announced the opposition between the pastoral and the piscatorial at the beginning of the poem: 'Vencida al fin la cumbre, | del mar siempre sonante, | de la muda campaña' [Vanquishing at last the peak | to the always sounding sea | and countryside ever mute] (*Soledad primera*, lines 52–54) (Góngora 2012: 11). Whereas the land is peacefully quiet, the sea tends to be noisy and much more aggressive.[12] Góngora might have decided on the change of setting for a simple reason: the sea illustrates better than the countryside how nature is not only a provider but also a taker. The Freudian duality of Eros and Thanatos, the instincts to create and to destroy, are irretrievably fused throughout the poem, but especially in its second part. Violence is necessary to complete the portrayal of the natural world, as death is the last link in the chain of life (Smith 1965: 230–31).

In terms of narrative discourse, this ekphrasis displays the course of things to come, like its counterpart of the *Soledad primera*. The seascape is a site of awe and imminent violence. Indeed, the ocean is the setting where brutal fishing scenes will take place immediately after the description (*Soledad segunda*, lines 425–511). Góngora's nature is Darwinian: he depicts most creatures as either hunters or prey, as the angler witnesses from the cliff. However, the seascape will also become the stage for two young fishermen, Lícidas and Micón, who will perform an amoebean love song (lines 542–611).[13] Having heard the ballad, the protagonist will intercede for them, obtaining his host's approval for their marriage to two of his other

---

12   *Soledad segunda*, lines 23–24: 'a la violencia mucha | del Padre de las aguas [...]' [to the immense violence | of the father of waters] (Góngora 2012: 85).

13   According to Ponce Cárdenas (2013: 86), the names of the fishermen are probably inspired by Sannazaro's (1966) first piscatorial eclogue.

daughters: Leusipe and Cloris (lines 635–51). Thus, apparent minutiae such as the 'vulgo nadante' are necessary to show that not even the most elusive creatures can escape death, while the panoramic view highlights the solemnity of the future marital union. The description of the ocean may be read as an early hint of both the fatal and the joyful events to follow, in fulfilment of a proleptic function.

The passage can serve this purpose because Góngora combines teichoscopy with an attention to detail that, *a priori*, would seem more appropriate for a still life. However, the technique of writing in small scale contributes to the visualisation or *enargeia* by producing an illusion of accuracy and thoroughness (Blanco 2012b: 285–87). In this respect, Góngora's *scrittura particolareggiata* might reflect a new empiricism or a modern mentality in the making. Obviously, to omit nothing in a text is neither possible nor conceivable. Only Funes, Borges' famous character with total recall, could perhaps produce such writing, which would be as useless as the Borgesian map that replicates reality. Nevertheless, by including elements such as the 'vulgo nadante' in his description, the poet showed that teichoscopy is not necessarily at odds with (partial) minuteness of detail.

In fact, various old masters had preceded Góngora in the successful combination of the panoramic gaze with the *Kleinmalerei* [painting of the small].[14] To an artist such as Jacques de Gheyn (c. 1565–1629), 'the map was the obverse of the drawing of a fly' (Alpers 1983: 133). Indeed, the globe appears in its entirety in maps, which provide us with a *Totalperspektive* that would be otherwise unreachable. Likewise, the *Kleinmalerei* brings before our eyes the world in its completeness, including tiny items we would not otherwise notice. From the largest to the smallest: Gheyn made maps and drew flies; Góngora described both panoramic views and whitebait.

Unlike the landscape of the *Soledad primera*, the seascape is not explicitly divided into different levels, possibly due to the lack of a river or a path that could guide the beholder through them. However, the match between teichoscopy and *scrittura particolareggiata* entails the simultaneous visualisation of multiple elements by the elderly angler, each one presumably more distant than the last, yet all of them clearly portrayed. In this respect, Góngora deploys a poetic equivalent of the pictorial technique called foreshortening: to depict an object as closer than it really is. So sweeping is the view from the 'escollo al mar pendiente', that the angler even mentions the shipwreck of vessels sailing to or from the 'New World': 'cuanto en vasos de abeto Nuevo Mundo | (tributos digo américos) se bebe'. The lines are noteworthy pictorially because they link the ekphrasis with a classic subgenre of seascapes (Peeters' *Shipwreck on a Rocky Coast* — Figure 2.2) and thematically because they provide the ocean with spatial and temporal context.

As noted by Hall (1912: 29–30), Sannazaro's innovation with the piscatorial eclogue was based on a geographical shift from the pastoral landscape of Arcadia to the Sicilian shores more familiar to him. A comparable evolution can be observed in Góngora. The ideal landscape of the *Soledad primera* offered an antithesis to existing reality by describing a utopia in an uncertain location. Conversely, the seascape

---

14   I refer to Figure 2.1, and to El Bosco's *The Garden of Earthly Delights* (1500–1505), which at the time was already renowned in Spain.

FIG. 2.2. Bonaventura Peeters, *Shipwreck on a Rocky Coast* (c. 1640),
© Philadelphia Museum of Art.

reveals that the action of the *Soledad segunda* probably takes place on the Atlantic coast of Andalusia, an area from which it was actually possible to see ships returning from the Americas (Jammes 2001: II. 476). Moreover, by providing the scene with a temporal context, the allusion to the shipwrecked vessels highlights the importance of the seascape: it is not just any sea that he describes, but the ocean through which, before Góngora's lifetime, Spain had sent its troops to conquer the 'New World'.

This dimension of the seascape can also be approached from the viewpoints of the piscatorial tradition and *conceptismo*. As noted by Grant (1965: 212), a feature of Sannazaro's poetry is the mingling of classical and contemporary, of artfulness and realism. This trait fits in the Baroque understanding of poetry as a means to surmount the wall that separates the past from the present, the distant from the close, enabling the reader to experience simultaneously the literary essence of different periods and places within the nutshell of a poem (Cacho 2012a: 86). In this respect, Góngora's texts often contain a syncretic flavour that reflects this kind of *agudeza*. In the seascape studied, mythical/historical, past/present, fictive/real facets of the Atlantic Ocean coexist without encroaching on each other, like a palimpsest in which all layers were simultaneously readable and reciprocally enriching.

Indeed, in Góngora conflicting forces often pull simultaneously in opposite directions. Although the ocean captivates the senses with its abundance of fish, the other facet of such fullness is ominous: 'ese voraz, ese profundo | campo ya de sepulcros [...]' (*Soledad segunda*, lines 402–03). Humankind has designed fishing devices and ships in order to dominate and exploit the seas. However, this hubristic desire often ends in disastrous failure. Nature does not submit to men's attempts at control but instead exacts retribution and punishes the sacrilege of seafaring.[15] Indeed, when the sea displays its might, human artfulness is swiftly removed from its surface, which then returns to its unadulterated original state. Unlike architecture, which at least can leave behind a memento in the form of ruins, shipwrecked vessels disappear without any permanent trace. Góngora compares the ephemeral foam they produce with burial mounds (*Soledad segunda*, line 406): 'en túmulos de espuma paga breve'. This unbearable lightness reminds us that nature remains unchanged and unmoved by human tragedies.[16]

In this sense, ekphraseis not only contribute towards shaping a setting or a character, but also towards portraying a worldview that sheds light on the plot (Lizcano 2003: 81). It is often said that one of the reasons why the *Soledades* appears so modern is that Góngora did not submit the whole of it to any moral or didactic purpose. However, this does not mean that the *silva* is void of moralistic components. Although the poet does not expressly disapprove of techniques to adapt the environment to human purposes, the ekphrasis reflects a certain preoccupation with the exploitation of nature. As highlighted by Magris (1986: 168–71), our morals are based on an inevitable distinction between humans and the environment: we cannot treat all animals and plants from a Kantian perspective, as ends instead of means. Therefore, it is impossible to live without at least partially destroying nature. This dichotomy obliges culture, which strives for human well-being, to erect the building of civilisation on the foundations of the exploitation of natural and animal resources, trying to soothe their shared hardships but resigned to not being able to remove them completely.

Although uneasiness in culture is far from being made entirely explicit in the *Soledad segunda*, the seascape conveys the message that the plenitude attainable through marine exploitation might be detrimental to humankind, at least when the environment is not paid its due respect. This idea is even clearer when set against the background of the Spanish conquest of the Americas, which entailed not only the coercive utilisation of nature but also of other human beings.[17] All of these connotations are consonant with the pictorial tradition of seascapes with a political dimension, since pictures of wild seas defending themselves from human presence constitute a gesture of defiance towards what is perceived as an oppressive, expansionist civilisation (Andrews 1999: 156) — Figure 2.2. In this sense, Góngora's allusion to the shipwrecked vessels may constitute the emblem of the triple crisis — political, economic and moral — of a decaying imperial Spain.

15   To paraphrase Ingram (2008: 37).
16   In this respect, the Atlantic Ocean may also be read as a graveyard due to the victims of slave trade who died en route to the 'New World'.
17   Góngora had already criticised the greed of the conquistadores in the *Soledad primera* (lines 366–502). According to Beverley (1980: 2), this passage pictures the discovery and conquest of the Americas 'as a misfortune, an act of tragic vanity'. The poet possibly draw inspiration from the old man of Restelo's speech in *Os Lusíadas*, IV. 94–104 (Camões 1834: I. 154).

Shipwreck(s) with Spectator(s)

The interpretation suggested above is supported by the fact that, for Spain, this was not only a time of crisis but also of awareness of crisis (Elliott 1977, and 2002: 300). With the hindsight of four centuries, one can easily appreciate the atmosphere of *desengaño* [existential disillusionment] provoked by a perception of decline in many works of the Spanish Golden Age (notably, Cervantes' *Don Quijote* and Calderón's *La vida es sueño* [*Life is a Dream*]). Likewise, the tone of the *Soledades* is not triumphal but melancholic. The poem betrays nostalgia for an irreversible loss. There were no major conquests in the seventeenth century. Hence, the historical trauma: the high point of imperial power had been left behind. *Conceptismo* might be an expression of this anxiety. Naturally, within the poem, little of this is apparent to the elderly angler, for whom the world of politics and international affairs is remote. Nonetheless, he alludes significantly to the sinking vessels (*Soledad segunda*, lines 404–06): not a long description but the message is clear. In any case, though aware of the ships, the angler is obviously more concerned about the immediate destiny of his daughters: Filódoces, and especially Éfire, are also in danger of shipwrecking.

The topos of the shipwreck with spectator was familiar to Golden Age writers, who learned it from the classics.[18] This could help explain the similarities between Góngora's ekphrasis and a poem by Horace (2004: 50–51). Like the poetic speaker in the latter's ode to the ship of state, significantly represented by a ship on the verge of sinking — I.14, lines 2–3: 'O *quid agis? Fortiter occupa portum*' [O, what are you doing? Make bravely for the harbour!] — the angler exhorts his daughter Éfire to return her boat to haven (*Soledad segunda*, line 453: '¡Cuántas voces le di!' [How many cries I uttered!]) (Góngora 2012: 113). Indeed, both spectators can perceive the circumstances of the ships more clearly than the sailors on board because they are at a higher standpoint. Thus, they intervene to call for a return to land.[19]

However, the common ground between the two poems ends here. While Horace's poetic speaker is concerned with actual real dangers (e.g. waves, wind, damage already suffered by the ship), Góngora's dismisses eventual attacks by sharks or swordfish and reveals that his greatest preoccupation is his daughter's virginity, which could be threatened by a water satyr (*Soledad segunda*, lines 453–64). As mentioned, the young woman had been compared with Diana, the goddess of chastity, in line 420. This mythic apprehension, which might appear odd if seen without a context, actually links the ekphrasis with both the piscatorial tradition and the visual arts.

Indeed, abduction by a sea creature or by the sea itself is a recurrent motif in fisher idylls. For instance, in the fourth eclogue of Sannazaro (1966: 177–83), Proteus tells the story of the huntress Nesis who, trying to escape from a lustful suitor, ended up being swallowed by a horrible sea seething with '*Neptunia monstra*' [monstrous fish] (Ravasini 2014: 400). Even closer to the *Soledad segunda* is the above-mentioned

18   For example, Quevedo's *silva ¿Dónde vas, ignorante navecilla...?* [*Where Are You Going, Ignorant Small Ship...?*] emulates Horace's ode I. 14. The topos also appears in contemporary paintings (Figure 2.2).

19   This paragraph is indebted to Blumenberg (1995: 53–54).

FIG. 2.3. Albrecht Dürer, *The Sea Monster* (c. 1498), © Dallas Museum of Art.

Alceo by Ongaro (1998: 52), in which Lesbina explains how her fellow fisherwoman Eurilla was abducted by Triton when she was fishing: 'uscì del mare un mostro, | E se la tolse in spalla, e via portolla' [a monster emerged from the sea, | And put her on his shoulder, and took her away].[20] In fact, the topos was also pictorial, as reflected in Dürer's *The Sea Monster*, which could almost be an illustration of the passage studied: the engraving portrays an old, powerless man witnessing from the shore the kidnapping of a young woman by Triton (Figure 2.3).

The elderly angler knows that fishing in the Atlantic Ocean entails risks not only for his children's life, but also for their *honra* [honour/virtue]. However, he appears to be more concerned with the latter than with the former. He goes to the hilltop and tries to monitor the whole process, succeeding at least regarding the fishermen. Just as shafts of sunlight hit the panoramic landscape, the 'inciertas formas de la Luna' before dawn illuminate the ocean. From the lunar phase he knows which fish are likely to be found, and thus which nets the young men will require: with more or fewer knots, depending on the size of the prey (Serrano de Paz 1673b: 288[v]; Pellicer 1630: 564–65). Consequently, the young fishermen make the best of nature's creative power, as suggested by the watercolour line 413, which describes them pictorially winnowing the sea to fish tuna: 'que, el mar cribando en redes no comunes'.[21] Unlike their submissive brothers, Filódoces and Éfire (particularly the latter) do not obey their father. Paradoxically, the loss of control takes place when the elderly angler is enjoying a *Totalperspektive*: his gaze from above reshapes nature and thus should entail order, an approach to the vision/power of God. In this sense, the father could be deemed the ultimate *artifex* of the picturesque scene, the director of a marine *Festspiel* on a grand scale. His efforts to reach the summit of a high 'escollo' are comparable to those of the artist who strives for control/creation. Some characters (i.e. the brothers) follow his instructions, as if they were taking part in a moveable *tableau vivant*. Other elements (i.e. the daughters/shipwrecks) are beyond his influence, as is often the case with creative works. Indeed, both art and literature are territories where the unexpected happens. Nevertheless, the angler has chosen the setting and determined most of its components, in an attempt to configure the seascape to the greatest extent possible.

Strictly speaking, the *tableaux vivants* or living pictures were motionless and did not appear in Europe until the eighteenth century. However, in a broad, transhistorical sense, the French notion refers to the moment in which the body, not necessarily alluding to any specific work of art, poses against a background and thereby converts it into — and itself becomes — a picture ('le moment où le corps [...] fait tableau') (Vouilloux 2002: 31). As mentioned above, the choice of a topic in which people interact with nature was, in early modern painting, a way of highlighting the importance of the landscape (Blanco 2006: 131). This is precisely

20   Claudian, a Latin poet who greatly influenced Góngora, included in his *Epithalamium of Honorius and Maria* a scene of Triton's attempted rape of a nymph (Platnauer 2014: I. 252–53). This might well be another of the sources of the passage (Serrano de Paz 1673b: 325[v] and 327[r]; Ponce Cárdenas 2013: 108).
21   Philostratus the Elder (2014: 55–59) wrote a similar scene of tuna fishing directed by a character from a high standpoint in mainland (*Imagines* I. 13).

what happens here, at least from the pilgrim's viewpoint: the input he is given is the description of a man who, having trained his offspring to interact with the ocean, through them transforms sea into seascape.

All these implications are conceivable because the pilgrim through whose eyes we see the story is relatively detached from the action. In the passage studied, his role is limited to listening. However, while hearing the pictorial description, he can arguably imagine the seascape as if it were a living picture. As in Calderón's *La hija del aire* [*The Daughter of the Air*], where this analogy is expressed with great originality, in Góngora's *Soledad segunda* the tongue of the elderly fisherman metaphorically becomes a paintbrush, his words pigments, and the ears — and the imagination — of the pilgrim, a canvas.[22]

In fact, the perceptions of the angler and the pilgrim are not quite the same. Although the sensory input of the former is more detailed — he directed the *tableau vivant* and witnessed the scene — his appreciation is less comprehensive. Land becomes landscape only when the beholder looks at it without a practical purpose, enjoying the view for its own sake (Ritter 1978: 18). Conversely, those for whom land is livelihood do not perceive it as landscape. They relate to it as insiders (Andrews 1999: 20). This is the reason why the elderly angler cannot see the seascape as the pilgrim does. The ocean is not only his home environment but also the background of the fishing scenes performed by his own children. Being so familiar with that shore and having witnessed so much violence, he cannot bridge the gap between sea and seascape. Not that landscape must necessarily be an eventless space, but actions are arguably what hold his attention. From his perspective, the ocean is, rather than a picturesque seascape, a venue, i.e. the setting of and the theatre for (line 401: 'ese teatro de Fortuna') the events involving his offspring and the sinking ships.[23]

Once more, a game of oppositions shows Góngora's alignment within *conceptismo*. His poetry is not an empty artefact ('La poesía barroca siempre dice' [Baroque poetry always says something], Egido 1990: 26) but tends towards content that is preferably paradoxical, at the limits of the thinkable (Blanco 1988: 28). On the most elemental level, the topos of the shipwreck with spectator contrasts the stability of the land (a space of life) with the dangers of the water (a space of death) (Echavarren 2012: 46). This metaphor fits into the opposition between the pastoral and the piscatorial that allows the arrangement of the *Soledades* in two parts. Nevertheless, Góngora's intellectual game goes further than that, as can be seen if we compare the seascape with the landscape. The pilgrim was not able to behold the panoramic view due to the atmospheric conditions. He had to imagine it. His poor visual input inspired an inner kind of view: the mental representation of an Idea of beauty.

Like its forerunner, the seascape delivers an *agudeza paradoja* [paradox conceit] related to (lack of) vision and imagination. In fact, the trope is double. The elderly

---

22   Calderón (2009: 117): 'Y así, me has de dar licencia | para pintártela, siendo | hoy el lienzo tus orejas, | mis palabras los matices | y los pinceles mi lengua' [And thus, you must allow me | to paint it for you, being today | the canvas your ears, | the colours my words, | and the brushes my tongue].

23   This paragraph draws from Lefebvre's (2006a: 20) insights on cinema settings.

angler faces no visual obstacles before the marine scenery. However, since he always sees the sea, he cannot seize the seascape. This is the first paradox, but not the most interesting. What makes the passage enthralling and links it with the panoramic landscape of the *Soledad primera* is the fact that, having heard the description by his host, the imagination of the pilgrim 'creates' the ekphrasis (that is, the scene appreciated as a 'painting'). Indeed, the angler's account stimulates in the pilgrim the only kind of view that the former is denied. The poet's literary display of wit is revealed in the exploration of this paradox.

We may resort again to Gracián's compliment (2001a: I. 79) — Góngora as an 'águila en los conceptos' [eagle of conceits] — to sustain that, from the viewpoint of *conceptismo*, the seascape seen from a bird's-eye perspective is also a conceit, one that inverts the logic of its predecessor and complements it with a 'twist'. On this occasion, the beginning (of clear sensory input perceived by the angler) is paradoxically the end (of his appreciation of the setting, which he only sees as sea), yet marks a new beginning (for the pilgrim himself, who may then picture the seascape).

We could draw an outline of the cliff and the sea defined against the sky as two perpendicular lines intersecting to form a right angle. If we added a diagonal line from the hilltop to the sea in order to represent the view of the beholder, then the whole scene would be pictured geometrically as a triangle. This is precisely the conceptual figure used to represent an *agudeza*, following on Sarbiewski's definition of a conceit (Blanco 1992: 176). In this case, the angles of the triangle of wit are formed by the angler (A), the pilgrim (B), and the panoramic scenery (C). The conceit explores the possibility of combining two divergent viewpoints — (A) and (B) — on the very same object (C), i.e. the scene that is seen as both sea (A → C) and seascape (B → C).

This is, in Deleuze's terminology (1988: 5, 1993: 3), a Baroque territory of contemplation for the mind, an image that may be described with the metaphor of infinite folding: 'Le Baroque [...] ne cesse de faire des plis [...] il courbe et recourbe les plis, les pousse à l'infini, pli sur pli, pli selon pli' [The Baroque [...] endlessly produces folds [...] it twists and turns its folds, pushing them to infinity, fold over fold, one upon the other]. Góngora treats the universe as if it were origami, emphasising the endless capacity of vision, narration and imagination to fold back in upon themselves.[24]

In this sense, the angler's and the pilgrim's respective involvements with the setting represent two sides of the same fold. While the former personifies the Horatian committed spectator (ode I.14), who tries to intervene in the course of events to make sure no harm comes to anyone, the latter is closer to Lucretius' ideal of the detached witness of a shipwreck, who observes other people's suffering to mark the evils he himself is spared (*De rerum natura*, II. 1–4). Those evils were close to the protagonist, shipwrecked by the harrowing sea at the outset of the *Soledad primera*. However, within the safe walls of his own fantasy, the fishing scene can be pictured as distant and harmless. Thus, the pilgrim faces no impediments to

---

24   To paraphrase Kaufman's (1998: 12) reading of Deleuze and Bohm.

FIG. 2.4. Annibale Carracci, *River Landscape* (c. 1596),
© National Gallery of Art, Washington, D.C.

recreating nature as a moral theatre for his own leisure, as if he were a dilettante *Deus pictor.*

In fact, the topoi of *Deus pictor* and *theatrum mundi* go hand in hand because the canvas of the world is a complex, changeable setting for the passing of everyday human events. In the late sixteenth century, the Baroque painter Carracci had created a type of landscape evocative of a theatre set, as his views seemed to reproduce constructed scenes with parallel planes representing nature (Carracci's *River Landscape* — Figure 2.4). Like a stage designer, Carracci presented human fates evolving against a background especially created to highlight the actions of the characters. The view implicit in such a conception was that settings exist for the sake of man (Rossholm 1990: 31–34, 98). Similarly, Góngora strengthens the link between his ekphrasis and early modern landscape art with the above-mentioned allusion to the 'teatro de Fortuna' (*Soledad segunda*, line 401), designed, in his case, not just as an arena for events but also as a moral locus, loaded with ethical connotations related to the fishing scenes and to the shipwrecks.[25]

By directing in his imagination the 'play' provided by the angler, the pilgrim conveys the message that, no matter how dramatic or terrible a motif may seem, it can always be appreciated as a work of art — when properly represented. Beholders like himself, seated at the loge level of the theatre, enjoy the spectacle from the distance conferred by teichoscopy. Indeed, the safer spectators feel, and the greater the perils they contemplate beneath them, the more they will immerse themselves

---

25   Góngora also mentions a 'festivo teatro' in the previous landscape (*Soledad primera*, line 188), referring to the Faunalia festivals of ancient Rome. However, the moral significance of that passage (if any) is far less clear.

in the performance. If we had to choose an image to represent a classic tragedy and its audience, that could well be the shipwreck with spectator (Blumenberg 1995: 50).

In the passage studied, the heroines of the (potential) tragedy are the sisters Filódoces and Éfire. Like Sophocles' Ismene and Antigone, the angler's daughters have much in common with one another (as evidenced by the double hypallage of lines 419–20). However, one of them respects patriarchal authority, while the other does not, risking her own life. Needless to say, the consequences of disobeying the angler have nothing to do with those of defying Creon, the ruler of Thebes who condemns Antigone to death for her defiance. In fact, the angler is secretly proud of his daughter's courage and does not consider disciplining her. In any case, Góngora conceived of the scene as an heroic moment of disobedience with strong Greek connotations (Blanco 2012b: 289).

The narrative of epic is structured not just by daring deeds but also by the gazes of those watching them: gods on Olympus and/or old men on the walls (Lovatt 2013: 1).[26] In this sense, the poet's allusion to epic teichoscopy could not be clearer: the patriarch observes his daughters 'desde los muros destas rocas' [from the ramparts of these rocks] (line 418), as if he were in a fortress. Furthermore, when Filódoces later kills a seal with her harpoon, the blood splashes 'las almenas | de las sublimes rocas [...]' [battlements of sublime rocks] (lines 441–42) (Góngora 2012: 112–13). Clearly, these are not endeavours of the pastoral world. The protagonist of Tansillo's third piscatorial song (1996: I. 220) proudly affirms that he is not a 'vil pescator' [miserable fisherman] with a rod, but someone who heroically hunts seals and orcas with a trident ('ma seguo col tridente e foche ed orche'). Likewise, the fisherwomen of the *Soledad segunda* convert the humble task of fishing into an exalted fight against dangerous sea dwellers (Ravasini 2014: 400).[27]

A scene with these epic undertones would not fit into a bucolic background. When Góngora wrote the *Soledades*, centuries of literature and art had already tamed the pastoral setting. The natural world it evokes is too idyllic to elicit any tragic feelings. A more untameable element is required if we are to be confronted with our own vulnerability: the sea fulfils this role (Mottet 2006: 76). Among the elements human beings fear, it is the one with which we are least at ease. The sea is the sphere of the unreckonable and lawless, and often stands for all-devouring matter that takes everything back into itself. It is thus no wonder that the poet describes it with the adjective 'fiero' [savage] (*Soledad primera*, lines 47 and 445; and *Soledad segunda*, line 174). Moreover, it is hard to see the monstrous creatures that the ocean hides until they come to the surface. They are farthest from the familiar face of nature, and seem to have no knowledge of the world as a well-ordered cosmos (Blumenberg 1995: 14–15).

---

26   As pointed out by Covarrubias (1943: 956), the Latin noun *theatrum* comes from the Greek noun θέατρον, and this from the verb θεᾶσθαι, i.e. to see. The beholder is as important as the spectacle itself.

27   Both enormous sea creatures ('*cete*') and horrendous seals ('*informes horrenti corpore phocas*') are mentioned in Sannazaro's first fisher idyll (1966), probably a common source for both Tansillo and Góngora.

FIG. 2.5. Michelangelo Merisi da Caravaggio, *Medusa* (c. 1598), Galleria degli Uffizi.
Source: Wikimedia Commons.

This is how Góngora portrays the Atlantic Ocean, necropolis of countless corpses and potential burial ground of the fisherman's own children: not only dangerous in itself but also nest of nightmarish monsters. The poet describes the seal killed by Filódoces as a 'marino toro' [sea bull], later as an aggressive 'bestia' [beast] (*Soledad segunda*, lines 427 and 441). As for the creature that Éfire dispatches, he portrays it as a 'fiera (horror del agua)' [beast, horror of the water], and 'monstro' [monster] (lines 490 and 509) (Góngora 2012: 114–17).[28] Against this background, the only remains of the Idea of the beautiful reside in the godlike appearance of the sisters.

28   The word 'monstruo' or 'monstro' was defined in the fourth volume of the *Diccionario de Autoridades* (1734: 598–99) as 'cualquier cosa excesivamente grande' [anything exceedingly large], and also as 'lo que es sumamente feo' [what is extremely ugly].

Like exterminating angels descending from the Empyrean, they merciless slay the horrid beasts in a Sisyphical attempt to purify the ocean.

The comparison with Sisyphus is pertinent because Filódoces's and Éfire's task can never be completed. Evil is not extraneous to the order of the universe for Neoplatonism. Evil is rather the result of that order, a necessary and even desirable part of the cosmos, since there could be no good without it.[29] From the viewpoint of the beholder, it is as though humankind could not distinguish good (beauty) from evil (ugliness) except by experiencing both, and could entirely enjoy the former only after having been exposed to the latter. This may explain why Góngora found a place for monstrosity in the otherwise lofty vision of nature experienced by the pilgrim. Much has been written about the poet's will to ennoble humble aspects of the rural world. This is not, however, the issue at stake here, as Góngora rather focuses on offering a poetic representation of ugliness. This was one of his great achievements, which in the arts was also Caravaggio's (*Medusa* — Figure 2.5): nothing is so ugly that art or literature cannot redeem it (Praz 1970: 132). Indeed, when developing his theory of mimesis (*Poetics*, 1448b), Aristotle had already pointed out that we enjoy looking at representations of things that are revolting to see in real life, such as obnoxious beasts.

Nevertheless, as noted by Lessing (1984: 127–32), poetry may have an advantage over painting. In a canvas, ugliness exerts all its force at one time and thus has an effect almost as strong as in nature itself. For instance, a painting of two sea creatures like those described by Góngora might be almost as disgusting as their appearance in real life. Conversely, in a poem, the repulsive effect of ugliness is softened by the change from the coexistent to the consecutive. This might be one of the reasons why an aesthete such as Góngora, who *prima facie* may have felt repelled by the motif, opted for the addition of monstrous creatures to his seascape. The way he describes them, they become projections of humanity's fears of nature and of animal otherness as uncanny.[30] Nevertheless, these distressing feelings are quickly mitigated by other factors: the ekphrastic embellishment of the scene and the annihilation of the beasts by the forces of good. Thus, Góngora's approach does not damage the aesthetic pleasantness of the seascape. Quite the opposite: the Idea of Beauty re-emerges triumphantly after the vanquishment of its nemesis.

The Concentric Spheres

The setting of the *Soledades* is not only seen for its own sake but also as a commentary on the human condition, split by the gulf between beauty and ugliness, cosmos and chaos. Hence, the evolution from the pastoral towards the piscatorial, the latter having stronger epic connotations.[31] However, Góngora does not

29   Ebreo's *Dialoghi d'amore* [*Dialogues of Love*] (2009: 113): 'In the same way, among the Platonic ideas there are also some principles of good and virtue, and others that are principles of evil and vice, because the universe needs one and the other for its preservation'.

30   I borrow this idea from Ingram's (2008: 90) study of ocean fauna in cinema. This page also follows the insights on Neoplatonism of Robb (1935: 82) and Hadot (1993: 103–04).

31   Line 958 of the *Soledad segunda* encapsulates this combination of genres: 'Glauco en las aguas, en las hierbas Pales' [Glaucus in the waters, Pales in the grasses] (Góngora 2012: 146–47).

limit himself to portraying these tensions. No matter how great his linguistic inventiveness may be, all his skills converge, like projections of parallel lines, at a vanishing point that transcends them. Góngora is a *conceptista*. His episteme, to use Foucault's terminology (1966: 32–91), is anchored in the belief that the universe is crossed by countless threads of wit that connect every point with every other. Thus, his ultimate purpose is not to mimic the world but to confront it with — or even, Borgesianly, to replace it by — a cosmos of language based on the mental association of objects.

Góngora's conceptual net will appear more clearly if we consider the interaction between the seascape and the landscape. The *Soledades* is not made up of insulated compartments: its passages are conversant with each other. Earlier, I quoted Gracián's analogy between the *agudeza compuesta* [compound conceit] and a constellation. He also compared this form of wit with architecture (Gracián 2001a: I. 63): 'composición artificiosa del ingenio, en que se erige máquina sublime, no de columnas ni arquitrabes, sino de asuntos y de conceptos' [artful composition of wit, in which a sublime mechanism is erected, not of columns or architraves, but of subjects and conceits].

Given that a conceit has the sphericity of that which is self-sufficient, Gracián's theory to create texts of compound wit has been deemed unsatisfactory. In Blanco's graphic words (1992: 305), and continuing with the architectural simile, one cannot build a wall with ball-shaped bricks. Nevertheless, as noted by Cacho (2012a: 30), given that the centre of a conceit projects lines in all directions, the conceptual figure envisaged by Gracián in his discourse IV may be pictured as a sphere of wit. Following this logic, an *agudeza compuesta* could be abstractly represented by concentric spheres, extending out equally in all directions from a common centre, their respective radii being partially superimposed.

From this viewpoint, the mechanism of the compound conceit allows for a comparison with physics. Just as the structure of a subatomic particle resembles that of a solar system (a central core/sun and orbiting electrons/planets), the structure of a conceit resembles that of an *agudeza compuesta*. According to Gracián (2001: I. 64), a 'concepto' is formed by a centre ('el sujeto sobre quien se discurre y pondera') [...the subject matter that is discussed and pondered] girded by adjuncts ('cualquiera otro término correspondiente') [...any other corresponding term]. The *agudeza compuesta* follows a similar logic. Although the Jesuit defined this form of wit in somewhat vague terms,[32] the key idea is that there should be a close correlation (that is, a broader conceit of correspondence) between the different parts of the discourse and/ or the conceits that underlie them. Thus, an *agudeza compuesta* is a macro conceit that structures the subconceits throughout a poem (Blanco 2012c: 339).

In this respect, the lines of thought traced by the landscape from the teichoscopic centre of vision to the first layer of adjuncts (frame | landscape as art | multi-

---

32   Gracián (2001a: II. 167–68): 'La [agudeza] encadenada es una traza, es aquella en que los asuntos [...] se unen entre sí como parte, para componer un todo artificioso mental' [The compound conceit is a trope in which the subjects [...] are linked with one another as a part, to compose an artful, mental whole].

layered stylisation | landscape as map | *varietà*) are prolonged by those traced by the seascape from the same centre to a second layer of adjuncts (human beings | Greco-Latin deities | animals | *scrittura particolareggiata* | shipwrecks). This arrangement increases the volume and density of the scheme of wit that englobes both passages by permitting the two types of connections described by Gracián (2001a: I. 64): the centre with the adjuncts, and these with each other ('valos careando de uno en uno con el sujeto, y unos con otros, entre sí') [one links each of them with the subject matter, and each of them with one another]. Firstly, all the radii link teichoscopy with different facets of the ekphrasis, enriching the relationship between the two motifs in a myriad of ways. Secondly, as we saw when we compared the human, divine and animal presences within the landscape and the seascape, salient adjuncts from the piscatorial sphere of conceits can be connected to implied adjuncts from its pastoral counterpart, which then become more noticeable.

Furthermore, the broader correspondence required by Gracián for compound wit is reinforced by a comprehensive *agudeza paradoja* [paradox conceit], which provides the common axis of rotation for both concentric spheres.[33] In the landscape, the paradox resides in the apparent conflict between teichoscopy and ekphrasis, which forces the pilgrim to resort to an Idea; in the seascape, it lies rather in how each beholder perceives the scenery, for the pilgrim arguably 'sees' in his mind's eye more than the fisherman who witnessed the scene. The title of Gracián's discourse LIV ('De la acolutia y trabazón de los discursos') [On the symmetry and consistency of discourses] (2001a: II. 183) points towards symmetry as a means of constructing an *agudeza compuesta*. In this respect, due to a structural paradox, both spheres of wit rotate around an axis between vision and imagination.

The importance of this form of wit can be linked to Sarbiewski's understanding of the *agudeza* as an 'alianza de lo acorde con lo discorde', i.e. a *concordia discors* (Woods 1995: 19; Sydor 2006: 587). Although the scope of this definition was limited to a sentence that combines harmonious and discordant elements (that is, what Gracián would later term an *agudeza simple* [simple conceit]), Sarbiewski's conceptualisation could also be applied to a compound conceit. One of the basic tenets of Góngora's poetry is precisely the composite of elements 'confusamente acordes', to use his own expression (*Soledad segunda*, line 351). Baroque is the art of wonder, and nowhere else is this aim better achieved than in the blend of *a priori* irreconcilable elements. Gongorism is a confusion of harmonies: the language of infinite combinatory possibilities, including those that seem to contradict one another.

Interestingly, this poetic goal is in line with a comparison offered by another cosmographic work: *De rerum natura* (I. 196–97): '*ut potius multis communia corpora rebus | multa putes esse, ut verbis elementa videmus*'.[34] Lucretius deploys the noun

---

33   Gracián (2001a: II. 188): 'No basta la unión del texto para que hagan compuestos asuntos; es menester que digan alguna correlación entre sí y se encadenen en alguna circunstancia o predicado universal a todos ellos' [The consistency of the text is not enough to produce compound conceits; there must be some correlation between its components, which should be linked in a circumstance or universal predicate common to all of them].

34   Lucretius (2001: 8): 'as there are many letters common to many words, so there are many elements common to many things'.

elementa, i.e. letters of the alphabet, as a synonym for atoms. The link can be explained as follows: just as atoms assemble into ordered structures, thereby constituting everything we perceive, letters assemble into words, equally shaping our worldview. From this perspective, the *Soledades* could be read as an attempt to portray all the arrangements of things that are conceivable: not only the world as it actually is but also all the ways it could be. To this end, the poet stretches Spanish almost to breaking point. As Wittgenstein (2001: 68) famously said, the limits of my language mean the limits of my world. Thus, by exploring every combination that language allows, thereby trying to depict every ontological possibility, the *Soledades* describes the limits of reality.[35]

In the *Carta en respuesta* [*Letter in Response*] (1613), attributed to Góngora, there is certain self-complacency concerning his own achievements: 'que el mundo está satisfecho que los años de estudio que he gastado en varias lenguas han aprovechado algo a mi corto talento' [for the world is satisfied that the years of study I have spent learning several languages have served my limited talent in something]. No doubt, the poet's erudition enabled him to find countless links between manifold objects, thereby multiplying the *conceptista* net of wit. This letter also shows awareness of the younger writers who were starting to imitate him: 'me holgara de haber dado principio a algo; pues es mayor gloria empezar una acción que consumarla' [I would be pleased to have started something; for there is more glory in starting an action than in completing it] (Carreira 1999: 2–3).

Indeed, as parodied by Lope (*La Dorotea*, act IV, scene 2) and Quevedo (*Receta para hacer Soledades en un día* [*Recipe to Make Solitudes in a Day*]), many Spanish authors embraced Gongorism. That was also the case in the Viceroyalties of Peru and New Spain. Sadly, the poet did not live long enough to realise the extent to which his words were prophetic. Although Góngora's impact in the 'New World' has been exaggerated since Carilla's *El gongorismo en América* [*Gongorism in the Americas*] (1946), there is no doubt that his work influenced literati of the viceregal elites from the early seventeenth century onwards. Camargo and Sor Juana were two of the few Creoles who succeeded in deploying Gongorism to produce works of the highest calibre. In a certain sense, both rebuilt the remains of the ship(s) that had wrecked in the *Soledades*. Their respective poems resemble this model while swerving from it in significant and different ways. It is on them that I will focus in the next chapters.

---

35   This paragraph is indebted to the BBC Radio 4 'In Our Time' program on Wittgenstein <http://www.bbc.co.uk/programmes/p0054945>.

PART II

Camargo's *San Ignacio*: The Ekphrasis of Ecstasy

FIG. 3.1. Convento de Santa Clara la Real in Tunja, Colombia. Photograph by the author. The foundation of this convent appears in both Juan de Castellanos' *Elegías de varones ilustres de Indias* [*Elegies of Illustrious Men of the Indies*] (1589), a key viceregal epic of the Renaissance, and in Juan Rodríguez Freyle's *El carnero* [*The Sheep*] (1638), the landmark chronicle of the New Kingdom of Granada. The references can be found in Castellanos (1857: 203) and Rodríguez Freyle (1979: 53 and 117–18).

CHAPTER 3

The Crucifix of Manresa

Góngora did not write much on religious subjects. However, some of his followers did. To this end, they adapted and transformed motifs from the *Soledades*. The shipwreck with spectator offers an example of this creative process. As we will see later, this topos can help explain a Creole poetic representation of a recurrent image in Western art: the crucifixion of Christ. Interestingly, the first Spanish painting accounted for in the New Kingdom of Granada was a banner entitled *Cristo de la Conquista* [*Christ of the Conquest*].[1] Peninsular art arrived in the 'New World' primarily as a means of evangelising Native Americans. For this reason, during the three centuries of Spanish rule, the vast majority of viceregal paintings and sculptures were produced under the patronage of the Church and/or devoted to religious topics (Gil Tovar 1989: 239–42).

The influence of the Counter-Reformation and particularly of the Jesuits on viceregal art was intense. The Society of Jesus requested placements for European artists such as Bernardo Bitti and Diego de la Puente throughout the Viceroyalty of Peru and promoted the dissemination of devotional images through the printing press in Lima (Tord 1989: 204). The Jesuits also founded schools and seminaries in budding towns/cities such as Quito, Cartagena and Tunja. During the second half of the sixteenth century, Tunja became one of the cultural centres of the region thanks to the work of the Italian artists Angelino Medoro and Francisco del Pozo, among others. Buildings such as the Convento de Santa Clara la Real (Figure 3.1) attest to its artistic richness.

With the sole exception of Lima, the priest Hernando Domínguez Camargo (1606–1659) lived in all the above-mentioned places (Bogotá, Tunja, Quito and Cartagena). A native of New Granada, he would become one of the greatest Creole Gongorist poets. In the course of his life, which became quite nomadic after his expulsion from the Jesuit order in 1636, he developed a strong penchant for the visual arts. His testament evidences, for instance, that he owned two books of engravings and twenty-seven artistic items.[2] Camargo was a close friend of Jacinto

---

1   Apparently, it was produced c. 1538, nine years before the establishment of the New Kingdom of Granada. Throughout the sixteenth and seventeenth centuries the kingdom was a captaincy general within the Viceroyalty of Peru.

2   The testament mentions five paintings ('Nuestra Señora de Chiquinquirá'; 'San José'; 'Magdalena'; 'Concepción'; 'Salvador del Mundo') [Our Lady of Chiquinquirá, Joseph, Mary Magdalene, the Immaculate Conception, the Saviour of the World] twelve 'sibilas' [sibyls], one 'Santo

FIG. 3.2. Gregorio Vásquez de Arce y Ceballos, *Regreso de la huida a Egipto* (1657). Source: <http://artecolonialamericano.az.uniandes.edu.co:8080/artworks/16178>. Photograph by Gustavo Mateus Cortés. The template for this painting is an engraving by Cornelius Galle after J. B. Paggi (Sebastián 1965: 128). Vásquez de Arce y Ceballos' canvas was last seen in the Templo de Santa Clara de Asís in Tunja, Colombia. Sadly, its current location is unknown. I owe this information to the art historian Marta Fajardo de Rueda.

de Rojas, an artist whom he hired to paint devotional paintings and figures of sibyls (Acuña 1964: 54; Mendoza 1969: 13). Since the poet spent the last years of his life in Tunja (1657–1659), he may have met the young Gregorio Vásquez de Arce y Ceballos (1638–1710), who would later become the most important painter of New Granada. The artist produced his first known canvas, the *Regreso de la huida a Egipto* [*The Return of the Flight to Egypt*] (1657) (Figure 3.2), precisely in this town (Acuña 1964: 61).

Both Vásquez de Arce y Ceballos and Camargo produced works that were eminently religious, with a special interest in Ignatius of Loyola (Carilla 1948: 19–20). In the case of Camargo, his major poem is the monumental — 8,928 lines — but unfinished *San Ignacio. Poema heroico*, which he wrote over a period of almost thirty years (c. 1631–1659) (Meo Zilio 1967: 33 and 228). Divided into twenty-four cantos, this epic tells the biography of the saint from his birth (1491) until the death of his disciple Diego de Hoces (1538), two years before the Society of Jesus obtained the papal approval (1540). Camargo's death prevented him from covering the final period of Ignatius' life (1539–1556).

The *San Ignacio* (1666) was posthumously published in Madrid but caused no impact whatsoever. This work was forgotten for almost three centuries. Góngora's rediscovery by the Spanish generation of 1927 was followed by that of his Latin American followers, including Camargo. However, unlike other viceregal Gongorist writers (e.g. Sigüenza y Góngora, Espinosa Medrano and especially Sor Juana), the poet from New Granada has not received much critical attention.

A controversial issue amongst the few scholars who have approached the *San Ignacio* is its genre. On the one hand, as noted by Bernucci (1998: 273), its initial lines announce that the subject matter, contrary to what Camargo had done before, would be heroic this time (book I, canto I, I.2: 'heroica ahora'). The title of the poem (*Poema heroico*), its protagonist (a saint, i.e. a universal hero for Catholicism), structure, metrics, style, tone and topoi, are all elements that show the poet's conscious desire to adhere to the norms of epic discourse (Meo Zilio 1967: 176–77; Echavarren 2012: 35). In fact, one Spanish peninsular poet — the Jesuit Antonio de Escobar y Mendoza (1613) — and two viceregal poets — Luis de Belmonte Bermúdez (1609) and Pedro de Oña (1639) — had already published epic works devoted to Ignatius of Loyola. Camargo's *San Ignacio* draws on some of these predecessors. Moreover, I will highlight various similarities with another viceregal epic: Diego de Hojeda's *La Cristiada* [*The Christiad*] (1611).[3]

On the other hand, the impact of Góngora impelled Camargo to write a poem of a hybrid nature (Carilla 1948: 11). Just as the pilgrim's journeys were often a pretext for the pastoral/piscatorial representation of nature in the *Soledades*, the saint's travels seem to play an equivalent secondary role in the *San Ignacio*. Camargo

Cristo de bulto' [sculpture of Christ], one 'lámina' [print] of 'Nuestra Señora' [Our Lady] and one of 'Verónica' [the Veronica], one 'relicario y cruz de naranjo' [reliquary and cross made of orange wood], five 'guadamecíes traídos, al óleo' [oil-painted leather wall hangings], and one sculpture of 'San José' [Joseph] with baby Jesus (Torres Quintero 1960: cix–cxvi).

3   All quotations from this poem about the Passion of Christ will follow the edition by González (2002). As for the *Ignacio de Cantabria*, I will use Oña (1992).

abandons the protagonist with surprising frequency in order to describe banquets, buildings, landscapes, animals, clothes and many other items. The shell of the poem might well be epic but its kernel is descriptive (Mora 1983: 60). This is precisely where Camargo shines for his prodigality, clarity of vision and original reworking of the *Soledades*. The *San Ignacio* is not always, as has been argued, Gongorism *a lo divino* [religious contrafactum of a secular source], but often a hagiography *a lo profano* [secular contrafactum of religious sources].

In this respect, two Gongorist features distinguish Camargo's ekphraseis (Mayers 2009: 4): their unusual prevalence over the primary narrative and their indulgence in fabulous metaphorical detail. The poem is rich in descriptions of imaginary religious architecture and works of art, especially of devotional objects. One of the longest and most impressive of these ekphraseis is the depiction of the crucifix that Ignatius places on an elevated 'balcón' [ledge] inside the cave of Manresa (book II, canto IV), where he wrote his *Ejercicios espirituales* [*Spiritual Exercises*] and practised asceticism during most of 1522. The passage illustrates Camargo's inversion (low to high) of the teichoscopic arrangement that we saw in Góngora (high to low). Indeed, Ignatius' vision of the crucifix from below emphasises the reverent submission of the character to God.

Moreover, I shall explore the relationship between the ekphrasis and the third of the literary traditions — besides religious epic and Gongorism — to which the passage belongs: devotional poetry. The seventeenth century saw a surge in interest in the subject of the Passion of Christ, as the publication of the spiritual *romanceros* [collections of ballads] by José de Valdivielso (1612) and Lope de Vega (1624) shows (Mayo 2013: 253).[4] Camargo also draws on this tradition of devotion to the humanity of Jesus, which was studied by Ricard (1964: 239). However, since Valdivielso and Lope tend to write about the actual Christ on the cross, they often reach a balance between his divine and human nature, a duality which was essential to the development of their religious works (Mayo 2007: 79).

This is not the case with Camargo, who describes a mere icon in the passage studied. His approach alters the content (and loosens the decorum) of the ekphrasis if one compares it with its Italian (Marco Girolamo Vida), viceregal (Hojeda) and Spanish (Valdivielso, Lope) predecessors. Indeed, when describing a work of art instead of Christ himself — in other words, when introducing a (poetic) representation of a (sculptural) representation, i.e. an ekphrasis in Spitzer's (1955: 207) *sensu stricto* — the duality (man | divinity) traditionally offered by Passional poetry is no longer possible. According to the kenotic theology of the cross, Christ renounced — at least in part — his divine nature in the Incarnation.[5] This feature is especially noticeable in an ekphrasis of Christ made flesh where God has been elided.

Camargo examines the bodily manifestations of Jesus. By describing the physical effects of the crucifixion, the poet underlines Christ's humanity. Thus, the realism of the image and its emphasis on suffering produce a crucifix consonant with

4   I will follow these editions: Valdivielso (1984) and Vega (1941).
5   Camargo's *San Ignacio*, book II, canto III, C.8: 'Dios se viste de Hombre' [God dresses as Man].

the *crucifixi dolorosi*, which emerged in the early fourteenth century and were still promoted by art theorists of the Counter-Reformation (Pereda 2017: 322–23). In fact, the torment of Christ may also be interpreted as an early warning of the penances to follow for Ignatius. Moreover, Camargo takes advantage of the fact that he is not describing Christ, but an icon of Christ, in order to add two further components. First, an aestheticised sense of the world, which is typical of Gongorism. Second, extravagant details such as the fauna that interacts with the crucified. The passage studied will thus serve to determine the extent to which Camargo deployed Gongorism to enrich the aesthetic dimension of his ekphrasis without betraying its post-Tridentine religious substance. Kluge's notion of diglossia (2014: 4–5) to describe how early modern authors tried to reconcile their spiritual and artistic goals will be of help.

A Counter-Reformation Christ

After his visit to the Abbey of Montserrat (March 1522), Ignatius went to Manresa in order to spend the rest of the year at the Hospital de Santa Lucía and in a nearby cave.[6] His life in the village constitutes the subject of book II, canto IV, of the *San Ignacio*. As usual, Camargo devotes several lines to describing the scenery, including the cave (stanzas CVII–CVIII), river (CIX–CXII) and fauna (CXIII–CXVI) of Manresa. Then, the poet introduces the crucifix on which I shall focus (CXVIII.1–4):[7]

> Tesoro antiguo de su casa era
> un crucifijo, que condujo, escudo
> en que pudiese rebatir severa
> flecha letal de Leviatán sañudo.

> [Ancient treasure of his house was
> a crucifix, which he carried, as a shield
> with which he could deflect the severe
> lethal arrow of the enraged Leviathan.]

As evidenced by the decrees of the twenty-fifth session of the Council of Trent (3–4 December 1563), which include a section about sacred images, the defence of the pastoral function of art was a response to Protestantism (particularly, against Calvinist iconoclasm) and its rejection of religious imagery as idolatrous.[8] Unlike Luther, Calvin even repudiated the use of the crucifix. In this contentious context,

---

6   Nieremberg (1645: 6): 'De allí partió a Manresa, donde por espacio de un año hizo en el Hospital de Santa Lucía, y en una cueva cerca del río, rigurosísima penitencia, y vida santísima' [From there he moved to Manresa, where during a year in the hospice of Saint Lucy, and in a cave near the river, he did very rigorous penance, and had a very holy life].

7   In this chapter, when I only quote a stanza (e.g. CXVIII) and lines (e.g. 1–4), this means I am referring to book II, canto IV. I will specify when I quote from other books and/or cantos. All quotations from Camargo follow the edition of his complete works by Torres Quintero (1960). This is still the best edition available, despite its shortcomings (Arellano 2016).

8   The idea was that sacred paintings would help to instruct people and reinforce their faith ('*erudiri et confirmari populum in articulis fidei commemorandi*') (Waterworth 1848: 233–36). The third Council of Lima (1582–1583), which applied the Tridentine decrees to the Spanish Americas, also emphasised the devotional importance of the images of Christ, the Virgin Mary and the saints (Lisi 1990: 112–13).

it is worth noting that Camargo uses the noun 'escudo' to describe the 'crucifijo'. The word reveals the link between the icon and the tradition of epic poetry, which has in the shield of Aeneas its paradigm of the ekphrasis that summarises the political content of an entire poem. Inscribed on that shield there is an ideology of empire that informs the *Aeneid* and that Virgil bequeathed to subsequent literary epic (Quint 1993: 21). The 'escudo' of Ignatius, equally, contains an ideology of religious empire (i.e. the universal triumph of Catholicism, as if it were predetermined and inevitable) that infuses the *San Ignacio*. Indeed, saints have a will to power, and their worldview is imperialistic in the most absolute meaning of the term: the space they seek to conquer is not only the earth but also the heavens (Cioran 1995: 45).

In this case, there is a powerful reason for describing the crucifix as a shield: the icon is a model for the new life that Ignatius wants to begin (in CXXVIII.3, the poet says 'para dechado de su nueva vida'). Thus, as a sacred image, the ekphrasis serves a didactic-protective purpose, offering a visual regime closely linked to Counter-Reformation contemplative practices (Gimbernat de González 1987: 575; Mayers 2012: 65). From that moment onwards, Ignatius will deploy the cross to defend himself from the arrows/temptations of the Devil ('flecha letal de Leviatán sañudo').[9] The poet's initial promise to make his protagonist a warrior like Mars (book I, canto I, I.7: 'que el vizcaíno Marte es tan guerrero') acquires a new meaning as soon as we start book II. Like Jesus' battles, those of Ignatius are fought on a different ground, where his enemies are himself (before his conversion), Protestantism and the Devil (Bernucci 1998: 280). This is the reason why he uses the crucifix as a shield. The cross is a symbol of victory: not of the victory of Caesar but of the victory of God (Wright 1996: 610).[10]

In the light of its importance, the fact that the icon is placed by Ignatius at a lofty vantage point is hardly surprising. The crucifix must be in a high location to preside over the whole cave and approve of the saint's penances. If I may coin a neologism, the passage presents an anascopy (from ανα — upwards — i.e. looking up from below), a perspective that constitutes a clear counter to the teichoscopy studied earlier. See CXXVIII.1–4:

> Aquesta efigie Ignacio, dolorida,
> en un balcón del risco mal volado,[11]
> para dechado de su nueva vida,
> con aseo estudioso ha colocado.

> [This sorrowful effigy, Ignatius,
> high up on a ledge of the rough-hewn rock
> as a model for his new life,
> with studied care has placed.]

9   In Valdivielso's *Décimas a la cruz* [*Song to the Cross*] (1984: 248–53), the cross 'a mí me sirve de escudo' [serves me as a shield] (line 110).
10   Lope's ballad (Vega 1941: 139–41) on Ignatius at Montserrat encapsulates this idea: 'la espada al altar ofrece | porque se quiere ceñir | armas que conquisten almas' [he offers the sword to the altar | for he wants to carry | weapons to conquer souls] (lines 13–15).
11   This line is inspired in line 193 of the *Soledad primera*: 'verde balcón del agradable risco' [green balcony to the pleasant crest of reef] (Góngora 2012: 18–19).

Writers of manuals for meditation used a variety of techniques to evoke a sense of divine presence. In the case of Camargo, his bodily viewing of Christ's Passion owes much to the tradition started by the *Ejercicios espirituales*. Meditation, for the Jesuits, involves an imaginative participation in the events of Jesus' life. To paraphrase Nowakowski (1994: 44), one must close the gap between the present and the past of the historical Christ by engaging as a witness in the drama of the Passion. This is the reason why the *Ejercicios espirituales* always start with a *composición de lugar* [mental representation of the place] that helps to visualise the setting of the episode. In this sense, by highlighting that the crucifix is located on an elevated, prominent 'balcón', Camargo seems to obey the injunctions of the Jesuit meditative manual on how to address God. Just as the soul has to lift its 'eyes' to behold Him, Ignatius has to raise his gaze to observe the lofty figure of the crucified (Mayo 2007: 32 and 114).[12]

Ignatius feels overwhelmed by the sacrifice of the Messiah, which he contemplates from the ground of the cave with reverent awe. When describing the crucifixion, the historical saint was more moderate in gritty details than his medieval predecessors. However, in the field of art theory, the Italian Cardinal Paleotti (2002: 173) would later criticise for lack of verisimilitude the paintings that depict Christ on the cross with a soft white body. Arguably following this kind of advice, Passional Spanish and viceregal art of the seventeenth century frequently portrays Christ with blood, gushing profusely from his wounds (Figure 3.3). The motif became commonplace in Baroque representations of Christ's Passion. In some instances, blood was added to early viceregal paintings as later sensibilities found them wanting in this regard (Hughes 2010: 45).

Camargo's vision of the crucifixion reveals a similar taste. In fact, the poet's gory artistry outdoes that of writers such as Vida, Hojeda, Valdivielso and Lope.[13] There is, no doubt, a historical basis for his approach. Certain studies contend that shock brought on by dehydration and loss of blood is the only plausible medical explanation for the death of the crucified Jesus (Brown 1998: II. 945–51 and 1092). The numerous lines that Camargo devotes to this motif are consistent from this viewpoint, although his motivations are arguably more ideological than historical. Like its medieval forerunners (Nowakowski 1994: 50), the *San Ignacio* provides a wealth of graphic detail in order to render the account closer to that of an eyewitness and to evoke greater compassion for the suffering Saviour.

---

12   Loyola (2013: 164–66): 'la composición será ver con la vista de la imaginación el lugar corpóreo donde se halla la cosa que quiero contemplar [...] Imaginando a Cristo Nuestro Señor delante y puesto en cruz' [the mental representation will be to see with the sight of the imagination the corporeal place where the thing that I want to contemplate is located [...] Imagining Christ Our Lord before me and placed at the cross]. A few pages later, Loyola (2013: 171) adds: 'alzado el entendimiento arriba, considerando cómo Dios nuestro Señor me mira, etc., y hacer una reverencia o humillación' [having elevated the mind, and considering how God our Lord looks at me, etc., to take a bow or humble oneself].

13   Camargo's earlier description of the siege of Pamplona offers another example of his gory aesthetics: 'de cuerpos ya sin el vital oficio | sangrienta se ha erigido una montaña' [of bodies already without the breath of life | a bloody mountain has been erected] (book I, canto III, CLVIII.3–4).

FIG. 3.3. Pedro de la Rosa, *Crucificado del santo Hermano Pedro* (1657), Calvario de Antigua, Guatemala. Photograph by Rafael Ramos.

FIG. 3.4. Juan de Mesa, *Jesús del Gran Poder* (1620), Basílica de Jesús del Gran Poder de Sevilla. Photograph by Jesús Argudo García. Archivo de la Hermandad del Gran Poder de Sevilla (A.H.G.P.S.).

There are three main sources of blood in the body described by Camargo: the pierced limbs, the wounds produced by the crown of thorns and the bruises originating from previous lashing. When portraying these features, the poet seems to follow the advice of early modern art treatises. Firstly, although four nails were more common in early Christian art, the number of three eventually became standard — a nail for each hand, and a third for the feet (Brown 1998: II. 951). Francisco Pacheco reacted against this tradition in both his writings and his paintings, through which he tried to restore the so-called *Cristo de cuatro clavos* that, to his mind, was historically more accurate (Pacheco 1956: II. 363–99). These four-nail crucifixes would also arrive in the Americas (Figure 3.3).[14] In this sense, Camargo states clearly that four nails produce four torrents of blood from the body of Christ (CXX.1 and 8: 'Cuatro lo fían de obstinado acero' | 'cuatro raudales lo desatan rojos').

Secondly, Pacheco also wrote extensively about the crown of thorns to argue that 'no solo rodeó las sienes, como se pinta de ordinario, sino cubrió toda la cabeza' [Not only did it surround the temples, as is ordinarily painted, but it covered the whole head] — Juan de Mesa's *Jesús del Gran Poder* (Figure 3.4) offers an example

14   Pacheco's proposal was followed by numerous artists, including Francisco de Zurbarán (Pereda 2017: 71 and 117). Three four-nail crucifixes by this Spanish painter were identified in Peru, although one of them is now in a private American collection. I owe this information to the art historian Akemi Herráez.

akin to what Pacheco envisaged. This 'helmet-crown', as it were, so hurt the head of Christ that his 'ojos, orejas y barba quedaron bañados de nuevo en sangre' [eyes, ears and beard were bathed again in blood] (Pacheco 1956: II. 283 and 400).

Likewise, Camargo describes the crown piercing Christ's head deeply and thoroughly (stanza CXXII), as if he sought to create a shocking eidetic image for his readers. Using, as he often does, an image from the animal world, Camargo compares the thorns with two animals that evoke atavistic fears to death: a snake and a scorpion (lines 4 and 6: 'complicado de juncos un serpiente' | 'de agudos escorpiones a su frente'). Then, the poet concludes with a reference to the streams of blood that flow from the tortured head (line 7: 'que en los hilos que brota carmesíes').

Thirdly, as mentioned above, Paleotti (2002: 173) had complained about the Passional paintings of Christ that show no sign of bruising or whipping. In this respect, Camargo is aware that the previous torments with which the Passion started must have left traces on his body.[15] The way the poet approaches this motif is insightful because not only does stanza CXXIII mention the physical injuries, but it also hints at the mental anguish that accompanied them. He first describes the endless lashing: 'la copia aleve | que las violentas manos le imprimieron' (lines 3–4). Then, in the only reference of the ekphrasis to characters other than Christ, Camargo alludes (with a metaphor) to the anonymous crowds that insulted and spat at him (lines 6–8):

> ...sí llovieron
> desde las nubes de profanos labios
> borrascas de salivas y de agravios.[16]
>
> [...there rained
> from the clouds of profane lips
> squalls of spit and insults.]

Crucifixion was a powerful symbol with a clear and frightening meaning in the Roman world. It was not just a means of liquidating undesirables or rebel leaders; it did so with the maximum degradation (Wright 1996: 543). In this respect, Camargo could choose between two Gospel traditions when portraying this form of torture: John (19:25–27), who softened the emotional suffering by mentioning the presence next to the cross of people who were close to Jesus, including his mother and Mary Magdalene; or Mark (15:29–32) and Matthew (27:39–44), according to whom Jesus was abandoned by his disciples and mocked by all surrounding the cross. Camargo followed Mark and Matthew. This eschatological tradition fits in with the poet's *crucifixus dolorosus*, which is not limited to mere bodily injuries. The *San Ignacio*

---

15   He explains this in the *Invectiva apologética* [*Apologetic Invective*]: 'es mucha nieve para tantas llagas y cardenales' [it is a lot of snow for so many sores and bruises] (Torres Quintero 1960: 453). The *Invectiva*, Camargo's only text in prose, was written in 1652 and published posthumously by Jacinto de Evia (1676: 323–406).

16   The metaphor is similar to that in Paravicino's *Romance a la pasión de Cristo* [*Ballad on the Passion of Christ*] (lines 167–68): '¿Injurias, aún no escampáis? | Lloved, como halléis adónde' [Insults, do you ever let up? | Find somewhere else to rain down on] (Torres Quintero 1960: 418).

emphasises not only Christ's physical suffering, but also his psychological torment: he dies surrounded by enemies who target offensive language at him. The cross means to suffer and to die as one who is rejected as an outcast (Moltmann 1974: 55).

However, Camargo is not narrating the entire story of Christ's Passion but only describing a crucifix. Thus, the fact that his ekphrasis includes none of the characters who play a role either as torturers or as witnesses is entirely logical. The main source we have to infer the poet's reading of the Passion is his portrayal of Christ. Camargo evokes compassion for Christ's physical and mental suffering by allowing the eyes to linger over the evidence of his pain, the ears over the voices that were shouting insults at him. Only Christ appears in bodily likeness; only his tortured body will provide us with a map of his suffering. To paraphrase Nowakowski's (1994: 48–49) insight on Julian of Norwich, the poet delivers his vision as a picture rather than as a story. He takes great care in describing the image to impress it on the minds of his readers.

It was, after all, failed Messiahs who ended up on crosses; the historical Jesus must have had to wrestle with the serious possibility that he might have been deluded (Wright 1996: 606). According to Mark (15:34) and Matthew (27:46), his last words were sombre: 'My God, my God, why have you forsaken me?'. The Passion narrative of these two evangelists is indeed a tragic drama, for nothing shows God acting on the side of Christ while he is alive.[17] No one answers his question; silence is his last experience of God in this world. Christ died with the signs and expressions of a profound abandonment by his Father (Moltmann 1974: 147). In the tradition of devotional poetry, however, Christ on the cross is more often silent since the sinner, from his position of poetic subject, usually prays to a crucified who is already dead (Mayo 2007: 140). This is Camargo's approach: although the historical Ignatius affirmed that he could hear Jesus in some of his ecstatic visions, the poet might have thought that, on this occasion, the tortured corpse was eloquent enough: *res ipsa loquitur*.

The way in which Jesus would defeat evil (that is, by letting it do its worst to him) was consistent with the deeply subversive nature of his own kingdom-announcement. While his contemporaries expected a military victory over Israel's enemies, he offered them a model that was the opposite of, say, a Judas Maccabeus. Camargo understood that suffering was the means through which the apocalyptic drama attained its goal. Thus, his ekphrasis does not portray the powerful Christ whom the faithful had worshipped for centuries. Quite the opposite: the Christ of the *San Ignacio* is depicted in terms of atonement. No detail of pain and torture is omitted. In the absence of words, the poet offers a powerful image to describe the godlessness and godforsakenness of one who has plumbed the depths of the abyss and is enveloped in darkness (CXXI.5–8):[18]

---

17   Loyola (2013: 199): 'considerar cómo la Divinidad, que parecía esconderse en la pasión' [to consider how God, who seemed to hide Himself during the passion]. The last line of Quevedo's (1998: 49) sonnet *A Jesucristo, nuestro Señor, expirando en la cruz* [*To Jesus Christ, our Lord, Expiring on the Cross*] expresses a similar thought: 'dudara, gran Señor, si tenéis Padre' [I would doubt, great Lord, that you have a Father].

18   This paragraph is indebted to Wright (1996: 565–77) and Moltmann (1974: 243–44).

> El pecho esconden, cuando el rostro niegan,
> enmarañadas ondas del cabello,[19]
> que cuando crespas la cerviz anegan,
> se derraman inciertas en el cuello;
> bajeles sus dos ojos las navegan,
> y en lo sangriento naufragó lo bello:[20]
> las luces turbias, que el naufragio agota,
> en niña y niña se aparecen, rota.

> [Concealing the chest, covering the face,
> tangled waves of messy hair,
> which when they drench the neck
> spill precariously around it;
> his two eyes are vessels that sail his hair
> and beauty was shipwrecked in the bloodiness:
> the murky lights fade in the shipwreck,
> and appear in his sunken pupils.]

In other parts of the poem, Camargo deploys the topos of the shipwreck with spectator following literally its traditional features (for instance, in book III, canto I, stanza LIII) (Echavarren 2012: 45–46). However, the lines transcribed are more original, since it is the actual face of Christ where the shipwreck takes place: Jesus' eyes, metaphorically transformed into ships, sail through the 'enmarañadas ondas del cabello'. The torture/shipwreck dims ('naufragio agota') the murky lights ('luces turbias') of his pupils ('en niña y niña'), which represents the life that is ebbing away. The last word of the stanza ('rota') evokes the idea of apparent defeat: Christ's pupils are 'broken', i.e. destroyed, without brightness, without sight.[21] The whole scene is partly seen, partly imagined, by the penitent Ignatius.

Having witnessed so much suffering, Ignatius' reaction is strong. Like the poetic speaker in Horace's (2004: 50–51) ode to the ship of state (I.14), and the elderly angler of Góngora's *Soledad segunda*, the spectator (Ignatius) is completely absorbed by the shipwreck (the death of the Messiah). In this case, three aggravating circumstances make the spectacle even more painful for the witness. First, he can do nothing to prevent Jesus from suffering and dying. Second, he shares the collective guilt of humankind for that deed. Third, unlike other saints such as Francis Borgia and Teresa of Ávila, Ignatius had sinned gravely during his youth. His conversion was the result of a hard and painful effort, a profound crisis and prolonged meditations (Ricard 1964: 149–52).

---

19   Note the similitude with Hojeda's *Cristiada*, VII. 149. 3–4: 'Y el cabello [...] | Enmarañado ven, y escarnecido' [And the hair [...] | They see it tangled and scorned] (González 2002: 409).

20   There are comparable lines in Hojeda's *Cristiada*, VIII. 90. 7–8: 'Y anégase la eterna hermosura | En el mar rojo de su sangre pura' [And the eternal beauty drowns | In the red sea of his pure blood] (González 2002: 438). Vida's *Christiad* (2009: 299–301) could well be the source of both Hojeda and Camargo.

21   Camargo also uses the metaphor of the shipwreck when Ignatius arrives home after being gravely wounded at Pamplona: 'Del cuerpo augusto el breve esquife roto, | naufragante vacila en un mar muerto' [From the august body the slight broken skiff | risks shipwreck adrift in a dead sea] (book I, canto IV, CCXXIX.1–2).

FIG. 3.5. Benedictus van Haeften, 'Christo confixus sum Cruci', in *Regia via crucis* (1635).
Source: HathiTrust Digital Library.

Camargo understood that, in Manresa, Ignatius needed an atonement for his sins. The crucifix would inspire him in this respect.[22] In Christianity, the Passion of Christ has often been understood and relived as a mysticism of suffering. By performing acts of self-mortification, believers have drawn closer to the torments of Christ, have participated in them and felt them as their own (Moltmann 1974: 45). The cross is the place chosen to force self-examination and repentance, the site where one discovers the consequences of previous wrongdoing. Haeften's emblem (Figure 3.5) delivers a visual representation of the Christian thirst for pain, a strong longing that also appears in other Baroque poems (Holloway 2017: 93).

In this respect, the death of the crucified is self-explanatory and serves to stimulate awareness in Ignatius, who wants to change his life radically in order to attain the salvation of others and his own (Mayo 2007: 85–86). Before the crucifix, the saint will weep tears both of regret (for himself) and of compassion (for the Passion of Christ). Thus, a specular relationship emerges between the icon and the protagonist. Ignatius feels a compulsion to repeat throughout his own body the strokes of Christ's blood that are already 'written' on the crucifix (Gimbernat de González 1987: 575–76). Like the poetic subject of Valdivielso's (1984: 154) sonnet *De un pecador arrepentido* [*From a Repentant Sinner*],[23] the protagonist of the *San Ignacio* understands that, although the ultimate benefit of the penances will be spiritual, physical imitation of Passional suffering will facilitate the action of the intellect and the emergence of affections (Mayo 2007: 82). This is the reason why the ekphrasis fulfils a proleptic function: like Jesus, the penitent will shed his own blood in the hope of redemption.

Although the saint was relatively moderate when giving advice for self-mortification,[24] Camargo prefers to take a hyperbolic line. The source material he uses is historical, as Ignatius was praised in his litany for being 'constant in the practice of corporal penance'. However, the poet surpasses the toughest theorists of the time, arguably to highlight the importance of this devotional practice for the future of the Society of Jesus: hardship builds character and that, in turn, builds empire (Quint 1993: 94). In Camargo's hands, history has acquired a malleable property that is made to convey an orthodox religious message in a typical Counter-Reformation manner. The poet devotes no fewer than thirteen stanzas to the penances of Ignatius (CXXIX–CXLI).[25] What fascinates Camargo is the saint's thirst for pain and his

---

22   According to Nieremberg (1645: 6), at Montserrat, Ignatius already had 'una cadena de hierro con que se había de ceñir para afligir su cuerpo, y otras cadenas más delgadas, para disciplinarse cruelmente' [an iron chain which he strapped to himself in order to punish his body, and other thinner chains to cruelly discipline himself]. Loyola's (2013: 164) spirituality is also relevant in this respect: 'La demanda ha de ser según sujeta materia [...] si es de pasión, demandar pena, lágrimas y tormento con Cristo atormentado' [The request must agree with the subject matter [...] if it is of passion, ask for grief, tears and torment as with the tormented Christ].

23   Line 11: 'y pues herido estáis, Señor, heridme' [and since you are wounded, Lord, wound me].

24   He said that only 'cuerdas delgadas' [thin strings] should be used because they produce just 'dolor y no enfermedad' [pain and not disease] (Loyola 2013: 172).

25   Conversely, Oña's *Ignacio de Cantabria* (1992: 221) contains just four lines about Ignatius' penances at Manresa: 'Con tal rigor allí su cuerpo trata, | que lo reposa helado en dura tierra; | tres veces la matiza de escarlata | a costa del humor que rojo encierra' [There, he treats his body with

resilience in enduring it, i.e. the voluptuousness of suffering, to borrow Cioran's expression (1995: 9). Ignatius punishes his body to such an extent that his blood covers the ground of the cave and raises the level of the nearby river (CXVII.7–8 and CXXIX.7–8). He feels infinite compassion for Jesus but behaves without any mercy towards himself: 'y en el Cristo, a quien voces da devotas, | nuevas imprime llagas con sus gotas' [and on the Christ, whom he addresses with devout expressions, | he imprints new wounds with the drops of his blood] (CXLI.7–8). Having seen the cruel treatment that Christ received, he offers him his own pain trusting that it will soothe, to some extent, the physical and emotional distress of the crucified (Mayo 2007: 101).

The direct address to the well-to-do reader in the next section of Camargo's description (stanzas CXLII–CXLV) provides an example of another technique to encourage imaginative participation in the events of Christ's life. The ekphrasis aims at changing not only the protagonist within the text, but also the readership outside it.[26] There must be a 'chain reaction' from the Saviour to the reader, as it were. Just as Ignatius, who was born in a well-off, aristocratic family, dismissed that wealth and background in order to follow the path of Jesus, readers should take as an example the sacrificed life of the saint, and then examine their own conscience, acknowledge their sins, repent, confess and perform acts of penitence.[27] Moreover, although autobiographical references are conspicuous by their absence, there could be a subtle self-reproach in the passage, for Camargo's refined lifestyle was at odds with his poetic preaching (Meo Zilio 1986: XLIV).

Thus, the death of Jesus, as represented in the ekphrasis, paradoxically brings life. The oxymoron 'vivamente muerto' [vividly dead] (CXIX.8) can be understood in this sense. In fact, as noted by Gracián (2001a: II. 221), the transformational impact of Christ on the cross is a conceit: 'El verdadero Orfeo es aquel señor, que teniendo estirados sus sagrados miembros en la lira de la cruz, con aquellas clavijas de sus duros clavos, hizo tan dulce y suave armonía que atrajo a sí todas las cosas' [The true Orpheus is that lord, who having his sacred limbs stretched out on the lyre of the cross, with those tuning pegs of his hard nails, made such sweet and gentle harmony that he attracted all things to himself]. Camargo's approach is less tender but shares with Gracián the belief in the power of the icon. Furthermore, what is theologically more important is the faith that the poet's gory aesthetics reflect, which could be encapsulated in an *agudeza paradoja* [paradox conceit]: Christ brings help through that which, from the human point of view, is his impotent suffering (Moltmann 1974: 46). Indeed, by means of his own torment and death, the crucified brings God to Ignatius.

---

such harshness, | that he rests it frozen on hard earth; | three times he stains the earth with scarlet | from the loss of the blood from his body] (VI. 490.1–4). I borrow the argument about the Counter-Reformation from Darst (1998: 134).

26   I borrow this idea from Nowakowski (1994: 46). Camargo's approach is in line with Paleotti's (2002: 82) account of the impact caused by paintings of the crucified Jesus, as reflected in his examples of conversions experienced before these icons.

27   I paraphrase Darst (1998: 95), who writes about self-directed conversions.

Although Camargo's ekphrasis satisfies the Counter-Reformation demands concerning sacred images, there are also other traditions from which the poet draws inspiration. The poetic crucifix is clothed beneath layers of an aestheticised sense of the world, linguistic complexity and boundless imagination (e.g. the extravagant animals of the cave) that complement the spiritual message in an original and creative way. As we shall now see, these 'supplements' to Camargo's religious agenda cannot be explained without his Gongorism.

An Aestheticised Christ

Both the crucifix and the religious hero of the *San Ignacio* embody quintessential features of the Counter-Reformation. Camargo, who worked for the Inquisition in Tunja towards the end of his life, was familiar with the theological and moral functions that art had to fulfil according to Catholic orthodoxy (Meo Zilio 1967: 58–61).[28] However, many lines in the *San Ignacio* suggest that his poetic interests were broader than that. Although the epic poem constitutes the bulk of his corpus, he was not a spiritual writer in the manner of, say, a Saint John of the Cross. Camargo was a follower of Góngora, who was well known for sublimating natural motifs into ideal representations of beauty. Having this background in mind, the viceregal poet perhaps felt that the *crucifixus dolorosus* did not satisfy his aesthetic leanings completely.

As a creator, Camargo was not only interested in religion but also in beauty. Góngora could not offer many examples of devout poetry. However, his corpus had a wealth of topoi and techniques to embellish reality, make it more enthralling and bring it closer to a work of art. These were all purposes Camargo wanted to fulfil, even when writing about the crucifixion. Thus, he focused on projecting his Gongorist aesthetics onto the crucifix to convert it, despite all the wounds and suffering represented therein, into an aesthetically precious object. This is the reason why the ekphrasis works so well as an illustration of the Baroque tension between Counter-Reformation orthodoxy and secular experimentation, two substantive strains that were not easily reconcilable. As we shall see, the outcome is a doublespeak or diglossia, which illustrates 'the conflict between theological and artistic intentions' (Benjamin 1977: 177).

Camargo idealises the crucifix in four ways. First, he explains that the icon was so accomplished that people wondered whether art could produce such a lifelike effect. Second, he deploys maritime metaphors that end up converting the portrait into a seascape. I touched upon this idea when examining his approach to the shipwreck with spectator. I shall now examine the topos from another perspective, focusing on the description of Jesus' hair. Third, he portrays the blood of the crucified using a rich Petrarchan lexicon of precious stones, flowers, fire and fruits.

---

28   In the *Invectiva apologética*, Camargo even threatens to denounce the author of an anonymous poem about the Passion of Christ to the Inquisition: 'este verso [...] tiene cara de hereje' [this line [...] has the face of a heretic] (Torres Quintero 1960: 470). The first canto of book V of the *San Ignacio*, which is entirely devoted to attacking 'la herejía de Lutero' [Luther's heresy], is also indicative of Camargo's religious worldview.

These three features distance the description from the *crucifixus dolorosus* and bring it closer to an idealised Christ who, while denying peace or calm, at least radiates beauty. Camargo's fourth and most striking innovation is the extravagant, lengthy depiction of various animals that try to heal the wounds of the crucified.

Let us begin with the artistic merits of the icon. Having explained that Ignatius took the crucifix from his family treasures, Camargo introduces it with the following praise (CXVIII.5–8):

> en cuyo vulto el arte así se esmera,
> que dudan del pincel y escoplo agudo,
> los que en el Cristo admiran sentimientos,
> si del primero fueron instrumentos.

> [in whose face craft so excels itself,
> that those who admire the feelings in the Christ
> wonder whether the brush and sharp chisel
> were instruments of art.]

Camargo may have included these lines to bring his description closer to the kind of ekphrasis at which Góngora excelled. The Cordovan poet tends to convert every artefact he describes into a prodigy, regardless of its intrinsic qualities. One of his ways of doing so is by explaining the origin or process of creation of the item portrayed (Blanco 2012b: 277). Praise for the artist's mastery would also help elevate the allure of the ekphrastic object (Pineda 2000: 261–62). In this respect, craft so excels itself that the spectators, who see feelings vividly portrayed, can hardly believe their eyes. They wonder whether art can produce such an impact with mere material instruments (i.e. the chisel and the brush). The crucifix is an outstanding work, the sculptural and pictorial achievements of which arouse *admiratio*. Indeed, the combination of the art of the wood carver and that of the painter or gilder of images achieves a life-like effect. The spectators forget the tools of craftsmanship while immersing themselves in a powerful illusion of reality.[29]

Moreover, according to the ekphrasis, art exceeds itself particularly on Christ's face ('en cuyo vulto [i.e. face, a typical Gongorist Latinism] el arte así se esmera'). Interestingly, this quality is hard to perceive because the hair of Christ is a tangle that covers the front part of his head. This is how Camargo describes it (CXXI.1–4):

> El pecho esconden, cuando el rostro niegan,
> enmarañadas ondas del cabello,
> que cuando crespas la cerviz anegan,
> se derraman inciertas en el cuello.

> [Concealing the chest, covering the face,
> tangled waves of messy hair,
> which when they drench the neck
> spill precariously around it.]

---

29   In his ballad XVIII, Lope (Vega 1941: 98–101) also merged the ideas of gore and artistry: 'a la Cruz, de quien pendía | un rojo y sangriento lienzo' [to the Cross, from which | a red and bloody canvas hung] (lines 17–18).

As noted by Mayo (2013: 257–65), many Golden Age authors (e.g. Garcilaso, Quevedo) had previously likened the hair of (often female) characters to waves. Thus, the metaphor, as such, is not particularly original. In fact, the lines transcribed evoke the liquid sinuosity of Polyphemus's hair and beard, which Góngora compares to both the sea and a river.[30] Apart from the motif of the shipwreck studied above, what makes Camargo's approach original is the way he uses the metaphor to dignify a 'sea' which, in fact, is formed by a mixture of hair, blood, sweat, tears and dirt. If one accepts the invitation to see the portrait as a seascape with a storm, then the ekphrasis can produce the effect of a verbal painting in which each element (e.g. wounds, bones, eyes) finds its nautical counterpart (e.g. shores, cliffs, ships) (Colombí-Monguió 1986: 275).

However, by adopting a vertical perspective, the description also enables the reader, for a moment, to imagine the hair as a curtain of water rather than as sea. Metamorphosis is, indeed, a key feature of Camargo's ekphraseis, which often find in transformations the essence of all things and beings (Cancellier 2000: 35). The head of Christ falls onto his chest so that, when contemplated from the front, his face cannot be seen completely.[31] This position is both physiologically natural after death and typical of the visual arts, since many artists (e.g. Velázquez, Zurbarán) resorted to it in order to circumvent the challenge of portraying the face of God as a dead human looking straight into the beholder (Ramos 2013: 299 and Figure 3.3).

Therefore, the waterfall races down in a series of cascades that cover not only the face ('el rostro niegan') but also the chest of Christ ('El pecho esconden'). Given its object, the ekphrasis remains equally ominous but gains in visual suggestiveness and appeal at the expense of abandoning all plausibility. According to John (19:28), the penultimate words of Christ on the cross were: 'I thirst'. There is a certain paradox in the attempt to describe a dehydrated corpse with torrential metaphors of water. Nevertheless, this example shows how Camargo approached the topic as a poet and not as a historian. Perhaps the physiological cause of the death of Jesus was indifferent to him when writing the ekphrasis. What did concern him was a *conceptista* understanding of beauty, the cornerstone of which was to find unexpected connections between disparate elements, even when this entailed mixing the sacred (the crucified Jesus) with the profane (a seascape).

The tendency to describe the divine with a secular lexicon is even clearer in the portrayal of Christ's body, especially his blood. This is the third way in which Camargo idealises the corpse. His vocabulary consists primarily of words taken from certain lexical families (e.g. gemstones, flowers, fruits) that are typical of the Petrarchan tradition. Most of them allude to the colour red which, as such,

30   *Polifemo*, lines 57–58, and 61: 'Negro el cabello, imitador undoso | de las obscuras aguas del Leteo [...] | un torrente es su barba impetüoso' [Black hair, wavy imitator | of Lethe's dark waters [...] | his beard is an impetuous torrent] (Ponce Cárdenas 2010: 157).
31   One can find the same image in Hojeda's *Cristiada*, XII.134.7–8: 'Y el alma despidió y dejó suave | la cabeza inclinada al pecho grave' [And he breathed out his soul, and left | His head softly inclined on his heavy chest] (González 2002: 607). According to Pereda (2017: 420), the artfulness of concealing facial expressions of pain alludes to a Plinian topos (*Natural History*, book XXXV, chapter 36).

is mentioned just three times in a description of eighty-eight lines (CXX.8, CXXV.7 and CXXVII.3). Although Petrarch is relatively restrained when using this aestheticised lexicon, Camargo's exuberance is common among Gongorist poets: a colour is not represented abstractly by its corresponding signifier but suggested by a precious object that is associated with it. The object thus substitutes the colour (Meo Zilio 1967: 189).

For instance, the ekphrasis contains six references to gems or precious stones — three to 'rubíes' or 'rubís' (CXX.6, CXXII.8, CXXV.3); one to 'pórfido' and 'jaspes' (CXXIV.5–6); and one to 'zafiro' (CXXVII.6) — and four to flowers or corals: two to 'rosa' or 'rosas' (CXXIII.1 and 6); one to 'alelí' (CXXIII.3); and one to 'corales' (CXXV.5).[32] Christ's vital fluid undergoes an almost kaleidoscopic transformation through various shades of red, purple and black. Camargo uses these nouns in order to exalt symbolically the brightness, purity and beauty of the blood — and thus of the wounded corpse that it covers. The red rose, for example, evokes exquisiteness and delicacy, although the flower is paradoxically covered with thorns like the crowned Jesus. The blood enhances the beauty of Christ, which is based on the greatness of his love. This aesthetic is Platonic and its notion of beauty directly proportional to the intensity of the atonement.[33] This is the reason why a bloodstained corpse can serve as a springboard for a series of images of great lyrical value (Mayo 2007: 103).

After the first seven stanzas of the ekphrasis (CXVIII–CXXIV), Camargo evolves from the imagery of precious stones and flowers towards the depiction of a torch (CXXV). This transitional metaphor reinforces both the purifying function of the blood within the text, and the theory of the poet's familiarity with the Petrarchan tradition outside it. Indeed, as noted by Mayo (2007: 94–101), the image of the flame that burns without consuming, that is renewed inexhaustibly, is typical of Petrarch and was widely used in amatory poetry during the sixteenth and seventeenth centuries. Góngora himself linked the love motif to the phoenix when describing the bride at the end of the *Soledad primera*.[34] Although Camargo does not mention the mythological bird, he applies the topos of the flame to the crucified Jesus, thereby suggesting the idea of divinity by means of the light emanating from his body. Like the phoenix, Christ suffers a transitory death by fire (line 1: 'Sangrienta

---

32   Valdivielso's poem *A las llagas de Cristo nuestro señor* [*On the Wounds of Christ our Lord*] (1984: 67–68) describes the wounds similarly as 'flor y fruto que ha dado | la tierra de promisión' [flowers and fruit given by | the land of promise] (lines 15–16).

33   Camargo encapsulated a similar idea in line 53 of his ballad *A la pasión de Cristo* [*On the Passion of Christ*]: 'Feo hermosamente el rostro' [Beautifully ugly face]. This brings to mind his *Invectiva apologética*: 'esas sus deformidades eran sus mayores hermosuras' [his wounds were his greatest beauty] and 'lo explique tan hermoso, que parezca como lo es, paraíso de los ojos' [[the poet] should present an attractive Christ, who looks just as he is, a paradise for the eyes]. (Torres Quintero 1960: 395, 444 and 490 respectively).

34   In the poem CCXLI of the *Canzoniere*, Petrarch (1999: 982) describes his love as 'l'incendio che m'infiamma' [the blaze that burns me] (line 13), which nothing can extinguish. I also refer to the *Soledad primera*, line 948: 'cual nueva Fénix en flamantes plumas' [like a new phoenix dressed in plumes] (Góngora 2012: 72–73).

antorcha el corazón se vía').[35] Warm blood (line 3: 'turbias llamas de rubís hervía') slips down his chest, and thus is compared to the ashes that are thrown out of the dying embers of a fire (line 7: 'rojas cenizas'). Nevertheless, he will be reborn from his ashes to grant sinners eternal life.

When representing the final triumph of Christ over death, Camargo moved towards yet another lexical family: fruits, first a pomegranate (CXXVI) and then a vine — grapes — (CXXVII). The choice of the pomegranate is unsurprising, since the poet included this fruit in two of his poetic still lifes in order to link it with the pelican: the mythological bird that plucks at her own breast, spills her blood on her dead offspring, and restores them to life.[36] Moreover, in early modern art, the pomegranate is a symbol often associated with baby Jesus as a prefiguration of his death (Figure 3.6).

The crucified body has virtually burst — the chest is broken open: 'Abierta en dos mitades la granada | del pecho' (CXXVI.1–2) — due to the scourging, blows and punches. The crucifixion stretches the body and makes it 'rest' on the joints of wrists, arms and shoulders. Therefore, Christ resembles an open pomegranate, the (displaced, separated) seeds of which echo his dislocated bones. The bright red colour of the fruit's juice is reminiscent of blood (Mayo 2007: 54). Moreover, although Camargo does not mention the pelican, he may have had the myth in mind when writing these lines, since the parallel is obvious: like the bird, Christ emanates the blood of salvation.

This key image can be appreciated more clearly in the next metaphor of the vine. Jesus himself, in prophetic style, identified during the last supper the bread with his own body and the wine with his own blood. He spoke about these in language that echoed the connotations of Passover: sacrifice and covenant (Wright 1996: 559). The metaphor of stanza CXXVII becomes transparent if one has this background in mind: the 'vid' (body of Christ) is full of 'racimos' (wounds), the grapes of which can be pressed to make wine, a precious liquid, like the blood of the crucified (Mayo 2007: 66).

Then, the shining blood of the icon attracts, as if it were real, several creatures to the crucifix.[37] The poet describes eight animals in total: a snake (CXLVI), a spider (CXLVII), a firefly (CXLVIII), snails (CXLIX), a lizard (CL), a butterfly (CL), ants (CLI) and bees (CLII). Osuna (1969: 18) points out that most of these creatures appear in Adrián de Prado's *Canción real a San Jerónimo* [*Royal Song to Saint Jerome*]

---

35   The phoenix myth's Christological associations were prevalent in the early modern Hispanic world (Holloway 2017: 109).

36   Book I, canto I, LXVI.1 (repeated in book IV, canto III, CXIX.6): 'Pelícano de frutas, la granada' [Pelican of fruits, the pomegranate]. Lope's ballad XIX (Vega 1941: 102–06) called Jesus 'Pelícano amoroso' [Loving pelican] (line 37). Valdivielso also described Christ on the cross as a pomegranate in five ballads of his *Romancero espiritual* [*Spiritual Ballads*], including the *Romance al Santísimo Sacramento* [*Ballad on the Blessed Sacrament*] (1984: 147–49): 'Es su corazón de fuego, | cuyas amorosas llamas | hicieron al noble pecho | reventar como granada' [His heart of fire, | whose flames of love | made the noble chest | burst like a pomegranate] (lines 21–24).

37   Likewise, Petrarch (1999: 79) had compared his love for Laura with insects' attraction to light in his sonnet XIX.

FIG. 3.6. Sandro Botticelli, *Madonna of the Pomegranate* (1487), Galleria degli Uffizi.
Photograph by Miguel Hermoso Cuesta. Source: Wikimedia Commons. License:
Creative Commons Attribution–Share Alike 4.0 International.

(1619), arguably one of the sources of the passage.[38] Some of them (snake, snails,
butterfly, ants and bees) are also typical of Gongorist imagery.

Like the penitent Ignatius, most of these animals want to share the pain of Jesus.[39]
The spider, for instance, covers with its web the bleeding wounds of his head: 'y
en esconder la sangre persevera' (CXLVII.6). The snails try to remove the nails in
order to take the place of the crucified: 'porque quedar en su lugar pretende[n]'

38   The poem can be found in Blecua (1945: 207–19).
39   A similar idea is expressed in Valdivielso's *Romance de un alma a los pies de un crucifijo* [*Ballad of a
Soul at the Foot of a Crucifix*] (1984: 24–26): 'Heridas tenéis, mi vida, | y duélenvos, | tuviéralas yo, y
no vos' [You have wounds, my life, | and they hurt you, | I wish I had them, and you did not] (lines
25–27).

FIG. 3.7. Cross as Tree of Life, apsidal vault (c. 1100–1130), Basilica di San Clemente al Laterano, Rome. Source: Wikimedia Commons. License: Creative Commons Attribution-Share Alike 3.0 Unported.

(CXLIX.8). The lizard closes the wound in Christ's side with its own teeth: 'el costado con diente y diente sella' (CL.8). The ants and the butterfly also cover various injuries with their bodies (CL.5–7 and CLI.1–6), and the bees sweeten Jesus' lips with their honey: 'nadan los labios dulces ambrosías' (CLII.8).

Such animal attitudes towards a human corpse, summarised in CLI.7–8 ('que en los brutos ha hallado y en las peñas, | su Criador caricias halagüeñas') [for in the beasts and in the rocks their Creator | has found loving caresses] are, needless to say, wishful thinking. In fact, Brown (1998: II. 948) contends that crosses in ancient Rome were often low enough (perhaps only a foot off ground) for animals to ravage the feet of the crucified. Camargo's representation of these animals is thus his fourth and last way of idealising the crucifixion.

As if this were not enough, two of the creatures undertake actions that are completely unwarranted: the snake coils around the forehead of Christ (CXLVI.5–8), and the firefly, in lines that constitute the most graphic statement of Camargo's extravagant visual imagination, introduces itself into the eye sockets of the icon: 'los ojos muertos de la efigie dota | y en pupila y pupila donde habita, | fulgores late cuando luz palpita' (CXLVIII.6–8).

The symbolic use of animals is common in sacred art, as evidenced by the paintings of the Annunciation from the Renaissance onwards, or by Medieval crucifixions such as the apse mosaic at San Clemente in Rome, where the apostles are represented by doves that adorn the cross (which is surrounded by vines) and by sheep flanking the Lamb of God (Figure 3.7).

Unlike the animals of this mosaic, which make immediate sense from a theological viewpoint, the disgusting insects and beasts that cover the bleeding wounds of Camargo's crucifix do not appear to have support in the scriptures. I concede that what seems a frenzy of fantasy may conceal a rather refined symbolism, the holistic meaning of which escapes me. For example, the religious significance of the snake is obvious; the butterfly appears conspicuously in several *Madonne delle farfalle*; the snail can be read as a Christly figure (Feuillet 2008). Admittedly, one could find an explanation for each item. However, despite Baroque culture's predilection for symbols, the amalgam is so bizarre that a consistent allegoric meaning seems unlikely. I do not know of any crucifixion with such profusion of unpleasant creatures. Artists often worked under the supervision of very demanding theologians; this does not seem to have been Camargo's case. Although undeniably original, his image could well have appeared distasteful.[40]

Were the topic different, this could be yet another example of Camargo's humoristic ekphraseis (e.g. his poetic still lifes), which often offer an anticlimactic parenthesis immediately before or after an extraordinary episode such as a wonder or an ecstatic vision (Ponce Cárdenas 2012: 189). However, the *San Ignacio* is always respectful with the tenets and symbols of Catholicism. Counter-Reformation writers typically deploy no paradox, irony, indeterminacy or contingency regarding their doctrinal message (Darst 1998: 11). In fact, in the *Invectiva apologética*, one of Camargo's accusations against an anonymous poem about the Passion of Christ is that it treats this subject with neither respect nor devotion (Torres Quintero 1960: 427). This is the reason why humour does not seem to be the point here.

Therefore, my contention is that the passage must be seen in relation to the address to uncompassionate readers that I examined earlier (stanzas CXLII–CXLV). Since even bugs and vermin (the basest of all creatures) feel sorrow over the fate of Jesus, human indifference to his torture and death appears even more scandalous.[41] However, despite this plausible interpretation, the truth is that Camargo was carried along by his powerful visual imagination far beyond what was necessary to convey this moral message. Inspired not only by Góngora but perhaps also by viceregal art (e.g. the murals at the Gonzalo Suárez Rendón house in Tunja, which depict the sheer variety of fauna — Figure 3.8), the poet wrote a sub-digression (the animals) within a digression (the crucifix), an exercise in excess that does not serve the biography of the saint in the slightest.

When an ekphrasis encapsulates the multivalent meanings of an epic poem through *mise-en-abyme*, the outcome is often a shorthand version for the work's complexity. This is particularly the case with ideology, which ekphraseis tend

---

40   In Icelandic sagas, similar 'evil' creatures such as adders, frogs and toads actually crawl from the corpses of pagan idols once the illusion of their divinity has been broken (Clunies 2010: 78).

41   This is clearly expressed in CLIII.1–2: 'Las piedades del risco Ignacio admira, | cuando impiedades de los hombres llora' [Ignatius wonders at the compassion of the cave, | when he weeps for men's lack of compassion].

FIG. 3.8. Ceiling frescos in the main hall (sixteenth century), Casa del Fundador Gonzalo
Suárez Rendón in Tunja, Colombia. Photograph by the author.

to simplify (Quint 1993: 23). However, Camargo did not write a quintessential
description of Jesus' death (i.e. the Passion synthesised in the crucifixion). Rather,
he partly diluted the doctrinal content of his ekphrasis beneath exuberant tropes
and extravagant features, as if he were unable to accommodate his creative excess.
At this point in the *San Ignacio*, the appearance of the animals saturates the Baroque
grotto. Camargo experienced a poetic *horror vacui* akin to that of Góngora.

Typically, the ekphrasis serves as an ornamental brooch pinned to an epic
cloak. However, if the *San Ignacio* is a cloak, it is so profusely decorated with
ekphraseis that it is undone by their weight (Mayers 2009: 4–7). Their abundance
slows the narration to the point where the reader loses sight of Ignatius. Indeed,
these digressions compete with and even threaten to displace the epic plot. If the
unbearable lightness of the pilgrim in the *Soledades* was puzzling for contemporary
readers, the frequent 'disappearance' of the protagonist of the *San Ignacio* must have
been astonishing in no lower degree. In fact, the poem's meandering narrative is
completely at odds with the straightforwardness of Saint Ignatius' own writings
(Loyola 2013).

As we saw earlier, the *Soledades* has moral and didactic components. However,
they are not the *raison d'être* of the poem. Moreover, religion is almost non-existent
in Góngora's *silva*. Camargo cannot secularise his work so drastically because he
is writing a Jesuit hagiography. Nevertheless, the passage studied shows that his

poetic agenda accommodates non-religious interests as well. On the one hand, the hardness of certain images based on both the Gospels (the crucifixion of Jesus) and Nieremberg's early biography (the penances of Ignatius) encourages a devout response in the reader. On the other hand, Camargo elaborates on the aesthetic ideas behind the production of the crucifix. He idealises reality and offers bizarre visual effects such as the animals interacting with the body of the crucified. There is an exuberance of artistry and life in his description of Christ, one that strives to produce an impression of wonder. Without deviating from Catholic orthodoxy, Camargo adds to the scene a strong taste of profaneness. Thus, the poet endows ekphrasis with a dual nature (post-Tridentine spirituality and Baroque euphuism), a diglossia in which Góngora's influence is unmistakable.

The Fragile Balance

According to the decrees of the Council of Trent, sacred images should not be worshipped for themselves because the honour which is shown them is referred to the divinity that they represent (Waterworth 1848: 234–35).[42] This means that an icon should not be considered a deity in itself, for in such case it would cease to be a symbol and become an idol. The formulation of the Council of Trent is similar to that of the Second Council of Nicaea (AD 787), which had also addressed the issue of the veneration of icons. However, the crucifix is different from other images. Given what it symbolises, many theologians[43] had overlooked Nicaea and taught that the crucifix must be the object not only of *dulia* (that is, veneration) but also of *latria* (adoration). Early modern Spanish figures such as the art theorist Francisco Pacheco, the Jesuit Martín de Roa and the inquisitor Luis de Páramo were of the same opinion (Pereda 2017: 109–16).

Would Camargo have agreed with them? Although he mentions 'Santo Tomás' in his *Invectiva apologética* (Torres Quintero 1960: 488), his ekphrasis does not reflect Thomas Aquinas' lesson. Interestingly, the poet writes as if his artistic choice (i.e. to describe a fictive crucifix instead of the actual crucifixion, the subject matter of many of his predecessors) gave him more room to manoeuvre in his aesthetic experimentation. Thus, Camargo ends up venturing into a territory of extravagance that would hardly qualify as *latria*.

At first, he deploys this liberty to focus on the bodily manifestations of Jesus that emphasise his humanity. The dispirited, bloody crucified figure who hangs dying over the cave of Manresa could be vicariously understood only by the sick and the unhappy: the suffering members of the Church. For instance, the native Americans surrounded by whom Camargo spent most of his itinerant life, who may have found

42   In the Latin original: '*sed quoniam honos, qui eis exhibetur, refertur ad prototypa, quæ illæ repræsentant*'. This lesson is expressed poetically in Hojeda's *Cristiada*, VII. 82. 5–8: 'Que no adoramos, no, las piedras duras | y tablas do parecen dibujados; | sino al santo en la imagen esculpido, | y a su dibujo con el santo unido' [For we do not adore, no, hard stones | and panels where they are drawn; | but rather the saint sculpted in the image, | and the drawing united with the saint] (González 2002: 396).
43   Including Saint Thomas Aquinas, as evidenced by question 25 in the third part of his *Summa Theologiae* (1505) [mid-thirteenth century].

consolation in the thought that the God that had been imposed on them had also suffered torments and had become flesh in a form as mistreated as their own.[44]

Nevertheless, unlike contemporary icons of a mortified Jesus, which may have attained a consolatory goal among broad audiences, Camargo's ekphrasis has a limited impact potential given its hermeticism. Moreover, the *San Ignacio* neither mirrors (in the slightest) its viceregal historical present nor includes any reference whatsoever to the living conditions of native Americans, which the poet must have known well (Cristina 1989: 276).[45] Camargo's extreme *crucifixus dolorosus* might have offended the refined taste of the courts of the 'New World'. However, when one takes into consideration the complexity of the *San Ignacio*, it becomes unsurprising that few people beyond the viceregal elites were able to understand it.

This could not be otherwise, since Camargo's poetic credo prevented him from targeting a large readership. Like Góngora in his attributed *Carta en respuesta* [*Letter in Response*], and Horace (2004: 140–41) before him — ode III.1.1: '*Odi profanum vulgus*' [I shun the uninitiated crowd] — the viceregal poet would have been satisfied if only a few knowledgeable readers appreciated his work. To lay bare the hidden mysteries and the secret intentions of the loftiest poetry, which lie concealed under the hard shell of *conceptismo*, what else could this be, to quote the above-mentioned letter, but to 'dar las perlas preciosas a animales de cerda' [cast pearls before swine] (Carreira 1999: 2)?

Perhaps therein lies the difference between the respective styles of Ignatius of Loyola and Camargo. The sacred is a mystery and thus needs no further embellishment. Conversely, in the words of Espinosa Medrano (2017: section II, paragraph 5), profane poetry is a human creation that starts from 'poco más que nada, que será una alusión a historia, costumbre o fábula, o en un equívoco, en una sal, en un concepto de donaire o gracia' [little more than nothing, which could be an allusion to history, custom or fable, or a play on words, a flash of wit, a conceit full of elegance or finesse] (*Apologético en favor de don Luis de Góngora*, Lima, 1662) [*Defence of Góngora*].

If literature *a lo divino* [religious contrafactum] is a process of spiritual conversion of the materials and forms used by secular writers (Darst 1998: 16), then Camargo moves in the opposite direction: his starting point is religious poetry (both epic and lyrical), which he enriches with a 'twist' *a lo profano* [secular contrafactum] inspired by Góngora. Once the emphasis is placed more on the artistry of the crucifix than on its doctrinal message; once the link between the religious topic and the divinity is broken; once the object, separated from the thing, is nothing but the instrument of a representation, then poetry cannot become mystery save by means of form (Picón-Salas 1944: 124; and Foucault 1966: 31).

As if he were foreseeing Keat's *Ode on a Grecian Urn* (1819), Espinosa Medrano (2017: section II, paragraph 4) drew an insightful parallel for the dichotomy between

44   This paragraph is indebted to Huysmans (1908: 207–08).
45   Unlike Rodríguez Freyle's *El carnero* [*The Sheep*], which is full of gossip about daily viceregal life, the *San Ignacio* shows little interest in the Americas as a literary subject. Camargo's references to the continent and its inhabitants are sporadic, often mere clichés (e.g. abundance, wealth) (Meo Zilio 1967: 184; and Castellví Laukamp 2015b).

religion and literature on the one hand, and artistic vases on the other, that illustrates this idea clearly: 'Pues decía el Apóstol viendo la opulencia de sacramentos que en tiestos de vocablos sin adorno ocultaban las *Escrituras sagradas*: tenemos el tesoro en frágiles vasos de barro; cuando al contrario toda la majestad de las letras seculares consiste en tener los tiestos en el alma y el oropel de fuera' [for Paul the Apostle said, seeing the richness of the sacraments, which the *Sacred Scriptures* concealed in vessels of unadorned words: we have the treasure in fragile vessels of clay; conversely, all the majesty of secular letters consists in having the vessels out of sight and the tinsel on the outside].

Poetically speaking, Camargo not only wanted to convey a doctrinal message but also to be, in his own words, the 'Apeles de esta imagen' [Apelles of this image] (Torres Quintero 1960: 435): the life of the saint provided him with a façade of respectability behind which the poet delved into his Gongorist aesthetics. In fact, in several lines of the passage studied, his voice manages to free itself from the Jesuit hagiographic tradition by writing *a lo profano* about the crucifix in a poem that, in theory, had to be primarily edifying and exemplary. Gongorism and its aestheticised sense of reality helped in this quest: all windows had to be opened to air the room of the post-Tridentine Baroque (Meo Zilio 1967: 61–62).

Thus, the ekphrasis studied could serve as an example of diglossia: the fragile balance between religious orthodoxy and artistic experimentation that was prevalent in Baroque poetics (Kluge 2014). I use the adjective 'fragile' because one cannot but wonder whether Gongorism was the most suitable style for a religious epic poem with proselytising intentions. Today, most propaganda practises the technique of inverting the relationship between difficulty and didacticism: the more the sender wishes to have the message received intact and properly interpreted, the clearer the message will be. Following a similar logic, Golden Age authors such as Lope denounced Góngora's *nuevo estilo* [new style] as incompatible with religious matters (Darst 1998: 24 and 169).[46]

However, this criticism misses a fundamental point of Baroque culture. Clarity of language to assure a precise, direct, understandable, unambiguous message may well be a hallmark of today's propaganda but was not a feature of Counter-Reformation proselytisation. Quite the opposite: if you could startle the recipients of your message into suspending their train of thought (*admiratio*), then you could more readily impose your message in their minds (Darst 1998: 170). To paraphrase Collins' (2002b: 111) reflection on Góngora, Camargo summons all his visionary powers to convey the elusive beauty and redemptive power of Christ's death by means of poetic wonderment. Hence, the four startling ways by which the poet idealises the crucifix (artistic/sculptural merits, sea metaphors, Petrarchan lexicon for blood, interaction of animals with the cross), which distance the description from the *crucifixus dolorosus* and bring it closer to a field where Góngora's followers felt at home: ekphrasis, or the description of dazzling works of art.

---

46   *Contra los que predican en culto* [Against Gongorist Preachers] (Vega 2003: 'Otros sonetos', sonnet 132): 'Dejad, oh padres, los conceptos vanos, | que Dios no ha menester filaterías, | sino celo en la voz, fuego en las manos' [Leave, oh fathers, the vain conceits, | for God does not need wordiness, | but rather zeal in the voice, fire in the hands] (lines 12–14).

Thus, in Camargo's hands, a Passional topic becomes profane, a static motif something intensely dynamic; a portrait is represented as a seascape, an ascetic cave as a 'procession' of compassionate animals... Perhaps a key factor for all these idiosyncrasies was the poet's self-perceived geographical marginality, which provided him with the intellectual freedom to combine different ingredients flexibly (Mayo 2013: 269).[47] Since Camargo undertook his poetic experimentation without questioning any basic tenet of the Catholic faith, he had little to fear from the Inquisition, which was more concerned with doctrinal religious texts and not very active in the vast rural territories of the Viceroyalty (Guibovich 2003: 63, 262–64). Indeed, Camargo's mannerisms were extravagant, but all he was doing was describing an icon that represented Christ's death and its spiritual effects on a believer. After the great pain of conversion, a voluptuous feeling of infinite plenitude comes to Ignatius. He who has drunk the cup of suffering to its last dregs can no longer be a pessimist (Cioran 1995: 58). In the next canto, God will reward his devotion with an ecstatic vision.

47   In the dedication of his *Invectiva apologética*, signed in Turmequé (New Granada), Camargo requests books to distract 'la soledad de estos desiertos' [the solitude of these deserts] (Torres Quintero 1960: 423).

CHAPTER 4

Ignatius' Ecstatic Rapture

The historical Ignatius enjoyed mystical experiences in the cave of Manresa; however, his longest ecstasy took place in a nearby chapel dedicated to Saint Lucy where, in December 1522, he was seized by a *rapto* that lasted eight days. This constitutes the main subject of book II, canto V, of Camargo's *San Ignacio*, on which I shall now focus.[1] Just as Ignatius symbolically elevated Christ by placing the crucifix on a 'balcón' [ledge] in the cave of Manresa (book II, canto IV), God reciprocates shortly thereafter by raising Ignatius' soul up towards Himself.

Before setting out my analysis of this episode, it is worth considering the available data about the historical rapture. Thanks to the more than fifty testimonies that were adduced during Ignatius' process of beatification, there is copious information regarding the external conditions in which the ecstasy occurred (e.g. location, duration, physical appearance of Ignatius, reactions of the witnesses) (Creixell 1914: 228). Moreover, three early biographers of the saint (Ribadeneyra, Maffei and Orlandini) explore these accounts. Illustrated hagiographies — Rubens and others (1622: 19 — Figure 4.1) — also depict the outward conditions of the rapture.

Yet, despite all these sources, we know nothing about the content of Ignatius' *rapto*. In the words of Benítez i Riera (1996: 27), 'no podem dir [...] de quina naturalesa fou el fenomen, i molt menys, què 'veié' Ignasi' [we cannot say [...] what the nature of the phenomenon was, let alone, what Ignatius 'saw']. The reason for this is simple: Ignatius never uttered a word about the rapture to his contemporaries.[2] His *Autobiografía* [*Autobiography*] and *Diario espiritual* [*Spiritual Diary*] do not even mention the experience.

Consequently, not only scholars but also poets felt the urge to fill this vacuum. For instance, in the early Mexican poem *Vida del padre maestro Ignacio de Loyola* [*Life of the Father Master Ignatius of Loyola*], Luis de Belmonte Bermúdez (1609: 64[r]) states: 'Que Dios le comunicó | grandes cosas que alcanzó | del misterio de la fe' [For God told Ignatius | great things he absorbed | about the mystery of faith]. The following two Hispanic epics devoted to Ignatius, Antonio de Escobar y Mendoza's *San Ignacio. Poema heroico* (Valladolid, 1613) and Pedro de Oña's *Ignacio de Cantabria*

---

1   Unless otherwise specified, all quotations of stanzas and/or lines will refer to this canto (Torres Quintero 1960: 157–72).

2   Ribadeneyra (1945: 64): 'con humilde y grave silencio siempre tuvo encubierta esta tan señalada visitación del Señor' [with humble and solemn silence he always kept to himself this remarkable visitation from the Lord].

*In mentis raptu septem ipsos dies persisten=
tem humaturi iam erant, nisi e tenuissima
cordis palpitatione vitae indicium deprehendissent;
a quo tandem raptu veluti a dulci somno,
nomen IESV suauiter ingeminans soluitur.*

19

FIG. 4.1. Jean Baptiste Barbé or Cornelis Galle (after Rubens' work), '*In mentis...*', in *Vita beati P. Ignatii Loiolae, Societatis Iesu fundatoris* [*Life of the Blessed Father Ignatius of Loyola, Founder of the Society of Jesus*] (1622). Source: DigitalGeorgetown.

(Sevilla, 1639, although written in the 1620s in the Viceroyalty of Peru), contain elaborate descriptions of the saint's mystical experiences in Manresa, including references to the rapture.

The importance of the *rapto de Manresa* helps explain why, like two of his predecessors (Escobar and Oña), Camargo felt that the episode deserved detailed poetic treatment. In the light of this corpus, the ecstatic vision might be considered a special category of ekphrasis. These authors developed it on the assumption that, in defiance of the inexpressibility topos, the artistry of the poet may well complement the testimony of the mystic. In fact, the biographical void allowed them to cultivate their imagination, following the Aristotelian idea of poetry as the genre that, unlike history, deals with things as they may have happened, rather than as they actually happened (*Poetics*, 1451a, quoted in the foreword to the *San Ignacio*).

To this end, Camargo could not resort just to the mimicry of so secular a poet as Góngora. Rather, he combined elements gleaned from various readings. Recurrent allusions to a poetic 'father' may point to one of many genealogical lines, yet the intertextual roots of a masterpiece tend to be more tangled (Greene 1982: 19 and 173). For instance, Camargo's treatment of the crucifix disclosed echoes of poets such as Lope, Valdivielso and Paravicino. Canto V on the rapture will reveal other sources, the importance of which had not yet become apparent: not only Ignatius' hagiographies in prose (Ribadeneyra, Maffei and Orlandini), but especially one in verse (Escobar).

Camargo deals with his own anxiety concerning influence[3] by confronting it on almost every page: he follows Escobar in the title of the poem (which is almost identical), the *dispositio* (the arrangement of the cantos is similar in both works), and the *inventio* (the historical facts, which he obviously draws from the biographies as well). Nevertheless, the Baroque genius is evident in his ability to enter an already existent genre and redefine it from within (Kluge 2014: 156). In this sense, my contention is that, although Camargo's starting point is the Ignatian hagiographies filtered through Escobar's poem, he deploys the style of Góngora (*elocutio*) and the imagery of Gongorism and Marinism (*inventio*) to innovate within and deviate from that tradition.

In this chapter, I will suggest parallels between the *San Ignacio* and the *Adone* (1623) of Giambattista Marino. This poet was less popular in the Hispanic world than earlier Italian writers such as Petrarch, Ariosto or Tasso. However, plenty of Spanish authors praised the *Adone*.[4] Gracián took a name from the poem for a character of the *Criticón*. Lope complimented Marino on several occasions. Notable Gongorists such as the Count of Villamediana and Pedro Soto de Rojas imitated and/or translated his works (Rozas 1978: 109–27). His name even reached the 'New World', as Espinosa Medrano (2017: section IX, paragraph 77) mentions Marino

---

3   To paraphrase Bloom's (1973) title.

4   Salcedo Coronel (1636: 158ᵛ): 'Redújola al idioma toscano Juan Bautista Marino en el *Adonis* con atención digna de su ingenio' [In his *Adone*, Marino rewrote the fable in Italian with a care worthy of his wit]. Saavedra Fajardo (1768: 46) admired the 'fertilidad y elegancia' [abundance and elegance] of the poem, although he admitted that Marino was 'más atento a deleitar, que a enseñar' [more interested in entertaining than in teaching].

in the *Apologético en favor de don Luis de Góngora* (Lima, 1662) [*Defence of Góngora*]. In the light of this fame, and given that the works of Camargo and Marino have common ground — to borrow Chapelain's expression (1988: 28), they both have 'plus d'accidents que de substance' [more digressions than plot] — I think that the comparison is worth consideration.

The influence of Gongorism and Marinism is especially noticeable whenever Camargo departs from Ignatius' experiences in order to elaborate on digressive descriptions. This is the reason why the ekphrasis is such a relevant motif. By absorbing key features of the *Polifemo*, the *Soledades* and either the *Adone* or the Marinist tradition, the *San Ignacio* defines itself through this rewriting and 'modernising' of the hagiographic genre. Keeping this focus in mind, the chapter will be structured in two sections.

Firstly, I will explore what I have termed the rapture *ad intra*, i.e. its content as portrayed by Camargo. Escobar and Oña wrote extensively (twenty-nine and 120 stanzas respectively) about the *ad intra* dimension not only of this rapture, but also of other mystical experiences of Ignatius in Manresa. Conversely, Camargo focused exclusively on the *rapto* and devoted just twenty-three stanzas to its content (CLXXXVI–CCVIII). Its threefold structure (dogmas of the faith, Creation and the future establishment of the Society of Jesus) is consistent with Ignatius' mysticism, but hardly original. As we shall see, Camargo's more interesting contributions are: (i) the development of the Marinist cult of *préciosité* (i.e. refinement of language, effects of grandeur, lavish metaphors... in a nutshell, an enthusiastic devotion to the ornamental aspects of poetry) (Priest 1967: xvi–xvii); (ii) his embracing of Góngora's style (*elocutio*), and holistic approach to nature, which becomes a source of wonder; and (iii) the relative brevity (vis-à-vis Ignatian forerunners) when dealing with ecstatic visions.

Secondly, I will also explore the rapture *ad extra* (that is, its context or setting) which, in the *San Ignacio*, is longer than the *ad intra* dimension (thirty-two stanzas, including twenty-six that have nothing to do with the historical episode). Camargo concentrated most of his Gongorist and Marinist imagery (*inventio*) on the outward aspects of the rapture: the arrival of the shepherds with their rustic banquet (CLXV–CLXXXIV) and a funeral procession of pagan deities (CCXI–CCXVI) respectively. Thus, he framed the opulent yet orthodox ecstasy within two imaginative descriptions that are as profane as they are extravagant. The final touch (CCXVIII) is the ekphrasis of a monument to the life of Ignatius: the needle-like obelisk that Bishop Juan de Cardona placed before Saint Lucy's chapel at Manresa in 1588. The poetic image is noteworthy because, while being rigorously historical, it also encapsulates in one symbol Camargo's familiarity not only with the Greco-Latin heritage but also with Góngora's imagery: the obelisk is a key motif in the *Soledades*.

Góngora never pretended to be a theologian. Like Petrarch's *Canzoniere* and Ariosto's *Orlando furioso*, his *Soledades* is (almost) completely profane. In this respect, Camargo's *San Ignacio* shows how the desacralisation of aesthetics reached even religious poetry. His poem also betrays the uneasy relationship between representation and that which is being represented through a common Baroque device: accumulation, where the piling up of various elements replaces harmony (González Echevarría 1996: 205).[5] In this respect, the production of lesser authors should be valued no less than those of the towering figure of their era, since the works of the former frequently contain the most eccentric features (Benjamin 1977: 58 and 178).

Given the subject matter of the *San Ignacio*, its attempts to reconcile poetic experimentation with a religious agenda are less harmonious than the hybridisation of pastoral, piscatorial and epic in the *Soledades*. Camargo's diglossia is extreme, for he seeks to counteract his indulgence in nature and mythology (rapture *ad extra*) with a spiritual message that would have been excessive for Góngora (rapture *ad intra*). As a result, Camargo goes further than his poetic mentor in both digressive boldness and doctrinal content.

The rapture *ad intra*

In his book about Ignatius in Manresa, Creixell poses the following rhetorical question (1914: 192): '¿Quién puede saber lo que pasa en el entendimiento o en el corazón de un extático o contemplativo, si este no toma la pluma y lo refiere fidelísimamente?' [Who can understand what happens in the mind or heart of an ecstatic or contemplative, if he does not take pen to paper to explain it faithfully?]. The answer, obviously, is no one. Oña understood this in his *Ignacio de Cantabria* (1639) which, following Ribadeneyra, narrates the external conditions of the rapture but does not speculate about its content.

However, Oña's attitude is inconsistent: he had already devoted sixty-two stanzas of book VIII (728–89) and thirteen stanzas of book IX (790–802) (i.e. 600 lines!) to describing imaginatively other visions that Ignatius enjoyed in Manresa, not to mention the episode in which three nymphs (*sic*) explain certain mysteries of the faith to the saint (IX. 815–854). Escobar (1613) was equally confident in his poetic skills to express the ineffable. He wrote two cantos (book II, cantos II and III) in which he described Ignatius' mystical experiences in Manresa. Even some early biographers — Maffei (1837: 57) and especially Orlandini (1614: 9) — speculated about what Ignatius might have seen, thereby distancing their works from history and bringing them closer to poetry in the Aristotelian sense (*Poetics*, 1451a).

Given this tradition, Camargo was compelled to accept his lack of prior status. Not that originality was particularly relevant in an age dominated by the poetics of *imitatio*, but no strong author wants merely to repeat what his predecessors have done. The rapture was so important for the saint that Camargo had to include it in the *San Ignacio*. In this respect, his threefold vision (dogmas of the faith, God's Creation of the world and the future Jesuit order) is indebted to the hagiographic tradition (especially to Escobar). However, Camargo deploys three techniques in order to keep repetition to a minimum and make a contribution to the subject: (i) unlike any other author of the Ignatian tradition, he deploys Gongorism to

---

5   Indeed, Camargo's poem offers an 'amontonamiento indiscriminado de objetos' [haphazard heap of objects], to borrow Marcaida's (2014: 47) definition of Baroque accumulation.

emphasise the mystery and wonder of the revelation; (ii) he expands his writing beyond the confines of the Spanish models (including Góngora) by following either Marino or his imitators in the sumptuous imagery of the ecstasy; and (iii) he devotes just twenty-three stanzas to the Manresan visions (CLXXXVI–CCVIII), which is less than Escobar and especially Oña wrote. To sum up, Gongorism, lavish ornamentation and conciseness are key features, in varying degrees, in Camargo's rapture *ad intra*. All of them are present in each of its parts. Nevertheless, the cult of *préciosité* is the dominant feature in the vision of the dogmas of the faith, Gongorism in that of Creation and conciseness in the proleptic stanzas about the Society of Jesus. This section will explore these three dimensions of the rapture.

The rapture starts when Ignatius' soul is borne upwards, as described in line CLXXXVI.1: 'Rompiendo nubes, cielos escalando' [Breaking clouds, climbing the heavens]. The soul ascends to the 'Empíreo' [Empyrean], where God constitutes its initial vision. Camargo conveys religious dogmas with a language which is heavy with material display. To paraphrase Priest's (1967: xxvi–xxvii) assessment of Marino, Camargo's notion of truth/beauty is one of decoration that is both elaborate and rich. In the foreword to his *Philosophia thomistica* [*Thomasian Philosophy*], Espinosa Medrano (1982: 327) argues that the Creoles of Peru 'son superados por los europeos en un solo astro [...] Falta la presencia del rey' [are surpassed by Europeans in only one aspect [...] The king is missing]. This worldview helps understand why Camargo presented God as a majestic king enthroned before his court: 'a la corte de Dios Ignacio vuela, | y al trono se presenta, venerando' [Ignacio flies up to the court of God, | and presents himself before the throne, venerating] (CLXXXVI.4–5). The comparison of the king with the divinity was frequent in Baroque literature, since it served to emphasise the exclusiveness of royal authority. Camargo inverted the topos: God is actually a king.[6]

Following this metaphor, Camargo portrays Ignatius' soul as a 'sumiller de Dios' (CLXXXIX.5), the sacred equivalent of a Sumiller de Corps, i.e. the elite officer in charge of the royal chambers who was responsible for giving the king the most immediate attention. Just as religious images were jealously guarded behind curtains to preserve their mystery, only to be revealed at the appropriate moment of the liturgy, Camargo's God is hidden under a canopy that only the 'Sumiller de Corps a lo sagrado' (CXCIII.8), taking advantage of his access to the intimacy of the monarch, can unveil.[7] Having done so, the soul solemnly declares (CXC.8): 'Visto he, mi Dios, la esencia como es ella' [I have seen, my God, the essence just as it is]. That essence is precisely God's Trinitarian nature (CLXXXIX.2: 'Deidad que es una y trina') [Deity that is one and trine]. The Trinity is the first religious dogma that Camargo presents in the rapture *ad intra*. Unlike contemporary artists such as

6   Hojeda's *Cristiada* [*Christiad*] offers another example of this analogy (II.30.1–2): 'Aquí llegaban ya los cortesanos | del rey supremo' [This is where the courtiers | of the supreme king arrived] (González 2002: 167).
7   These lines are indebted to Pereda (2017: 347–48). Camargo may have drawn inspiration from Marino's (1988: I. 448) description of the marriage bed for Venus and Adonis, ornamented with gold and precious stones, and hidden behind 'cortine [...] di porpora di Tiro' [curtains [...] of Tyrian purple] (VIII.92.2).

FIG. 4.2. Gregorio Vásquez de Arce y Ceballos (attributed), *Símbolo de la Trinidad* (seventeenth century), Museo Colonial de Bogotá. Photograph by Óscar Monsalve. Despite the censorship of the Church, the Trinity with either three heads or faces was common in viceregal art (Álvarez 2008: 91).

Gregorio Vásquez de Arce y Ceballos (Figure 4.2), the poet is far from introducing any doctrinal deviation.

The ekphrasis may seem abstract on this point, but it is entirely orthodox. Like Oña (VIII.746), Camargo focuses on the relationships between the hypostases: the Father begets the Son (CXCI.1: 'Vio cómo engendra el Padre'); they both engender the Holy Spirit; yet there is no hierarchy within them since the Trinity is a single, undifferentiated Godhead expressed identically in each of the three Persons (CXCI.5–8):

> ...ni excede
> el Padre al Hijo porque lo ha engendrado;
> y tan grande como ambos, es divina
> la que, de ambos, Persona se origina.

> [...the Father
> does not exceed the Son because he has begotten him;
> and as great as both is the divine Person
> which originates from them both.]

Having understood this dogma, and later the Eucharistic mystery (CXCIII.4–5: 'de aquella carne, a que se unió, divina, | en quien el pan la suya transubstancia') [of that flesh, to which God united Himself | into which the bread transubstantiates itself], the soul/Sumiller is given a golden key for the chamber that contains one of the most precious treasures for the faith (CXCIV.1–2): 'Dorada llave le concede a Ignacio | del camarín en que la fe se ciega' [He gives Ignatius a golden key | to the room where faith is dazzled].[8] Ignatius takes the key, opens the gates of heaven (CXCIV.4: 'abre el empíreo') and admires it in all its glory. Suddenly, the blinding flash of the celestial vision illuminates the chamber. Then, Camargo compares Ignatius to an eagle, which not only resists the light of God, but also absorbs all the rays (CXCV.5–6): 'y ave Ignacio real, en la lucida | copa, los resplandores le ha agotado' [and Ignatius the golden eagle, in the splendid | crown of the tree, has absorbed all the radiance].

For the period 1600–1700, the CORDE online database of the Real Academia Española (2019) shows 541 instances of 'resplandores', 426 of 'lucida' and eighty of 'camarín'. Indeed, the pompous imagery of the *San Ignacio* is common in seventeenth-century Spanish poets and in mystical writers or preachers. This corpus could well be the main source of inspiration for Camargo's *inventio*. However, his euphuism might also draw from Marino or the Marinist tradition. Priest (1967: xxvi) described the *Adone* as 'a proud representation of the spectacle of court splendours'. Given Camargo's elaborate descriptions, fantastically ornamented court and metaphors of shining, his empyrean domain could also be read as a transposition of Marino's palace of love (canto II) into a sacred context.

Nonetheless, this is just a hypothesis. Góngora is more clearly present, especially if one considers Camargo's style (*elocutio*). The Cordovan author explored the potential of a poetic language which is closed in on itself. Due to this feature, it

---

8   Carducho (1865: 49) explains the meaning of 'camarín': 'Tienen sus Altezas una tribuna, o camarín, donde guardan las más ricas y preciosas joyas de su Corona' [Their Highnesses have a chamber, or small room, where they keep the richest and most precious jewels of their Crown].

was hard to determine whether the *Soledades* hid a secret, profound meaning, or indulged in the delight of linguistic experimentation for its own sake (Kluge 2010: 138). Earlier, I justified Camargo's use of Gongorism for sacred purposes because the *admiratio* produced by his poetry would help to win the hearts and minds of his readers (mostly clerics at the time). This idea is still relevant here.

In fact, there may be an additional reason to use such an idiolect in his description of a rapture. Had Camargo written a *Carta en respuesta* [*Letter in Response*] as Góngora allegedly did, he might have defended the hermeticism of the passage by pointing to the relevance, loftiness and intricacy of the subject described. According to Saint Augustine, who is quoted in that letter, scriptural imagery was consciously designed to be esoteric, not only because it discloses an ineffable revelation but also because obscurity increases the mystery (Kluge 2010: 51).[9] This is precisely what Camargo tries to achieve with Gongorism. To borrow from Tamayo's reading of Espinosa Medrano (1982: xxxiii): 'las palabras son las que divinizan y prestan eficacia a la materia' [words deify and infuse the subject matter with eloquence].

Given the difficulty of the endeavour (i.e. not only to represent but also to enhance the invisible by means of the visible), the poet emphasises his own inability to cope with the subject: the object of his ekphrasis is beyond the understanding of the 'más agudo ingenio' [sharpest wit] (CLXXXVIII.4).[10] Nevertheless, as we have seen, Camargo has no qualms about portraying not only the divinity, but also some of the greatest mysteries of the faith (e.g. the Trinity, the Transubstantiation) with a wealth of detail that would have been inconceivable in Ignatius' own writings. Like Oña, Camargo is inconsistent in his apparent reluctance. The poet alludes to the inexpressibility topos to highlight that his ekphrasis will be a *tour de force* of technique: he will describe the indescribable, and will do so by deploying the most difficult style. Gongorism grows so dense in his hands that, while magnifying the mystery, it threatens to cloud the revelation. The line between unravelling a religious truth by stretching language to its limits and indulging in the shallow world of forms is razor thin.

As mentioned, one of the truths revealed to Ignatius is that of Transubstantiation (CXCIII). To draw a parallel, just as, according to this dogma, the bread and wine of the Eucharist are the body and blood of Christ, the Baroque claimed the world to be not like a theatre (as the traditional topos goes), but an actual stage (Kluge 2010: 210). In this sense, God offers Ignatius a theatrical vision of the world during its Creation (CXCVI–CCVI). Small wonder then that Camargo equates the cave of Manresa with a theatre (CCXVII.4: 'teatro la Cueva fue, aplaudido') [the cave was an acclaimed theatre].

9   Augustine (1958: 38): 'what is sought with difficulty is discovered with more pleasure'. I also refer to the *Carta en respuesta* (Carreira 1999: 3): 'en tanto quedará más deleitado en cuanto, obligándole a la especulación por la obscuridad de la obra, fuere hallando debajo de las sombras de la obscuridad asimilaciones a su concepto' [the reader's understanding will take more pleasure inasmuch as, forced by the difficulty of the work to speculate, it will go on approaching its meaning beneath the shadows of its difficulty].

10   Oña (1992: 81) expressed a similar idea: 'Es Dios allá otro sol, muy otro lumbre | — si lícito es hablar de lo inefable —' [God is therein another sun, another light | — if I am permitted to discuss the ineffable —] (I.14.1–2).

This is the second part of the rapture, where the poet mimics not only Góngora's *nuevo estilo* [new style] but also his holistic approach and attitude of wonder. Various authors with whom Camargo was likely to have been acquainted wrote extensively about Creation. For instance, Tasso's last significant poem (1607) is his seven-canto *Le sette giornate del mondo creato* [*Seven Days of Creation*].[11] Oña devoted 312 lines to the topic when describing Ignatius' Manresan ecstasies (VIII.751–89). Hojeda wrote two hundred lines about it in his epic about Christ (II.53–77). Although Escobar did not describe the Creation of the world *stricto sensu*, he touched upon Adam and Eve (1613: 64^r). Camargo possibly had these models at hand, together with the Bible, the obvious common source of them all. Nonetheless, he devotes just eighty-eight lines to the motif.

The goal of encompassing the whole globe at a glance belongs to an ancient literary tradition. The first ekphrasis in Western literature (the Homeric shield of Achilles) was already a physical encapsulation of the entire cosmos; its first circle portrayed the earth, the heavens and the sea, the sun and the moon, and all the constellations (*Iliad*, XVIII. 478–89).[12] Similarly, Góngora's panoramic landscape in the *Soledad primera* is not only a frame for the action but also a microcosm of the whole *silva*. Just as his landscape included *in nuce* all the subsequent rural views, Camargo's 'worldscape' encapsulates all the elements on which he will later focus. Thus, the viceregal poet takes the Baroque *mise-en-abyme* to its logical extremes. What appeared *prima facie* to be the prerogative of the divinity — '*Non coerceri maximo, contineri tamen a minimo, divinum est*'[13] [The divine is not to be confined by the biggest, but to be contained by the smallest] — may well be attempted by the writer who deploys *conceptismo* to deliver the most ambitious poetic representation possible, ranging from Alpha to Omega: the cosmos fits within a conceit.

As Espinosa Medrano emphasised in his *Apologético*, everything that is exists in language and hence can be represented (González Echevarría 1996: 220). Through various strategies of repetition — i.e. parallelism, and especially anaphora (e.g. CCII.1: 'Vio que al aliento de la sacra boca' [He saw that, in the breath from the sacred mouth]; CCIII.1: 'Vio que, fecunda la mullida espuma' [He saw that, the fruitful frothy foam]; CCVI.1: 'Vio, que vaheada del divino anhelo' [He saw that, given breath by the divine yearning])[14] — Camargo builds momentum into the eleven rhythmic stanzas and suggests the smooth travelling of the gaze throughout Creation.

Following Meo Zilio (1986: xlvi–xlvii), I will offer a summary of their content before moving on to my analysis. The themes covered by these stanzas are: (i) the Creation of the world in seven days; (ii) the birth of light, the sun and the moon; (iii)

---

11   According to Bellini (1991: 56), Camargo must have read Tasso, whose works were widely available in the Spanish Americas.

12   Camargo mentions Homer in his *Invectiva apologética* [*Apologetic Invective*] (Torres Quintero 1960: 487). Since the *Iliad* was available in Spanish America (Leonard 1992: 164), he might have been familiar with the poem.

13   Motto contained in a Latin epitaph to Ignatius (Bollandus and Tollenaer 1640: 280).

14   These lines seem reminiscent of Tasso's (1607: 270) opening 'veggio' [I see] (four times in seven lines).

celestial mechanisms driven by an angel charioteer; (iv) the effects of light scattered throughout heaven; (v) the concord of discordant elements; (vi) the separation of land and water; (vii) fish obeying God's hand; (viii) birds arising from sea foam; (ix) four rivers fertilising the earth; (x) terrestrial animals, both domesticated and wild; and (xi) Adam and Eve.

This taxonomy reveals a clear division: the first six stanzas (CXCVI–CCI) describe how chaos is transformed into cosmos or, *mutatis mutandis*, how the world arranges itself as a poem. The next five (CCII–CCVI) depict life starting in all its forms or, symbolically speaking, the poet coming into the world (Adam as the giver of names). In this respect, Camargo's 'worldscape' works as a Gongorist ekphrasis of nature *a lo divino* [religious contrafactum]. Earlier, we saw how the seascape of the *Soledad segunda* included not only pagan gods but also human beings and even sea creatures, for the portrayal of animals was part of the pictorial landscape tradition. In Camargo's Creation, the Catholic God has replaced heathen deities but the other two components (animals and humans) remain in sight.

Abundance is a Baroque theme par excellence. In this respect, there are here animals of the most varied kinds. The scenery also combines crops, carpets of flowers, torrential springs and trees. Like Góngora, the viceregal poet presents fertility as a key element of the ideal landscape. The sea is portrayed as equally rich and fecund, since it is the origin of life: 'o vulva fue sagrada, o dulce nido' [the foam was a sacred vulva or a sweet nest] (CCIII.2). However, Camargo diverges from the classic topos in one detail: Ignatius' soul has gained so much height that it can actually see the whole earth. Therefore, it is not this or that particular landscape that is presented as a fruitful *locus amoenus* but rather the entire globe, which has become a 'huerta del paraíso' [garden of paradise] (CCIV.4).

This helps understand the feeling of wonder conveyed by both the subject matter and the style of the passage. Camargo celebrates nature with reverence, as if he were seeing for the first time the splendour of Creation from the greatest to the smallest. In this respect, the poet follows Góngora in his combination of the panoramic gaze with the *Kleinmalerei* [painting of the small]. Indeed, when juxtaposing phenomena of unfathomable scale — the creation of light and the celestial objects (CXCVII), the concord of discordant elements (CC), and the separation of land and water (CCI) — with the depiction of the small — the 'hermosa flor' [beautiful flower], the 'dulce fruta' [sweet fruit] (CCIV) — Camargo imparts the message that there is a mutual attraction between created things by virtue of their common origin.[15]

Everything described is endowed with God's grace and beauty; each item of the 'worldscape' represents a divine gift that men will never be able to match. Even their artistic imitation is taxing. The ekphrasis does not mention the *Deus pictor* topos. However, the motif is arguably implied in the poet's reference to God as an 'arquitecto soberano' [supreme architect] (CCVII.2).[16] God, the first, major architect (thus a creator, an artist), designed a world of unattainable beauty. Like philosophy (Plato, *Theaetetus*, 155d; Aristotle, *Metaphysics*, 982b), both literature and art are born

---

15   To paraphrase Benjamin (1977: 93).
16   Orlandini (1614: 9) describes God as an *'architectus'* when portraying the rapture.

of wonder, a reverent awe before the mystery of Creation. Books and paintings are attempts to answer the question towards which this mystery leads: why this instead of nothingness? Nothing is truer in the case of Camargo, whose pursuit of totality when describing God's Creation heightens the sense of the marvellous, which is so typical of Góngora.[17]

It is thus no wonder that the rapture has an impact on the beholder. The poet portrays Ignatius as being 'en éxtasi süave, en largo olvido, | en rapto amable, en dulce parasismo' [in gentle ecstasy, forgetful of everything, | in sweet rapture, in a devotional trance] (CXCVII.3–4). The ecstasy feels like a foretaste of life in heaven. The saint notices that not only his environment but also he himself are joyfully being changed, renewed and purified, back to an environment and self once known and later lost (i.e. Adam before the Fall).[18] Indeed, the climactic moment of the vision is the Christian Creation myth. The event was popular among viceregal artists, perhaps influenced by the chronicles depicting the Americas before the conquest as a 'paraíso terrenal' [earthly paradise] and their inhabitants in a prelapsarian state (Las Casas 1984: 122; Holloway 2017: 168–69). I refer to the painting devoted to the first line of the Credo by the Ecuadorian Miguel de Santiago (Figure 4.3). As for Camargo, he depicts Adam and Eve in stanza CCVI:

> Vio, que vaheada del divino anhelo
> aquella argila se informaba, aquella
> única criatura a quien el cielo
> el pie llegó a besar, estrella a estrella:
> el hombre, emperador de cuanto el suelo,
> de cuanto el aire y cuanto el agua sella;
> a quien de su costilla, Dios le esmera,
> en letargioso sueño, compañera.

> [He saw that, given breath by the divine yearning,
> that clay took form, that
> unique creature whose foot the sky
> came to kiss, star by star:
> man, emperor of everything that earth,
> that air, that water holds;
> from whose rib God creates,
> in a dreamlike state, a companion.]

The myth is also present in the *Ejercicios espirituales* [*Spiritual Exercises*]. The '2.° punto' of the first week consists of reflecting on 'el pecado de Adán y Eva' [the sin of Adam and Eve] (Loyola 2013: 165). However, Camargo approaches the topic as a humanist. The ekphrasis focuses on propagating an anthropocentric worldview, rather than on lamenting original sin.[19] This point will become

---

17   Woods (1978: 103): 'This is precisely the attitude which one sees epitomized in the Spanish Baroque poet's fondness for *Cornucopia*. The desire to cram as much of the physical world as possible into their poetry, a sense of the wonder of nature, and at the same time an ardent curiosity which reflects itself in a concern for detail.'

18   I follow Laski's (1961: 104) description of Adamic ecstasies.

19   I refer to Rodríguez Freyle's *El carnero* [*The Sheep*] (1979: 34–36) for a viceregal example of this kind of lamentation.

FIG. 4.3. Miguel de Santiago (attributed), '*Credo in Deum patrem...*' (1673), Catedral primada de Bogotá. Photograph by T. Luke Young. This painting is based on a previous engraving by Johan Sadeler (Fajardo 2011: 199).

clearer after comparing Camargo with his predecessors. Vida (2009: 41–43, 193) and Oña (VIII.787–89) focus primarily on the tasting of the forbidden fruit and its consequences. For his part, Hojeda explains how Eve was created from Adam's rib, praises her beauty (II.31–32), but then concludes by remembering how the first man was expelled from 'la patria feliz que allí tenía' [the happy homeland he had therein] (II.77.6) (González 2002: 168 and 177).

Doubtless having Escobar (1613: 64^r) as the main model for this passage, Camargo devotes just eight lines to the myth: fewer than any of his forerunners. He does not even mention the infringement of God's commandment or the expulsion from the Garden of Eden. Quite the opposite: his aim is to ennoble and beautify Adam and Eve, who appear still unspoilt by original sin. At first sight, Camargo's portrayal of the couple seems almost a pretext for the display of physical perfection and his aestheticised sense of the world inherited from Góngora. Yet there is more to this than mere praise of beauty. At a deeper level, by bringing the Creation myth into the foreground, Camargo seems to ask himself an implicit question similar to that posed to God in the *Psalms* (8:4): 'What is man, that thou art mindful of him?'. The poet's unequivocal answer is enthusiastic praise of man as human being (CCVI.3–4: 'única criatura a quien el cielo | el pie llegó a besar, estrella a estrella') that distances him from Creation and brings him closer to the Renaissance ideal of man as the centre of the world.[20] Thus, the above-mentioned motif of wonder culminates with this Baroque embodiment of a Latin motto: '*Magnum miraculum est homo*' [Man is a great miracle].

Immediately after Adam and Eve, Camargo introduces the proleptic dimension of the rapture. Although prolepsis is key in Góngora's ekphraseis, on this occasion the model is Escobar (1613: 64ʳ). Indeed, the poet from Valladolid linked both visions in his poem, albeit somewhat clumsily, comparing Eve being born from Adam's rib with the Jesuits being born from Ignatius: 'Que duerma Ignacio así, no es maravilla | pues de él ha de salir otra Eva nueva' [Small wonder that Ignatius sleeps like this | for another, new Eve will be born of him]. Later Neogranadian art preserved this proleptic tradition. For instance, in Pedro de Laboria's retable on the rapture (Figure 4.4), an angel holding an open book represents the future Society of Jesus.

As usual, Camargo is not only more sophisticated but also briefer. He reduces Escobar's fifteen stanzas to just two: conciseness is the key feature of this third and last vision. Moreover, the *ordo rerum* of Creation will serve as a model for the future founding of the Jesuit order (Meo Zilio 1986: xlvii). In this sense, the ekphrasis expands in all directions, both spatially (the world-at-a-glance motif) and temporally (from the past to the time to come).[21] This is clear in stanza CCVII:

> La que armónica allí le rayó idea,
> el arquitecto soberano quiere
> que norma ya de aquella ilustre sea
> fábrica, a quien Ignacio se refiere
> artífice segundo, a quien arrea
> del orden sumo que de aquella infiere
> planta del mundo, cuando Dios le fía
> compañera en su nueva Compañía.

> [This is the harmonious idea that struck him:
> the supreme architect wants
> the mechanism of the universe to be the norm
> on which Ignatius bases himself,
> a second artificer, spurred by
> the highest order that he infers from the
> worldscape, with which God
> entrusts him for his new Society.]

20   According to Pérez de Oliva (1995: 138), man is 'la más admirable obra de cuantas Dios ha hecho' [the most admirable of God's works]. This idea is poetically expressed in viceregal poems such as the *Discurso en loor de la poesía* [*Speech in Praise of Poetry*] (1608): 'recopilar queriendo en un sujeto | lo que criado había, al hombre hizo | a su similitud' [wanting to gather in one subject | everything in Creation, He made man | in his image] (Chang-Rodríguez 2009: 89).

21   In this respect, Camargo's ekphrasis seems reminiscent of Marino's (1988: I. 562) spherical world map (*Adone*, X.172.8 and 175.8), an Aleph *avant la lettre* which covers not only all space ('quanto l'orbe contien del'universo'), but also all time ('col passato e'l presente, anco il futuro').

FIG. 4.4. Pedro de Laboria, *El rapto de San Ignacio* (1748), Iglesia de San Ignacio, Bogotá. Photograph by Gustavo Rico. I refer to Ramírez (1982) and Villalobos (2012: 104–11) for scholarship on this work of art.

Only one early biographer of Ignatius included a proleptic reference when describing the content of the rapture. However, he mentioned it as a '*pia* [...] *ac probabilis coniectura*' [pious [...] and probable conjecture], without giving many more details (Orlandini 1614: 9). Less prudent, Escobar (1613: 63^v–66^r) flamboyantly depicts the Jesuit order as being born from the mystical union between God's glory and Ignatius. The Society of Jesus, in the form of a 'doncella' [maiden], gives a speech before the saint that concludes with a list of its future achievements and martyrs. The tribute of repetition is pointless but any creative variation entails rejection (Greene 1982: 195). In this case, Camargo might have had mixed feelings when reading Escobar. On the one hand, he did not want to give up the proleptic material that his precursor had unveiled, for to mention the 'Compañía' would enable him to present Ignatius as a perfect man, whose life project was already clear in Manresa. On the other hand, given that the proleptic dimension of the rapture was mere conjecture, Escobar's ekphrasis seemed excessive not only in length but also in content.

The outcome of this thought process is two densely material stanzas (CCVII–CCVIII) with a vague prolepsis. Instead of Escobar's erotic/nuptial metaphors, Camargo includes a final image that fits in with the overall aesthetic of the passage. The Society of Jesus appears as a glorious bridge that links this world with heaven (CCVIII.7–8): 'puente, por donde el mundo ya seguro | halle pasaje al estrellado muro' [a bridge, across which humankind, now safe, | finds its way to the starry heaven]. Thus, the *rapto* closes with a vision loaded with euphuism in the manner of Marino,[22] a poet whose approach to the digressive ekphrasis will become as relevant as that of Góngora to understanding Camargo's rapture *ad extra*.

The rapture *ad extra*

Camargo was aware that the external conditions of the rapture were tangential to the sacredness of the episode. Thus, given his objective of innovating within the Ignatian hagiographic genre, the poet felt less encumbered by this tradition when portraying the rapture *ad extra*. This helps understand why he broke away from his religious agenda and moved towards an indulgence in food and mythology seen through the lens of Gongorism and Marinism. At some point his imagery seems to run wild and almost to go out of control, diluting the ekphrasis into flights of ideas.[23] Unlike Escobar and Oña, Camargo devotes more stanzas to the rapture *ad extra* than to the content of Ignatius' Manresan ecstasies (thirty-two versus twenty-three). Most of them have nothing to do with the historical facts. Indeed, having given real background information about the saint's religious scruples (CLIX–CLXI) and his seven day fast (CLXII–CLXIV), the poet describes the fictitious appearance of a group of *Soledades*-inspired shepherds who start playing music and sports (CLXV–CLXXIV) before setting up a rural banquet (CLXXV–CLXXXIV).

22 According to Priest (1967: xxvi–xxvii), the 'goal he [Marino] aimed for was an effect of grandeur'. Hence, his emphasis on linguistic decoration.
23 To paraphrase Benjamin (1977: 199).

The poet resorts to prosopopoeia in order to present their meal as a burlesque battlefield of flavours (Ponce Cárdenas 2012: 184). The main 'ave' is accompanied by a procession of vegetables (onion, leek, cress, mustard, radish, pepper, endive, lettuce, cucumber, aubergine, artichoke), dressing (salt, pepper, oil, vinegar), fruits (melon, pomegranate), chestnuts, bread and wine — all of them playfully fighting with each other. Given its abundance, the meal is compared with a cornucopia (CLXXXIV.8: 'cuanto Amaltea de su cuerno llueve'). Since the shepherds have more than enough, after noticing Ignatius' emaciated appearance, one of them offers him food (CLXXXV).

None of this can be found in either Escobar or Oña. The episode, a poetic still life, which is full of references to the *Polifemo* and the *Soledades*, and to works by Quevedo, comes under the category of amusing diversions; it does not contribute to the plot in the slightest. It does, obviously, add to Camargo's general purpose of presenting with the greatest variety (not only in the *elocutio* but also in the *inventio*) his imitation of the Cordovan model. Indeed, the passage constitutes one of the most explicit homages to Góngora in the poem. It is as visually surprising as it is biographically unsound, since the historical Ignatius was not precisely a gourmet.[24] Nevertheless, this fact constituted no obstacle to Camargo, who here is more poet than hagiographer.

A close reading of the food ekphrasis is beyond the scope of this chapter. However, I will offer a narratological analysis of the passage in connection with the ecstasy that comes immediately afterwards. From the viewpoint of decorum, devoting the same number of stanzas (ten) to an imaginary banquet as to the vision of the dogmas of the faith seems inappropriate. Carducho's criticism (1865: 265) of religious paintings that devote excessive attention to food could well apply here: 'cercados todos con tanta prevención de comida [...] que más parecía hostería de la gula, que hospicio de santidad' [the sacred figures were surrounded by so much food that [...] it seemed more like an inn of gluttony than a hospice of sanctity].

On religious grounds, the parallel drawn between the profane delight caused by food and the ecstatic vision might seem irreverent. Nor does early modern literary theory help justify the poetic still life. According to Cascales (1975: 134 and 143), the epic genre 'tiene por fin dar suma excelencia y gloria a la persona principal que celebra' [aims to bestow excellence and glory to the prominent person it celebrates]. Given this objective, 'digresiones fuera de la fábula' [digressions beyond the plot] are allowed in order to 'ampliar, engrandecer y deleitar' [expand, magnify and delight]. Nevertheless, they should not be 'tan fuera que parezca cosa ajena' [so alien that they look out of place].

In this respect, Camargo could have connected the food with Ignatius' ecstasy in many ways. For example, one of the witnesses to the rapture, Inés Pascual, thought that the saint had fainted. Therefore, she prepared chicken soup and offered it to the

---

24   Ribadeneyra (1945: 316): 'gastóse con los ayunos y excesivas penitencias [...] Había perdido de tal manera el sentido del manjar, que casi ningún gusto le daba lo que comía' [the fasts and excessive penance eroded his body [...] He had lost the sense of taste to such an extent that he hardly enjoyed anything he ate].

ecstatic hermit (Creixell 1946: 117–18). Ignatius himself explains in the *Autobiografía* that, in Manresa, he had a 'visión de la carne' [vision of meat] that persuaded him to give up vegetarianism (Loyola 2013: 44–45).

Nevertheless, Camargo's still life has no observable connection with the main plot. Therefore, setting aside religion and epic theory, the interpolation will be better understood if read in the broader literary context of the time. In early modern Europe, countless authors (e.g. Góngora with the *Polifemo*) followed the practice of retelling ancient myths with varying degrees of embellishment. The purpose was to display one's capability of expanding the bare narrative with new episodes as well as descriptive, dramatic and reflective passages, decorated with as many ornaments as fantasy could invent. This practice of expansion of the story was known as *copia*. One of the reasons of Marino's success was precisely his virtuosity with this amplification technique: the *Adone* managed to convert the Ovidian source about Venus and Adonis, which has fewer than one hundred lines, into the longest poem of Italian literature, with 41,000 lines (Priest 1967: xviii–xix).

Camargo, who also wrote a poem on the death of Adonis (Torres Quintero 1960: 386–90), faced a challenge comparable to that of Marino. Both hagiographic and mythological works are limited by the 'fixity' of the story. Indeed, most readers were already well informed about how the plot (e.g. the life of the saint or the Greco-Latin myth) would unravel.[25] In fact, Camargo was even more constrained than Marino in the sense that the readership would be more willing to accept variations in the love story of two pagan gods than in a hagiography based on alleged real facts. Small wonder, then, that he introduced his boldest innovations in the ekphraseis rather than in the main narration.

According to Renaissance theory, the perfect work of art cannot be altered, not even in the smallest detail, without destroying the beauty and meaning of the whole (Wölfflin 1964: 65).[26] This aesthetic is alien to Camargo. Like the interlude of the grotesque animals with Christ, the still life could be removed from the poem without damaging its central plot. In fact, its deletion would make the whole canto much clearer when it comes to the main topic (that is, the rapture *ad intra*).[27] Though very much overdone, the ekphrasis of the crucified surrounded by compassionate beasts could be explained, to some extent, from a religious viewpoint. The lengthy, burlesque *bodegón* seems instead even more out of place in a sacred poem.

Thus, one might criticise Camargo for merely padding his poem out. Some scholars have argued that the excessive length of the *San Ignacio*, which has a high proportion of stanzas devoted to ekphraseis, weakens its Gongorism (Figueroa 1991: 103). The Cordovan poet was, of course, also fond of the descriptive *excursus*. However, Góngora's ekphraseis have two defining features: (i) intensity when read

25   I refer to the section 'La struttura generale' [General Structure] in Pozzi's (1988) introduction to Marino.

26   Cascales (1975: 135–36): 'aquello que está compuesto de varias cosas ha de estar tan unido en ellas, que quitando o mudando alguna parte, quede el todo imperfecto y manco' [that which is composed of several things must be so coherent, that by removing or changing one part, the whole becomes imperfect and faulty].

27   Significantly, the prose summary of canto V only mentions Ignatius' religious scruples and visions (Torres Quintero 1960: 157).

as autonomous passages; and (ii) consistency when connected with the rest of the *Soledades*. These attributes appear as the opposite of Camargo's food description, which (i) seems to prioritise, with its more than twenty edible components, quantity over density; and (ii) once more dilutes the doctrinal content of the poem, particularly when contrasted with the ecstasy. However, a more sympathetic reading would classify Camargo's still life as an outstanding example of *copia*: Gongorist in its theme (the *bodegón*), Marinist in its philosophy (a liberal approach to the question of unity) (Priest 1967: xx).[28] In fact, the poetic still lifes are among the most famous passages in the whole *San Ignacio*; also among the ones that the anthologist will select and the reader will remember. Thus, the practice of augmenting the bulk of the poem by introducing descriptive subject matter should reveal something essential about Camargo's work.[29]

None of the previous epics on Ignatius is a model of directness. Belmonte (1609: 222^v–43) devotes an entire book to the fabrics portraying Jesuit martyrs woven by three Garcilasian-inspired nymphs; Escobar (1613: 141^r–42) indulges in pastoral episodes; Oña (1992: cantos VI and VII) describes the creatures from hell in detail. Nevertheless, these digressions attempt to fulfil, with more or less success, pious intentions, namely: to extol the sacrifices of the Society of Jesus, to provide background that will help understand an episode of Ignatius' life, or to emphasise the temptations that the saint faced. Though colourful and varied, the works by Belmonte, Escobar and Oña adhere more closely to the traditional motifs of Jesuit hagiography (e.g. miracles, fights with the Devil, the greatness of this religious order).

Obviously, these topoi are present in Camargo as well. However, the influence of Marino may have served as a springboard to design a poem made up from watertight compartments. Albeit never reaching the Italian's lack of self-restraint, Camargo developed a poetics of digression that is far more revealing of the ethos of his age than that of his predecessors. Borrowing Houellebecq's terminology (2010: 258–59), the poet appears to be more interested in the *world as juxtaposition* (that of lyric verse, or even painting) than in the *world as narration* (that of epic poetry in the manner of, say, a Marco Girolamo Vida). In this respect, Camargo's penchant for the visual arts could have influenced not only his style but also his structural approach to the epic genre. The resulting ambiguity of perspectives reflects the doublespeak of the *San Ignacio*, digressively descriptive in structure yet, at times, straightforwardly dogmatic. The principle that *prodesse* should be above *delectare* did not always match Camargo's creative concerns. Thus, his poem oscillates between proliferating, material ekphraseis (e.g. the animals, the still life) and religious, transcendental meaning (e.g. the crucifixion, the Trinity). This diglossia enables the *San Ignacio* to work as one of the finest examples of the conflict in Baroque poetic between the aesthetic and the theological functions of art.

---

28 Cabani (2005: 212): 'Góngora sta a Marino come la concentrazione e la densità stanno alla dilatazione, alla ridondanza, alla prolissità' [Góngora is to Marino what concentration and density are to expansion, redundancy, wordiness].

29 One of the 'rediscoverers' of the poem, Gerardo Diego (1961: 283–88), focused exclusively on its *bodegones*.

These inner tensions help explain the poem's tendency towards abrupt transitions. After the eighty-line poetic still life, one might be surprised at the unexpected arrival of the *rapto* in the same stanza in which Ignatius accepts the shepherds' food (CLXXXV). In the blink of an eye, we have been transported from the *bodegón* to the mystical vision. Later, another rapid juxtaposition — from the sacred to the pagan — will take place immediately after the ecstatic visions. As we saw earlier, the content of Camargo's rapture *ad intra* did not depart greatly from the official narrative of Ignatius' Manresan ecstasies. Conversely, his description of the witnesses' reactions (after the still life, the second component of the rapture *ad extra*) starts in a realistic manner, which is suddenly marred by a completely fantastic episode. Following Ribadeneyra, both Escobar (1613: 61^v) and Oña (VIII.859–66) depict the response from ordinary people to Ignatius' rapture: they gave him up for dead, and would have buried him had it not been for a witness who noticed that his heart was still beating.[30]

There is a trace of these historical facts in Camargo. Mystical experiences are usually depicted as pleasant. However, ecstatics often pay a high price in return, for the effects of a rapture can give the impression that death is supervening. In this sense, when the *rapto* arrives, everything seems to suggest that Ignatius' soul is losing in vital strength what it is gaining in divine contact (CCX.1–4):

> Robada la color, el cuerpo yerto,
> yace de sí olvidado, en Dios unido,
> Ignacio, a quien latiendo mal despierto
> el corazón, que le pulsó dormido...

> [The colour lost, the body stiff,
> he lies, forgetful of himself, in God united,
> Ignatius, whose heart in a trance-like state
> is beating, palpitating as he sleeps...]

Then, following Escobar, Camargo moves to a completely imaginative dimension of the episode. The Jesuit from Valladolid introduced an innovation into his account of the rapture (Escobar y Mendoza 1613: 61^v–62^v). Having portrayed the reactions of the Manresan people, he devotes six stanzas to explaining how each day of the week went by before the saint returned to his senses. This entails a description of seven deities/planets: the sun (Sunday), the moon (Monday), Mars (Tuesday), Mercury (Wednesday), Jupiter (Thursday), Venus (Friday) and Saturn (Saturday).

Earlier in the poem (1613: 20^v–28^v), 'Júpiter' was the designation used to name the Christian God, 'Mercurio' was used for Saint Peter and 'Vulcano' for the Devil. Belmonte (1609: 74^r–83^r) also deploys mythology for sacred purposes: his Proteus foresees the future heroic deeds of the saint and the martyrs of the order. Oña's *Ignacio de Cantabria* constantly refers to Greco-Latin deities in order to show them subdued by the presence of God, the Virgin, the saints or the angels (Rodríguez

---

30   Ribadeneyra (1945: 64): 'quedó tan enajenado de todos sus sentidos, que hallándose así, algunos hombres devotos y mujeres le tuvieron por muerto' [he was so deprived of his senses, that having found him in this devotional trance, some pious men and women thought he was dead].

1992: 42). Given their proselytising intentions, all of these poets deploy the humanist repertoire in order to appeal to the readers' taste.[31]

Following the Renaissance, writers made similar efforts to reconcile two worlds (antiquity and Christianity) separated by a lapse of centuries (Seznec 1972: 322). In the Hispanic Baroque, despite the admonitions of theoreticians such as Cascales (1975: 155–57), who argued for the expulsion of the pagan gods from epics, the hagiographic genre embraced Greco-Latin mythology. This assimilation took place either by (i) reshaping the pantheon to convey Counter-Reformation spirituality, often by means of rudimentary allegory, as evidenced by some of the above-mentioned examples (Leone 2010: 167–68 and 202–03);[32] or by (ii) deploying heathen deities for merely ornamental purposes: a marginal role that became increasingly frequent (Kluge 2014: 151).

Camargo epitomises Jesuit syncretism by amalgamating varied intellectual elements. In this respect, classic mythology, both allegorical and decorative, is a constant in the *San Ignacio*. One of the poet's driving forces was the desire to provoke *admiratio* by displaying his familiarity with sacred and secular culture. He gave to both kinds of erudition almost equal importance, as reflected in his advice to the anonymous writer against whom he wrote the *Invectiva apologética* (Torres Quintero 1960: 488): 'mire mejor lo que escribe y estudie un poco en Góngora y un mucho en Santo Tomás' [be more careful with what you write and study a bit of Góngora and a lot of Saint Thomas].[33] Camargo deploys mythology, within Gongorism, to provide his work with complexity, sophistication and even authority: that of the poet who masterfully combines higher — or even mysterious, arcane — forms of learning.[34]

With this context in mind, Camargo's *modus operandi* becomes understandable. He must have liked Escobar's planetary week, for he took the same celestial bodies and presented them in identical order (CCXI–CCXVI, also six stanzas). However, although the model is clear, Camargo's alterations are revealing. To borrow Bloom's (1973: 68) terminology, the poet swerves from his precursor as if he had not dared enough. His 'twist' makes the gods more stirring: his is not a mere chronological procession to emphasise the duration of the rapture but rather a funeral pageant. Perhaps inspired by Marino (*Adone*, canto XIX), who presented Adonis' burial procession as a grand parade with hundreds of mourners (including pagan deities such as Mercury and Venus), Camargo took the fact that Ignatius was initially thought to be dead as an opportunity to treat the obsequies in a melodramatic and lavish manner.

---

31   This applies also to Oña (1992: 128): 'a lo humano | mayor viveza da el pincel profano' [the secular brush provides human nature | with more liveliness] (III.165.7–8).

32   According to the *Discurso en loor de la poesía*, poetry makes use 'de los dioses antiguos de tal suerte | que a Cristo sirven y a sus pies los pone' [of the ancient gods in such manner | that they serve Christ and are placed at his feet] (Chang-Rodríguez 2009: 131).

33   Studying Góngora also means learning classical culture, as explained by the editorial annotation to book I, canto I, XXIV.8: 'Es de D. Luis este verso entero. Tomolo el poeta para honrar los suyos, pues él los toma de los latinos, de Horacio y Virgilio, en infinitos lugares' [This entire line is from Góngora. Camargo borrowed it to honour his own poetry, just as Góngora borrows lines from the classics, from Horace to Virgil, on countless occasions] (Torres Quintero 1960: 51).

34   This paragraph is indebted to Rodríguez (1992: 47).

Thus, just as the endless parade of food marched before our eyes, so a smaller but equally striking set of deities descends from Olympus. The sun 'lacrimosa lamenta' [tearfully laments] Ignatius' alleged death; so does the crescent moon, transformed into an 'urna' [urn] (CCXI). Mars, moved by the death of that other 'Marte' or former soldier, snaps his 'marcial bélica trompa' [war horn] in half and devotes himself to the funeral rites (CCXII). Mercury has a similar reaction since he brings his caduceus to the mound as an offering ('al túmulo consagra por tributo'), which he also breaks (CCXIII). Jupiter sobs inconsolably, in the process destroying clouds ('Las nubes de dolor despedazando') and moaning 'en sordo y sordo trueno' [with deafening thunder] (CCXIV). Although Venus was defeated by Ignatius' chastity, she also laments his death and offers her tears/pearls 'a su sepulcro' [to his sepulchre] (CCXV). Finally, Saturn interrupts the mourning when he realises that the saint is in fact alive: 'muerto lamenta al que define vivo' [laments the death of whom he finds alive] (CCXVI).

From a narratological viewpoint, the digression is more closely connected to the plot than the still life. However, as often with Camargo, the sacredness of an episode (in this case, Ignatius' 'funeral') is symbolised by an image of resounding sumptuousness and pomp (Latchman 1956: 11). The display of physical brilliance (e.g. 'zafir', 'perlas') is not as abundant and over-elaborate as that of Marino. Yet the gestures are so affected that the deities do not seem to mourn Ignatius but rather to worship artifice as their superior god. For this reason, the passage may not serve as an example of the transformation of pagan forms to convey sacred values. Indeed, Camargo opts more for delivering a stagy scene loaded with extravagant pomp than for conveying any spiritual message. His pagan gods 'maintain a mourning ostentation', to borrow a line from Shakespeare.[35]

The relationship between grieving and display, which was so brilliantly revealed in the Baroque *Trauerspiel* (literally, 'mourning play'), as Benjamin called it, has one of its manifestations here. Since the reader knows that Ignatius did not die during the rapture, this passage cannot possibly cause mourning. Rather, in these lines mournfulness finds satisfaction, as if the gods were performing a play within the poem.[36] In this sense, the passage exemplifies Bolívar Echeverría's (2008: 7) theory of the Baroque as the *'messinscena assoluta'* [the ultimate *mise-en-scène*]. Camargo's podium of pagan deities has emancipated itself from any service to a theatrical purpose (that is, the imitation of the world) and seems to inhabit an autonomous universe of its own creation. The stage is no longer staging something; rather than mimesis, what sustains interest is Camargo's *staging for its own sake*. Thus, his funeral pageantry adds to the trite assimilation of his precursor (deities/days) a wealth of hermeneutic potential.

Yet the influence of Escobar is also present in a remarkable final image. In 1588, Bishop Juan de Cardona placed before Saint Lucy's chapel in Manresa a needle-

---

35   Camargo wrote a mock counterpart to this passage in the *Invectiva apologética* (Torres Quintero 1960: 484), which suggests that he did not take these deities seriously as vehicles for religious allegory. Shakespeare's line can be found in *Much Ado About Nothing*, act IV, first scene, line 205 (Kamaralli 2018: 198).

36   These lines are indebted to Benjamin (1977: 81 and 119).

FIG. 4.5. Antiguo Hospital de Santa Lucía, Manresa, Spain. Photograph from c. 1890–1900 by unknown author. Source: *Recuerdos de San Ignacio de Loyola* [*Memories of Saint Ignatius of Loyola*], book preserved at the Arxiu Comarcal del Bagés, Manresa, Spain. The obelisk on the left of the image was destroyed during the Spanish Civil War (1936–1939).

like obelisk in memory of Ignatius (Creixell 1946: 52). After his description of the rapture, the author from Valladolid devotes sixteen lines to this funerary monument (Escobar y Mendoza 1613: 69^v). He approves of the memorial function of the obelisk, praises the virtues of Cardona, and describes the epitaph engraved in white marble. Then, he writes eleven stanzas that refer to other Spanish monuments dedicated to Ignatius and applauds their patrons.

Camargo's *San Ignacio* is full of bookish ekphraseis of cities (e.g. Rome, Venice) that the author never visited. When setting out to narrate the life of Ignatius, the poet undertook the challenge to describe a continent of which he had had no direct experience (Mayo 2014: 161). In this respect, he examined both biographical and poetic sources in order to describe Manresa. Doubtless Escobar inspired him when writing the stanza CCXVIII, which encapsulates three of the above-mentioned ideas (memory, courtly praise and epitaph) in a much briefer format:

> Aguja que de nubes se corona,
> donde el cincel memoria aró estudiosa,
> el doctor le erigió Juan de Cardona,
> electo ya Prelado de Tortosa,
> que este agonal primero le blasona
> triunfo, a aquella mente victoriosa

de Ignacio, cuyas letras siempre bellas
con rayo y rayo limpian las estrellas.

[Needle that is crowned with clouds,
where the chisel engraved a learned inscription,
the doctor Juan de Cardona, already elected
Prelate of Tortosa, erected it for him,
for this first monument emblazons
his triumph, celebrating that victorious mind
of Ignatius; the stars clean with their rays
its always beautiful letters.]

In early modern Spain, obelisks were believed to be ancient Egyptian monuments dedicated to the cult of the sun. Covarrubias (1943: 833) defined the word as 'una columna que se va rematando en punta, que por otro nombre se llama aguja [...] De estos obeliscos había muchos en Egipto, y créese haberlos dedicado al sol, representando en ellos alguno de sus rayos' [a column that tapers to a tip, which is also called a needle [...] There were many of these obelisks in Egypt, and it is believed they were dedicated to the sun, representing its rays].

Given their mysterious historical origin, decorative and symbolic potential, and splendid geometric simplicity, the *mirabile* nature of obelisks was fully in harmony with Baroque taste (Blanco 2012c: 435). From an allegorical viewpoint, an obelisk is a monumental needle or 'aguja' that stitches heaven and earth together, the ancient and the modern, the old idols with the crosses that in Rome — and in Manresa (Figure 4.5) — were placed at their apex. In the eyes of a Baroque poet, the obelisk, *conciliatio oppositorum* par excellence, could well represent a marble *agudeza* [conceit] of colossal dimensions. That was certainly the case for Góngora, who used the expression 'verde obelisco' [green obelisk] as a key paradigm that reconciles nature with artfulness throughout the *Soledades* (Blanco 2012c: 393–401). The Cordovan poet also used the synonym 'aguja' in other works such as the *Égloga piscatoria en la muerte del Duque de Medina Sidonia* [*Piscatorial Eclogue on the Death of the Duke of Medina Sidonia*], from whence Camargo took the first line of his stanza CCXVIII.

Unlike Escobar, who devoted eight lines to the epitaph, the viceregal poet is more interested in the appearance of the obelisk, that is, its strictly visual and sculptural dimension. In the context of courtly architecture, these pillars could be deemed a synthesis of artfulness, wealth, exoticism and ostentatious height. In this sense, Camargo starts by describing the 'aguja' as hyperbolically tall ('de nubes se corona'). It thus serves as an unmissable memory of Ignatius' 'mente victoriosa', which emerged in the ecstatic afterglow as almost invulnerable in the enjoyment of his creed, and ready to undertake projects of the greatest complexity. Moreover, the vertical, elongated and pointed shape of this — symbolically speaking — petrified sunray points at the stars which, as a sign of respect and as a token of reciprocity, 'con rayo y rayo' clean the letters of the inscription to keep them 'siempre bellas'.[37]

---

37   Camargo later adds that not only do the stars illuminate the obelisk at night but also the sun in the daytime (book III, canto I, XIV.5–8): 'cuyo globo le dora el rey del día, | y la noche le cuelga luminarias, | donde a los siglos deja encomendado | de Ignacio un epitafio bien hablado' [Whose globe the king of the day gilds, | and the night hangs luminaries on it, | where it leaves entrusted to the ages | an eloquent epitaph for Ignatius].

Like Góngora's 'verde obelisco' (Blanco 2012c: 460), Camargo's 'aguja' also has the function of initiating readers into his hermetic literature. From time immemorial, the most admirable creations of ancient Egypt (e.g. hieroglyphs, sphinxes, pyramids and obelisks) have been used in the West as depositaries of arcane mysteries. In this sense, the cave of Manresa, to which the *San Ignacio* shall not return, is left under the guard of the funerary monument which raises itself up as the symbol that reconciles (*conciliatio oppositorum*) the saint's hagiographies with Gongorism and the Greco-Latin heritage: three traditions that are key to the deciphering of the poem.

The Anxiety of Confluence

In 1629, Fernando Fernández de Valenzuela wrote *Laurea crítica* [*Critical Laurels*], a satire of Gongorism that is, as far as we know, the first play ever written in New Granada (Arrom and Rivas Sacconi 1959: 161). Don Velialís, a character in this *entremés*, portrays the 'águila' as follows: 'El ave reina, | la que albergando el obelisco escollo, | en el sol examina el tierno pollo' [The eagle, | which nested at the rocky obelisk, | examines the eaglet under the sun] (lines 325–27). This description is particularly appropriate, for it contains two key images of the canto studied: the eagle, to which Ignatius is compared for his resilience during the rapture *ad intra* (CXCV.5: 'ave Ignacio real'); and the obelisk, which encapsulates the poem's manifold mainstay in the rapture *ad extra*.

It was common practice in seventeenth-century literature to pile up fragments like this without any clear idea of a goal (Benjamin 1977: 178). In the 'New World', this tendency generated a thematic of estrangement that is consubstantial with the Baroque. At the end of Chapter 3, I analysed the impact of Camargo's self-perceived marginality on his eclectic imagery. On the one hand, the poet was eager to emulate the Spanish classics. The foreword is clear when it emphasises that Camargo's inspiration 'tiene su origen del Parnaso español, de la cultura castellana' [originates from the Spanish Parnassus, from Castilian culture] (Torres Quintero 1960: 36). On the other hand, Camargo had a sense of distance from his sources that facilitated the process of swerving from his precursors. Increasing differences were converting Creoles into a population ever more distinct from the Spanish, increasingly self-aware and conscious of their belatedness. Camargo's aesthetic stems from these preoccupations and the tropes that they generate.[38]

During the seventeenth century, the idea took hold in Spain that there was nothing new about which one could write. This feeling of 'tardiness' or 'belatedness' became more poignant still in the 'New World', even in authors of the calibre of Sor Juana.[39] Creoles were not only in a different place but also in another time. Espinosa

---

38   This paragraph and those that follow are indebted to González Echevarría (1996: 196, 1993: 157–64).

39   Gracián's *El Discreto* (2001b: 166): 'Estamos ya a los fines de los siglos. Allá en la Edad de Oro se inventaba: añadióse después, ya todo es repetir' [We have reached the end of centuries. People invented things in ancient Greece and Rome. More was added later. Now, all is repetition]. Sor Juana's *Pinta en jocoso numen...* [*She Portrays with Playful Inspiration...*] conveys a similar idea (Méndez Plancarte 1994a: 321): '¡Dichosos los antiguos que tuvieron | paño de que cortar' [Blessed were the ancients who had | cloth from which to cut] (lines 45–46).

Medrano (2017: foreword 'Al lector') summarises this idea of a double displacement: 'Tarde parece que salgo a esta empresa: pero vivimos muy lejos los criollos' [It would seem that I am late to the Gongorist party, but we Creoles live very far away]. His words reflect the pathos of the viceregal elites, who were acutely aware of occupying a 'secondary' position vis-à-vis the cultural 'centrality' of Spain (Bass 2009: 9). Thus, Creoles received the Western cultural heritage with admiration but also with anxiety. If a medieval genius such as Petrarch experienced unease before the great authors of the past, how would Camargo feel when reading, after Virgil, Góngora and Quevedo?

Creole writers saw themselves as epigones of the Renaissance. However, despite their anxiety over influence, they were not gripped by paralysis. Quite the contrary: they produced a literature that not only mimicked the genres and style of the Spanish Golden Age but also challenged the primacy of its masterpieces. According to Espinosa Medrano, Góngora outdid the Greco-Latin classics with his *Polifemo*.[40] His belief in the perfectibility of poetry encouraged other Creole writers to outdo Europeans. Hence, the pride expressed by the prologuist of the *San Ignacio*, who affirms that the 'New World' is 'no [...] menos fecundo de minerales ricos y preciosas piedras, que de aquilatados y sublimes ingenios' [no less rich in minerals and precious stones, than in precious and sublime wit] (Torres Quintero 1960: 35).

The simile shows the importance that Creoles attributed to the reception of their literature in Europe. The parallel was simple: Spain provided not only the technology to extract silver for the 'Old World' but also the intellectual raw material (Spanish and Latin with their respective canons) for viceregal poets to write works that dazzled Europeans as surely as gold (Vitulli 2012: 149). Camargo shared this worldview. Small wonder then that he absorbed his Spanish precursors with such gusto. The imitation of Góngora, the most prestigious peninsular model, was his way of seeking in the 'Old World' the recognition he was never granted in the 'New'.[41] In this sense, the prologuist trusted that, in Spain, Camargo would receive the literary glory 'que no consiguió del todo en vida entre los mismos de su patria' [that he did not fully achieve among his compatriots during his lifetime] (Torres Quintero 1960: 36).

This has not been the case. However, the *San Ignacio* deserves reappraisal and not just for Camargo's mimicry of Góngora — and arguably of Marino. As hinted by Espinosa Medrano, viceregal poets were not mere parrots that could only repeat back what they had heard — at least not the best of them.[42] One must concede that the Baroque had a heightened consciousness of the models' authority, particularly

---

40   Espinosa Medrano (2017: section V, paragraph 41): 'Solo este parece que escribió el *Polifemo*, porque solo en su estilo llegó a ser gigante aquel cíclope' [It looks as if only Góngora had written the *Polifemo*, for only in his style did the cyclops get to be a giant].

41   The resentment against his Neogranadian peers is noticeable in the *Invectiva apologética* (Torres Quintero 1960: 430): 'no escupe dulce el que es amargo y tiene la hiel en la boca' [He who is bitter and has a bile tongue does not spit sweetly]. He even puns with his own surname: (C)amargo [Camargo/bitter].

42   Espinosa Medrano (2017: foreword 'Al lector'): 'harto es, que hablemos: mucho valdría papagayo, que tanto parlase' [It is enough that we speak: a parrot who talked as much would cost a fortune].

in Hispanic America given its cultural subordination to Europe (Téllez 2012: 127). When confronted with Góngora, Marino, Belmonte, Escobar and Oña, it appears that Camargo did not suffer an anxiety of influence so much as an anxiety of confluence: an excess of an assumed belatedness.

Nevertheless, his work offers an ambiguous homage to these poets whose presence served as a springboard for the new. Poetic influence always proceeds by a misreading of precursors: an act of creative revisionism (Bloom 1973: 30). This was Camargo's task. The genre he chose (hagiographic epic) was foreign to Góngora, his paragon of *elocutio*. So was his style (Gongorism) to Escobar, who offered him the *dispositio*. These authors' aspirations were hardly reconcilable, yet Camargo even drew from their *inventio*, enhancing the hybrid strangeness of his poem. These are not signs of a lack of creativity or of servile *imitatio*. The oddity in the *San Ignacio* is not the unknown but the destabilising or decentring of the known. Thus, Camargo's mimicry of the European models — almost the same, but not quite (Bhabha 2004: 127) — works as a form of difference. Despite being a latecomer, he deployed Gongorism and Marinism to renew the hagiographic epic of the Counter-Reformation as no other Hispanic author before him had dared to do (Meo Zilio 1967: 61–62). Thus, the *San Ignacio* outdid its precursors in the genre because of its diglossia: the doublespeak that the poet developed as a response to the conflict between his theological and artistic goals. Similar tensions are present in Belmonte, Escobar and Oña, but none of them vented them as visibly as Camargo did.

On the one hand, when dealing with the sacred content of the story (e.g. Ignatius' penances, the rapture *ad intra*), the poet is eager to conform to accepted beliefs. In fact, like the pagan gods of Ignatius' 'funeral', Camargo betrays a strong tendency to overact as if he feared that his double displacement — and/or aesthetic strangeness — may cast doubts on his religious orthodoxy. This is the reason why the ecstatic visions are loaded with solemnity and pompousness. In a typically Baroque manner (Wölfflin 1964: 22), the will to create images of authoritative beauty leads the poet to lavish display when presenting dogmas.

On the other hand, Camargo's excursive boldness is more radical than that of his Ignatian predecessors. His daring would have astonished even Chapelain. In the foreword to the *Adone* (1988: 14–21 and 27), the French critic defends digressions as long as the subject matter of the epic poem remains 'illustre' (note his examples, so distant from Camargo's animals or still life: palaces, gardens, architecture and especially love), jokes are kept to a minimum ('modestes ou modestement dittes') [modest or modestly told], and there is no 'disconvenance' [incompatibility] between the 'principal événement' [main plot] and 'ses accidents' [its digressions]. In fact, Chapelain censures the mixture 'd'histoire sacrée avec de poésie profane' [of sacred history with secular poetry], which is one of the tenets of Camargo's aesthetic.

As we have seen, the paradigm-shifting novelty of the *Soledades* had a profound impact on the *San Ignacio*, which would pay no heed to these rules of decorum. However, despite their radical deviation from the plot, Camargo's ekphraseis are not superfluous. Quite the opposite: they provide a space where the aesthetic and ideological contradictions of the Baroque can be contemplated through a magnifying glass, an aperture that the main plot itself was incapable of providing. The ekphrasis serves as a meta-aesthetic tool for delivering a less dogmatic view of Ignatius' life and reality than that endorsed by the sanctioned Jesuit sources.[43] Hence, this motif emerges as one of the most successful yet elusive strategies to reflect — and expand — the cracks that began to run along the Counter-Reformation wall at the outset of modernity.

---

43   To paraphrase Kluge (2014: 99 and 242).

PART III

Sor Juana's *Primero sueño*: Ekphrasis Unbounded

CHAPTER 5

The Cosmographic Mirror-Painting

In 1703, Francisco Álvarez de Velasco, a writer from Bogotá, published a collection of poems addressed to Sor Juana Inés de la Cruz (1651–1695) entitled *Carta laudatoria* [*Letter of Praise*]. This work (Buxó 1993) evidences not only the communication between the New Kingdom of Granada and the Viceroyalty of New Spain, but also the special consideration accorded to *Primero sueño* [*First Dream*] (written c. 1685), the longest of Sor Juana's poems (975 lines), among early readers.[1] The Mexican nun was arguably the last major author of the Hispanic Baroque and the greatest poet of viceregal Latin American literature. In the Spanish Golden Age, there is nothing comparable to her *Primero sueño*.

The text pushes to its limits the human impulse towards knowledge by representing this longing in the course of a night. Sor Juana describes how the soul leaves the body (arguably her poetic *alter ego*) during a dream, as she strives to contemplate the universe and herself. At the end, the experience reveals the impossibility of fully comprehending not only the cosmos but also any of its components. Nevertheless, the pursuit of knowledge is presented as being worth the struggle (González Echevarría 1996: 223).

The poem was published originally in the second volume of Sor Juana's works (1692) under the editorial heading *Primero sueño, que así intituló y compuso la Madre Juana Inés de la Cruz, imitando a Góngora* [*First Dream, which Sor Juana Inés de la Cruz so entitled and wrote, imitating Góngora*].[2] Indeed, the nun followed Góngora's style and, equally importantly, chose the poetic genre that he had popularised in the Hispanic world: the *silva* (Sánchez Robayna 1991: 198). This elastic metre facilitated the introduction of lengthy excursuses.

Sor Juana wrote neither a pastoral nor an epic but a poem based on abstract reasoning (Paz 1982: 470). This helps explain why the plot of *Primero sueño* seems drier and less 'poetic' than that of the *Soledades* or the *San Ignacio*. When fashioning their source material into narratives, Góngora and Camargo had an easier task than the nun. Nevertheless, since her topic is much narrower, her poetic *amplificatio*

---

1   Including Sor Juana herself, as evidenced by the *Respuesta a Sor Filotea de la Cruz* [*Reply to Sor Filotea de la Cruz*] (Salceda 1994: 471; More 2016: 121): 'no me acuerdo haber escrito por mi gusto sino es un papelillo que llaman *El Sueño*' [I do not recall having written for my own pleasure except for a trifle they call *The Dream*].

2   Luiselli (2017: 178): 'Since 1692, Sor Juana's imitation of Góngora has been the most accepted critical premise about *Primero sueño*'.

through ekphrasis becomes more visible as well (Alatorre 1993: 123; Vossler 1946: 24).

Like her forerunners, Sor Juana may have felt attracted to descriptive poetry because of her interest in the plastic arts. This penchant is noticeable in her *Neptuno alegórico* [*Allegorical Neptune*]: she designed the triumphal arch and its eight paintings, and then wrote an ekphrasis for each of them. Moreover, Sor Juana produced fifteen descriptions or poetic portraits of women (Sabat de Rivers 1992: 207).[3] In *Pinta en jocoso numen...* [*She Portrays with Playful Inspiration...*], for example, Sor Juana deploys a pictorial lexicon such as 'regla' [ruler], 'pincel' [paintbrush], 'aparejo' [primer] and 'retoque' [retouch] when depicting Lisarda (Méndez Plancarte 1994a: 320), a stock name for the beloved in love poetry. Despite her humble disclaimer ('sin haber en mi vida dibujado') [without ever having drawn before], she might have been an amateur painter (Figure 5.1). Thus, it is unsurprising that Sor Juana incorporates into *Primero sueño* several terms and techniques borrowed from the fine arts (e.g. colour, form, dimension and perspective) in order to enhance visualisation (Nanfito 2000: 29; Olivares 1998: 119).

From the outset of the poem, the reader meets images of an ascensional nature. If book II of the *San Ignacio* ended with an obelisk, *Primero sueño* starts with a pyramidal shadow that rises from the earth towards heaven: 'de vanos obeliscos punta altiva' [the haughty tip of its great obelisks] (line 3) (More 2016: 45). If Camargo's monument reconciled the Ignatian biographies, Gongorism and Greco-Latin antiquity, that of Sor Juana keeps the last two traditions but replaces the first with the pseudo-Egyptian Hermetic background of the text.[4] Given a textual resemblance between *San Ignacio* and *Primero sueño*, Olivares (2014: 127) has suggested that Sor Juana knew Camargo's work.[5] Since his epic was published in Madrid, from whence there was a thriving book trade to Mexico City, this thesis remains plausible. In any case, the obelisk is singularly appropriate for both poems. To borrow Paz's expression (1982: 500), *Primero sueño* is an 'obelisco verbal' [verbal obelisk] made up with metaphors of height.

Álvarez de Lugo, an early commentator of Sor Juana's *silva*, argued that the 'obelisks' of the poem are 'sombras que carecen de cuerpo' [shadows that lack a body] (Sánchez Robayna 1991: 63). In fact, these needle-like shadows are just one of the many staffage components that are not made of matter. As soon as the poetic speaker falls asleep, the soul embarks on an oneiric trip. From that moment onwards, the sense of sight will prevail (Buxó 2006a: 15). The soul of *Primero sueño* will dare to examine the last and highest of all the mysteries of the world, taking

3   Poems 19, 41, 61, 71, 72, 80, 87, 89, 102, 103, 126, 127, 132, 145 and 214 in Méndez Plancarte (1994a). Written in 1680, the *Neptuno* was included in *Inundación castálida* [*Flood of the Castalian Spring*], the first edition of Sor Juana's collected works (Cruz 1689). This book was republished a year later with another title (Cruz 1690b).

4   Hermetism was codified in the *Corpus hermeticum*, which Sor Juana knew either first-hand or through the works of Athanasius Kircher (Beaupied 1997: 2). This doctrine was a key element of Neoplatonism from Ficino onwards (Terry 1993: 250).

5   In her opinion, Camargo's 'funesto así, pirámide del valle' [funereal as it is, pyramid of the valley] (book III, canto II, XVIII.2) resembles Sor Juana's lines 1–2: 'Piramidal, funesta, de la tierra | nacida sombra...' [Pyramidal, funereal, a shadow | born of earth] (More 2016: 45).

FIG. 5.1. Nicolás Enríquez de Vargas (attributed), *Portrait of Sor Juana Inés de la Cruz* (eighteenth century). Source: The Dr Robert H. Lamborn Collection, Philadelphia Museum of Art. This Mexican painting presents itself as a 'fiel copia' [faithful copy] after a self-portrait by Sor Juana which, if it ever existed, is not extant. Villaseñor (2016) studied the portraits of Sor Juana. The speculation that she painted is addressed in Perry (2012).

the whole cosmos as its subject (Pfandl 1963: 208). Sor Juana's use of three images to describe the lofty vantage point of the soul (the lighthouse of Alexandria, mounts Atlas and Olympus, and two Egyptian pyramids) is a good example of the *variatio* technique (Tenorio 2013: 175–76). In this chapter, I will analyse the cosmographic canvas painted by human fantasy, which Sor Juana compares to the mirror of the lighthouse, because this ekphrasis triggers the ascension of the soul. Chapter 6 will be devoted to her subsequent vision of the universe, which deploys the other two motifs of height (the mountains and the pyramids).[6]

My main thesis is that Sor Juana pushes the boundaries of ekphrasis in three directions. Firstly, her holistic approach is different from that of her predecessors: she aims at portraying not only everything visible (like Góngora), or Creation plus certain spiritual entities (like Camargo), but also everything invisible: that is, the intellectual foundations of Creation, be they abstract or Platonic ideas. Secondly, Sor Juana broadens another path opened up by her forerunners as regards the balance between vision and fantasy. Ekphrasis never entails mere perception through the senses but also through the imagination. In this respect, the nun goes one step further by making explicit that the ekphrasis is not drawn from direct visual perception, but from images that fantasy crafts in a dream. Thirdly, Sor Juana's ekphrasis also reveals a certain ambivalence. On the one hand, the base of *Primero sueño* is vaguely Christian, though the poet's religious agenda is not as explicit as Camargo's. On the other hand, due to its emphasis on knowledge and esoteric potential, the cosmographic canvas invites a reading within the traditions of the art of memory and Neoplatonic Hermetism. These inner tensions can be reconciled if one accepts Sor Juana's gnostic approach to the Catholic faith.[7]

Indeed, the painting, like the whole poem, is geared towards voicing the nun's thirst for omniscience (Méndez Plancarte 1951: xxxi). Having assimilated the readings of her legendary library, Sor Juana produced a work in which she poured out three leitmotivs of her life: ambition, failure and dignity. They all converge in the figure of Phaethon (lines 796–802), the model for the soul (Paz 1982: 498). No wonder the protagonist of *Primero sueño* is isolated. Not even Góngora's pilgrim, who is often aloof in the *Soledades*, reaches her level of withdrawal (Luiselli 1993: 167). In Sor Juana's *silva*, knowledge and self-knowledge are the main concerns. Perhaps for this reason, and given that *Primero sueño* is clothed with scientific undertones, the poet felt the need to portray the inner self in medical detail before embarking on the dream.[8]

---

6   Méndez Plancarte (1994a: 607–09) entitled these passages 'El sueño de la intuición universal' [The Dream of Universal Intuition] (lines 266–339) and '"Intermezzo" de las pirámides' [Intermezzo of the Pyramids] (lines 340–411).

7   Authors such as Sabat de Rivers (1976: 139), Paz (1982: 469–507), Luiselli (1993: 190) and Merrim (2010: 178–89 and 205–14) have supported this interpretation of the poem's approach to knowledge as Neoplatonic, Hermetic and/or secular. I refer to Luiselli's (2017) critique of scholarship on *Primero sueño*.

8   Kirk (2016: 110): 'Sor Juana's "dissection" of the body's organs provides a pathway for the soul's adventure, and anatomical science itself provided her with the knowledge of the existence of such a pathway'.

A Total Painting

After nightfall, Sor Juana depicts all creatures asleep, including a human being: her poetic *alter ego*. She also displays her medical knowledge by describing the inner activities of the body at rest. The stomach emits humid vapours. They reach the brain and give a boost to fantasy, which starts creating representations: a dream. Sor Juana's account of this mental process shows that the word 'fantasy' was not used in the seventeenth century with the same sense as today. Its connotation was more toward the rational aspect of imagination. Fantasy can reproduce in the mind's eye things previously grasped by the senses and stored in memory. Moreover, it can also create *ex novo* things that we have never perceived. Small wonder then that seventeenth-century discourses on the imagination deemed fantasy crucial to any creative endeavour (Serés 1994: 208; Wardropper 1970: 923).

In this respect, Sor Juana does not seem to be pondering on mimesis but on the latter attribute of fantasy: she introduces it as the main author of 'imágenes diversas' [diverse images] that do not come from memory. By doing so, she pays homage to the inventive power of the artistic imagination.[9] The passage on which I shall focus portrays the beginning of this oneiric activity (lines 266–301):

> Y del modo
> que en tersa superficie, que de Faro
> cristalino portento, asilo raro
> fue, en distancia longísima se vían
> (sin que esta le estorbase)
> del reino casi de Neptuno todo
> las que distantes lo surcaban naves
> —viéndose claramente
> en su azogada luna
> el número, el tamaño y la fortuna
> que en la instable campaña transparente
> arresgadas tenían,
> mientras aguas y vientos dividían
> sus velas leves y sus quillas graves—:
> así ella, sosegada, iba copiando
> las imágenes todas de las cosas,
> y el pincel invisible iba formando
> de mentales, sin luz, siempre vistosas
> colores, las figuras
> no solo ya de todas las criaturas
> sublunares, mas aun también de aquellas
> que intelectuales claras son Estrellas,
> y en el modo posible
> que concebirse puede lo invisible,
> en sí, mañosa, las representaba

9   Huarte de San Juan (1989: 395–96): 'De la buena imaginativa nacen todas las artes y ciencias que consisten en figura, correspondencia, armonía y proporción [...] Estas son: poesía, [...] pintar, trazar, escribir, leer' [All the arts and sciences that consist of figures, correspondence, harmony and proportion [...] are born of a good imaginative faculty. These are: poetry, [...] painting, drawing, writing, reading].

y al alma las mostraba.
La cual, en tanto, toda convertida
a su inmaterial ser y esencia bella,
aquella contemplaba,
participada de alto Ser, centella
que con similitud en sí gozaba;
y juzgándose casi dividida
de aquella que impedida
siempre la tiene, corporal cadena,
que grosera embaraza y torpe impide
el vuelo intelectual...

[...And just as on
the untroubled surface, crystalline portent
of Pharos, that uncommon refuge and port,
in the quicksilver mirror,
at vast distances one sees clearly almost
all the realm of Neptune, despite the expanse,
and the far-off ships that furrowed it, the size,
number, and fortune of bold vessels risked on
a shifting, transparent field,
while their light sails and weighty keels divided
waters and blustering winds:
so did serene fantasy
copy images of all things, the unseen
brush shaping, without light, bright mental colors
the figures not only of all sublunar
creatures but also of those
clear hues that are intellectual stars
and in the manner that the invisible
can be conceived, ingeniously represents
and displays them to the Soul.
She, meanwhile, transformed into
immaterial being and beautiful
essence, contemplated that
spark shared with highest Being and cherished it
deep inside, in His image;
and deeming herself almost separated
from the coarse corporeal chain that keeps her
ever bound and hinders the flight of intellect...][10]

In his early sonnet *Varia imaginación, que en mil intentos* [*Varied Imagination, Which in a Thousand Attempts*] (1584), Góngora resorts to prosopopoeia to describe the 'blando sueño' [mild dream] as an 'autor de representaciones' [author of performances] who, 'en su teatro, sobre el viento armado, | sombras suele vestir de vulto bello' [in his theatre, staged on the wind, | bestows shadows with beautiful visages] (sonnet 72 in Ciplijauskaité 1975). The imagination not only creates but also deceives (Wardropper 1970: 924). These lines emphasise the gulf between appearance and

---

10   All quotations from Sor Juana will follow Méndez Plancarte's edition (1994a: 342). Edith Grossman's translation can be found in More (2016: 51–52).

reality and thus can be linked to the notion of *desengaño* [existential disillusionment]. In the early seventeenth century, the senses were no longer deemed a source of knowledge but of errors. This mentality explains the success of visual illusions such as the trompe l'oeil in painting, the play within the play in theatre, and dreams and visions in literature (Foucault 1966: 65).

Nevertheless, it would be wrong to impose an artificial reading on *Primero sueño* to make it match Baroque poetics of disillusionment (Paz 1982: 498). The *silva* may have a component of epistemological scepticism but is not just about that. Like Góngora, Sor Juana introduces an 'autor de representaciones', which is human fantasy. However, the nun is not interested in the *décalage* between dreams and reality, or at least not in a straightforward way. In fact, she even praises the insights of her own dreams in the *Respuesta*.[11] Sor Juana's emphasis is rather (i) on the meaning of the representation as a whole; and (ii) on its fantastic/artistic nature.

At the outset of the dream, the poet compares the standpoint of human fantasy with the lighthouse of Alexandria. She also explains that, while enjoying that lofty view, fantasy 'iba copiando | las imágenes todas de las cosas | [...] y al alma las mostraba'. What did these images represent? In the first place, earthly beings or visible things ('todas las criaturas | sublunares'). Earlier, we saw how Góngora's holistic approach had an impact on the 'worldscape' of Camargo, who also aimed at portraying Creation in its entirety. Sor Juana follows here the same path. It is no coincidence that the ancient Greeks placed a similar feeling of awe — i.e. wonderment before the mystery of Creation — at the origin of all sciences (Vossler 1946: 26). This attitude is also at the heart of the nun's quest for knowledge, as evidenced in the *Respuesta* (Salceda 1994: 458; More 2016: 108): 'porque como no hay criatura, por baja que sea, en que no se conozca el *me fecit Deus*, no hay alguna que no pasme el entendimiento, si se considera como se debe. Así yo [...] las miraba y admiraba todas' [for there is no creature, no matter how low, in which the *me fecit Deus* (God created me) goes unrecognised, none that does not astonish the mind, if considered as it should be. And so [...] I watched and admired them all].

However, fantasy not only represents the observable world but also 'aquellas | que intelectuales claras son Estrellas'. The nature of these 'stars' has been the subject of much discussion. Vossler (1946: 116) stated that they are the angels who move the celestial spheres. Although some saints equated the term 'star' with 'angel' (Soriano 2000: 113–15), nothing in the text suggests that this is the meaning intended by Sor Juana. Méndez Plancarte (1994a: 591) affirmed that they are 'conceptos espirituales' [spiritual concepts] and added that the metaphor has a Platonic flavour. Nevertheless, Sor Juana uses the adjective 'intelectuales', not 'espirituales'.

---

11   The passage seems almost a proto-surrealist manifesto (Salceda 1994: 460; More 2016: 110): 'ni aun el sueño se libró de este continuo movimiento de mi imaginativa; antes suele obrar en él más libre y desembarazada, confiriendo con mayor claridad y sosiego las especies que ha conservado del día, arguyendo, haciendo versos, de que os pudiera hacer un catálogo muy grande, y de algunas razones y delgadezas que he alcanzado dormida mejor que despierta' [not even my sleep was free of this continual movement of my imaginative faculty; rather, it tends to operate more freely and unencumbered, examining with greater clarity and tranquillity the images of the day, arguing, and composing verses, and I could offer you a large catalogue of them and the arguments and delicate points I have formulated more successfully asleep than awake].

Having enjoyed the vision, fantasy paints these intellectual stars 'en el modo posible | que concebirse puede lo invisible'. These lines demonstrate Sor Juana's indebtedness to Neoplatonism (Paz 1982: 490). Within her oeuvre, they are redolent of the *Neptuno*, where the nun explains — quoting Pierio Valeriano — that the Egyptians used hieroglyphics as an arcane elite code because they realised that certain 'cosas que carecían de toda forma visible' [things that lacked any visible form] were 'imposibles de mostrarse a los ojos de los hombres' [impossible to depict for the eyes of men]. Thus, it became necessary to 'buscarles jeroglíficos que por similitud, ya que no por perfecta imagen, las representasen' [look for hieroglyphics, which being similar, yet not perfectly identical, would represent them] (Salceda 1994: 355–56).

Thus, although *Primero sueño* is obscure on this point, one thing is clear: the 'Estrellas' are not heavenly bodies. Sor Juana's aim here is to describe a reality that is *per se* invisible.[12] This is the reason why she chose fantasy as a painter. According to Philostratus the Athenian (2005: II. 155–57), Apollonius of Tyana affirmed that imagination is a better artist than imitation, for the latter can only depict what it knows, but the former also what it does not know. In this respect, the nun seems to follow the Plotinian theory that artists do not simply reproduce the visible, but go back to the principles where nature itself found its origin.[13] Her theme is the experience of a world that is not only beyond the senses but also beyond Christian mysticism. If read as the account of an ecstasy, the *silva* could not be more remote from the *San Ignacio*. Sor Juana may have been thinking of Plato's *Timaeus* (41d–41e), where souls and stars are connected.[14] Given her choice of adjectives ('intelectuales claras'), the so-called 'Estrellas' could well be purely abstract, possibly Platonic Ideas. Fantasy paints them so that the soul, like a second God, can see not only Creation but also its intellectual foundations.

In one of his poems to Sor Juana, the viceregal writer Álvarez de Velasco compares her literary skill with that of Sostratus, the Greek architect who built a slab bearing his name into the lighthouse of Alexandria with such deftness that, had it been removed, the whole tower would have collapsed.[15] Following this logic, the duality of *Primero sueño* between the visible and the invisible is consistent from the viewpoint of *conceptismo*. If threads of wit link every point with every other across the universe, then the perfect *conceptista* work is one that leaves no loose ends. Each element in this world mirrors its counterpart in the world of Ideas. The Baroque fold unfurls all the way to infinity (Deleuze 1988: 5, 1993: 3).

Sor Juana mentions neither the earthly beings nor the intellectual entities that her protagonist observes. She suggests that the soul sees everything without describing

---

12   Lope's *silva* to painting, originally published in Carducho's *Diálogos de la pintura* [*Dialogues of Painting*], affirms that art raises to heavens 'dando cuerpo visible | a la incorpórea esencia' [giving a visible body | to the disembodied essence] (lines 5–6) (Sánchez Jiménez 2015: 156).

13   These lines are indebted to Panofsky (1968: 16 and 26).

14   I refer to Kalkavage's (2001: 72) translation: 'And when he had combined all of it, he divided it up into souls equal in number to the stars and assigned each soul to each star.'

15   Buxó (1993: 199): 'Y bien cual Sóstrato supo | embutir en solo un jaspe | su nombre y que en su torreón | fuese indisoluble engarce' [And just like Sostratus she knew how to | engrave in a single slab | her name and build her tower so that | the slab would be the keystone].

what it actually is. Indeed, the artificiality of the Baroque is the outcome of the relationship between representation and that which is being represented. The abstract figures of *Primero sueño* endorse this statement: in the realm of Baroque art, the object of attention tends to be the representation in and of itself rather than the actual items portrayed (Benjamin 1977: 105).

To use a Borgesian comparison, when picturing a labyrinth, most will think of a complex, uneven network of paths. Therefore, by introducing a desert as a maze 'donde no hay escaleras que subir, ni puertas que forzar, [...] ni muros que te veden el paso' [where there are neither stairs to climb, nor doors to force open, [...] nor walls that block your way], Borges (1989: I. 607) deconstructed that idea. For her part, Sor Juana challenged common understandings of the Whole or *Gestalt* as represented in seventeenth-century poetry. Instead of accumulating different elements, she opted for a minimalist approach. This conceptual simplicity is effective for reasons that can be found in the visual arts. One of Sor Juana's objectives is to emphasise that the view afforded from the lighthouse is the product of fantasy, particularly of the artistic imagination: that is, not a vision of any 'real' or plausible reality. This aim is related to her holistic ambition for the following reason: in presenting the cosmos as a canvas, the fantasy of *Primero sueño* relies on the synchronous ontology of the visual sign.

By this, I mean that, unlike a text, which must be read line by line, a canvas is directly and entirely present to the eye. Thus, the visual image enjoys not only a certain completeness (since the whole is continually present) but also a privileged veracity and intelligibility. This is the case even when representing a multi-faceted subject (Lessing 1984: 86; Campo 1998: 80).[16] Conversely, such qualities are conspicuous by their absence in poetry. The temporal sequentiality of words imposes a delay on the representational process that readers may find confusing. Indeed, in cases of long descriptions, the reassembling of the parts into a whole in the mind's eye is not only extremely difficult but also tedious.

Moreover, the synchronous ontology of the image entails not only completeness but also harmony. A poem that aims at the representation of beauty has to describe separately each particular part that makes up the concordant whole (Campo 1998: 82). To use a comparison from Leonardo da Vinci (1817: 16), it is as if an angelical face were to be disclosed bit by bit with the part previously shown covered up. Our forgetfulness would prevent us from composing any harmony of proportions. Conversely, a canvas can render the whole at once and thus recreate the proportions of perfect beauty.

Therefore, given the above-mentioned limitations of verbal diachrony, human fantasy chooses to represent the cosmos as a canvas. The fifth entry of 'representación' in the *Diccionario de Autoridades* (1737: 584) is relevant in this respect: 'Figura, imagen o idea que sustituye las veces de la realidad' [Figure, image or idea that replaces

---

16   According to Leonardo da Vinci (1817: 9), a battle in paint always has more 'brevità e verità' [brevity and truth] than in words. Lope's above-mentioned *silva*, particularly lines 53–55 about the 'pinceles' [paintbrushes], expresses a similar idea (Sánchez Jiménez 2015: 162): 'con que más breve que las plumas sueles | cifrar el ornamento | del mundo superior' [with which, more readily than quills, you tend to | encapsulate the adornment | of the higher world].

reality]. This fantastic painting is a *mise-en-abyme* of the fantasy's and spectator's gaze, a cipher of the iconic potential of the image to replace 'real' reality (Sabat de Rivers 1976: 105). Earlier, I presented separately my first two arguments on Sor Juana's ekphrasis: the holistic approach and the prominence of fantasy or the artistic imagination. However, both facets converge in the *Deus pictor* topos. The theme, which was allusive/secondary in Góngora and Camargo, emerges in Sor Juana in all its magnitude.

The world as a book and the world as a painting are two topoi that go hand in hand. They link the sister arts by depicting God as an artist/writer who deploys the brush/quill to generate the universe from himself, thereby merging creator and Creation into a common whole (Cacho 2012a: 123–25). In this respect, Sor Juana was familiar with the former topos, as evidenced by the *Respuesta* (Salceda 1994: 458): 'aunque no estudiaba en los libros, estudiaba en todas las cosas que Dios crió, sirviéndome ellas de letras, y de libro toda esta máquina universal' [although I did not study from books, I did study all the things God created; those were my alphabet, and the whole universe was my book]. Since *Primero sueño* forms a pendant to the *Respuesta*, the appearance of the latter topos in the *silva* is unsurprising. Human fantasy is not God but rather a presence as shadowy as the obelisk mentioned at the beginning of the poem. Its brush (a 'pincel invisible') and canvas do not belong to the world of matter but to that of the mind. Nevertheless, there is a clear analogy between the 'fantasía' and the *Deus pictor*. Painters and poets — e.g. human fantasy within the *silva*; Sor Juana outside the text — are creative demiurges, for they produce chains of conceits that encapsulate a cosmos within a scheme of wit, be it pictorial or literary.

Buxó (2004a: 103–04) drew a parallel between the noetic and the visual dimensions of Sor Juana's episteme that can shed further light on this point. In the introductory *loa* to *El divino Narciso* [*The Divine Narcissus*] (1690), the character 'Religión' repeatedly employs visual vocabulary, including five references to sight (Brooke 2012: 153, and 2018: 77–80). Lines 401–05 are particularly eloquent: 'Que en una idea | metafórica, vestida | de retóricos colores, | representarla a tu vista, | te la mostraré' [First you | must know it is a metaphor, | an idea dressed in the colours | of rhetoric and visible | therefore to your eyes, as I shall | reveal to you] (Méndez Plancarte 1994b: 17–18; and More 2016: 79).

Setting aside the evangelistic context, the strategy of providing an abstract idea with a visual embodiment echoes that of human fantasy in *Primero sueño*, whose figures ('mentales, sin luz') merge the cognitive with the aesthetic.[17] For this reason, *conceptismo* plays a key role in Sor Juana's approach to the *Deus pictor*. The colours that fantasy deploys exist without light (*in potentia*) but will require light to be seen (*in actu*), an idea that fits in Aristotelian scholastic thought and can also be found in Kircher (Vossler 1946: 116). The cosmographic canvas is not only addressed to

---

17   This again brings to mind Lope's *silva* to painting, lines 24–25 (Sánchez Jiménez 2015: 160): 'pues en ideas aún apenas claras | a la imaginación colores formas' [for, through ideas in the making, | you prepare the colours for the imagination]. The 'painter' within the human mind helps to shape ideas.

the senses but also to the 'intelectuales bellos ojos' [beautiful eyes of intellect], to quote line 441 (Nanfito 2000: 75; More 2016: 55). This is where the lighthouse of Alexandria comes into play: its light — of intellect or reason — converts the invisible figures into visible allegoric paintings, a system of encoded signs that mirrors the universe (Buxó 2006b: 152 and 281).

According to tradition, a fire was built at night at the apex of the lighthouse; a mirror reflected sunlight in the daytime. An Arab legend says that its glass could even set enemy ships on fire (Reynolds 1980: 597–98). Sor Juana elaborates on this 'cristalino portento', where 'en distancia longísima se vían | [...] del reino casi de Neptuno todo'. Since a mirror is an instrument of self-contemplation as well as of reflection of the universe, the poet arguably evokes it to express metaphorically the nature of the artistic imagination (Nanfito 2000: 75–76). A mirror seemingly absorbs all external forms and contains them within it. However, this ersatz reality is misleading, for mirrors decompose and recompose the image reflected within an unreal, contracted, concave space (Foucault 1966: 23). Similarly, human fantasy appears to grasp the cosmos and to portray it faithfully. Nevertheless, since this Platonic artist aims at the largest model possible, the canvas cannot encompass the subject fully or perfectly. Moreover, fantasy paints neither directly from nature nor from images grasped by sight and stored in memory. Therefore, all it can offer is a looking-glass image as pale and distorted as the thing when compared to the Idea.

Thus, the artistic ambition of fantasy is excessive. The canvas admired by the 'intellectual eyes' of the soul does not match the original. There is a gulf between representation and the object represented. This *décalage* will become evident much later, when Sor Juana compares human fantasy with the magic lantern (line 873), an early type of image projector that was popularised by Kircher (Fernández 2006: 19). This device of visual illusion provided mere painted surfaces with volume, giving them a corporeal appearance that they lack in reality. Therefore, the analogy questions the ability of human fantasy — that is, the poet's artistry — to represent any object (Fernández 1996: 52). Sor Juana will present the unsuccessful oneiric journey as a search for a synoptic vision comparable to that fruitlessly aimed at by the painting. Her soul will try to visualise the essential hidden principle of all things in the external world and to attain self-knowledge within herself. *Primero sueño* is the poetic embodiment of this insatiable thirst for wisdom, an earnest intent to grasp the cosmos and the self in all their magnitude (Nanfito 2000: 112).

If the components of the universe are intertwined and understandable only by reference to the Whole, then only the holistic vision may boost one's knowledge to its highest extent. I mentioned above that the mental paintings merge the cognitive with the aesthetic. That is a key to Sor Juana's *Weltanschauung*. Despite her extraordinary learning, the nun was not a scholar; she was a poet. Therefore, she arguably did not want knowledge for the sake of it but rather as a means to attain her artistic goals. Since Sor Juana highlights the intellectual contents of the cosmographic canvas, the picture could well represent everything learnable. In a way, her erudition is an aesthetic manifestation of her holistic approach to knowledge, as evidenced by the *Respuesta* (Salceda 1994: 450; and More 2016: 101):

'Yo de mí puedo asegurar que lo que no entiendo en un autor de una facultad, lo suelo entender en otro de otra que parece muy distante; y esos propios, al explicarse, abren ejemplos metafóricos de otras artes' [As for me, I can state that what I do not understand in an author from one discipline I usually can understand in a different author from another discipline that seems quite distant from the first; and in their explanations, these authors offer metaphorical examples from other arts].

We may read this attitude in the light of Gracián (2001a: I. 55), who defined a conceit as an 'acto del entendimiento, que exprime la correspondencia que se halla entre los objetos' [act of understanding, which expresses the correspondence between objects].[18] From the viewpoint of *conceptismo*, erudition is desirable because it multiplies the objects within which the *ingenio* [wit] may build its networks of connections (Blanco 1992: 134). This is the reason why Gracián praised the 'docta erudición' [learned erudition] and the 'erudición noticiosa' [eclectic erudition] in his discourses LVIII–LIX. In this respect, Góngora, Camargo and Sor Juana are all *noticiosos*. The poetics of correspondences rely heavily on their authors' humanistic training, which provides them with abundant cultural references.

Given the 'unpoetic' subject of *Primero sueño*, erudition is crucial to Sor Juana (Buxó 2004a: 91). The nun poured out there all she had learned: theology, philosophy, history, law, painting, architecture, Egyptology, astronomy, astrology, optics, physiology, medicine and so forth... These varied fields are not deployed for the sake of smugness but in order to poeticise a philosophical, scientific and metaphysical discourse. Thus, rather than merely serving as an ornament, the cosmographic canvas — a work of art that contains a summa of all branches of knowledge — constitutes the structural and thematic foundation upon which the poetic text will be erected, and provides the means by which to amplify its minimal plot through erudition (Nanfito 2000: 36). *Primero sueño* produces beauty by displaying knowledge through art. The ekphrasis represents this poetic credo (Rodríguez Padrón 2005: 147–67).

When seen through the lens of the poem's display of erudition, the cosmographic canvas acquires a new dimension. Holism means seeing all things visible and invisible, thereby having access to all possible knowledge. Human fantasy represents the faculty of putting everything learned at the service of art. In this respect, Méndez Plancarte (1951: xxxi) calls the poem a 'válvula desahogante', which could work as a Spanish translation of the 'venting' function of ekphrasis. Sor Juana employs the trope as a meta-aesthetic tool to display the contradictions of her own life and her time.

Firstly, if we are to believe the *Respuesta* (see the caveat regarding biographical readings of Sor Juana in the Introduction), Sor Juana became a nun because she was gripped by an intense thirst for study. Given the 'total negación que tenía al matrimonio' [total antipathy I had toward matrimony], that career was 'lo más decente que podía elegir' [the most honourable decision I could make]. In the letter, she also reveals that she has been persecuted because of her predisposition to learn ('han llegado a solicitar que se me prohíba el estudio') [some have requested that I be

---

18   Sor Juana knew Gracián, for she quotes him in the *Respuesta* (Salceda 1994: 455).

forbidden to study] (Salceda 1994: 446 and 458; and More 2016: 97 and 108). Thus, the whole of *Primero sueño* — the cosmographic canvas with a particular eloquence, given its density — could represent the author's yearning to be able to learn and create with freedom, unencumbered by the prejudices and bigotries of her time. In this respect, Grossi (2007: 35) links Sor Juana's realisation of the impossibility of reaching complete knowledge with her discovery of the infinite potential of poetic writing.

Secondly, although Sor Juana embraced Gongorism, a style that was on the wane in Spain, her preoccupation with ideas, cosmological breadth and universal curiosity heralded the coming of the modern age in viceregal Mexico and in Hispanic America (Leonard 1971: x). In this sense, the ekphrasis reflects the polarity between a Baroque understanding of literature that aims at surprising and dazzling readers with a poetic *tour de force*, and a development of philosophical concerns that could almost fit in with eighteenth-century rationalism. The canvas shows us the x-ray of a period of transition that struggled to reconcile the Baroque taste for spectacle with an emergent 'pre-Enlightenment' consciousness.

Indeed, Sor Juana was torn between two worlds. This tension manifests itself in other facets of the passage studied. Despite the scientific undertones of *Primero sueño*, the goal of depicting the sum total of knowledge in a canvas is hopelessly unscientific. This is a somewhat Hermetic idea, the origins of which may be traced back to the classic art of memory. These two dimensions of the ekphrasis (mnemonic/Hermetic) reinforce its holistic/artistic approach, and prepare the ground for the later Egyptian digression of the poem.

In Search of All Knowledge

Fantasy is not the only human faculty that Sor Juana portrays as if it were an artist. Earlier in *Primero sueño*, she had expressed the belief that memory stores, sorts and retrieves material using mental images. Line 263 ('grabó tenaz y guarda cuidadosa') [that etched them, tenacious, and guards them with care] (More 2016: 51) describes how the 'memoria' carves within itself the 'simulacros' or visual input that it receives. Memory is an artist but also its own canvas, like the *Deus pictor*.[19] We must presume that it will try to preserve the cosmographic vision or *Weltbild* offered by the painting. For this reason, it is my contention that the canvas can be read as a Hermetic mnemonic *locus*: the whole universe that it contains is designed to be remembered. Thus, it should be linked to the art of memory.

This art had different branches in early modern thought (Rodríguez de la Flor 1988: 70). One was the mental representation of settings for religious purposes encouraged by saints of the Counter-Reformation. Neither Ignatius of Loyola's *Ejercicios espirituales*, which privilege his *composición de lugar* [mental representation

---

19   Cicero (2001: 221) had compared mental image-forming with the work of an artist. The analogy became a topos (Carruthers 2008: 91), as evidenced by this quotation from Velázquez de Azevedo (1626: 11ʳ): 'porque de la suerte que con la vista corporal, con solo mirar una tabla o pintura, se alcanza la noticia de ella, así en la memoria se conocen las imágenes' [just as sight perceives a panel or painting by merely looking at it, so does memory call images to the mind's eye].

of the place] nor Teresa of Ávila's *Las moradas*, with her portrayal of the soul as a castle, can be understood without the imagination techniques of the mnemonic art (Gómez de Liaño 2001: 25; Gerli 1984: 157–59). Another branch was the Hermetic tradition of authors such as Marsilio Ficino, Giordano Bruno and Athanasius Kircher, who believed that all knowledge could be synthesised through images in a magical system of memory places (Yates 1999b: 383).

The *Hermetica* that these humanists knew can be divided into two sets of works. All of them were ascribed to Hermes Trismegistus, a mythical Egyptian priest — known as Thoth in his homeland — who was believed to predate Christ and even Plato. Firstly, there is a corpus of Greek and Latin texts written in Egypt under the Roman Empire which contains religious and philosophical teachings. The *Corpus hermeticum* and the *Asclepius* are the most important of these works. They were deemed to be the distillation of ancient wisdom handed down to humankind by Trismegistus. After their rediscovery in the Renaissance, they had a seminal influence in early modern Europe. Armas (2006, 1997) has studied the impact of Hermetism on Spanish Golden Age authors such as Tirso and Calderón, whose works numbered among Sor Juana's readings.

Secondly, a different corpus of treatises on occult arts and pseudo-sciences such as astrology, magic and alchemy also went under the name of this 'ancient sage'. For instance, the *Picatrix*, a Medieval Latin translation of an Arabic grimoire that I shall later examine, quotes Trismegistus as if he had written a work on talismans (Bakhouche and others 2003: 163–68). Setting aside the differences between these two groups of texts, the idea to retain is that the religious/philosophical and esoteric/magical strands of Hermetism cannot be kept entirely separate from one another (Scott 1985a: 1–2; Yates 1999a: 44).

Given its syncretism, Hermetism is not easily summarisable in a consistent set of tenets. Despite the prevailing Platonism of the doctrine, both the setting and the religious emotion of the *Corpus hermeticum* and the *Asclepius* are Egyptian in nature (Scott 1985a: 8–11). Moreover, although Trismegistus is not an equivalent to Christ, a few Hermetic passages have a Judeo-Christian flavour. In fact, to Ficino, who published a Latin translation of the *Corpus hermeticum* in 1471, the piety of Trismegistus and his supposed prophetic allusions to Christianity made of him almost a Christian.[20] Late Hermetists such as Kircher upheld this belief throughout the seventeenth century (Yates 1999a: 402; Findlen 2004: 33).

Kircher's books, which are full of citations of Ficino's *Corpus hermeticum*, circulated widely in New Spain. He even had epistolary relationships with Creole Mexicans, and sent one of his magic lanterns to Puebla (Osorio 1993: xxi). Thus, this Jesuit played a major role in the introduction of Hermetism to the Americas. For the purposes of this chapter, Kircher is also crucial because he illustrates how the Hermetic tradition converged with the magical strand of the art of memory. It is no coincidence that his design for the Egyptian labyrinth of Hawara (Figure 5.2) shares common ground with Giordano Bruno's courtyards and palaces of memory

20   I refer to Copenhaver's (1992: 2) English translation of the *Corpus hermeticum*: 'The lightgiving word who comes from mind is the son of god'.

FIG. 5.2. Athanasius Kircher, Egyptian Labyrinth, in *Turris Babel* (1679).
Source: Cornell University Library, Digital Collections.

(Gómez de Liaño 2001: 15 and 103; Malcolm 2004: 302–03). These mnemonic constructions reflect a key feature of Hermetism: the gnostic emphasis on salvation by mystical enlightenment. The idea was that one could reach complete knowledge through memory by contemplating the cosmos within one's mind. Given its Hermetic core, Neoplatonism transformed the classical art of memory into an occult art (Yates 1999a: 4, and 1999b: 128).[21]

This magical goal is not alien to the cosmographic canvas of *Primero sueño*. Sor Juana was familiar with Kircher and Hermetism. The Jesuit introduced knowledge to his readers more as an art than as any science (Findlen 2004: 29). Sor Juana may have felt quite at home with this approach, and perhaps for this reason chose a painting as the summa of wisdom. She quotes Kircher in the *Respuesta* and alludes to him in *Primero sueño*. She also mentions his *ars combinatoria* in two poems that I shall discuss later. Furthermore, the nun includes Trismegistus in a list of relevant figures in her *romance* [ballad] 38 (line 86: 'qué Mercurio Trismegisto') (Méndez Plancarte 1994a: 108). Since Sor Juana was a philosophical poet with a strong artistic imagination, she might have felt attracted to Hermetism because of its emphasis on the visual dimension of thought.

Indeed, Giordano Bruno had expanded the *ut pictura poesis* [painting is like poetry] Horatian analogy to include philosophy, a branch of the humanities which he also conceived in terms of intense visualisation. In Brunian terminology, magus equals wise. The unity of knowledge that he represented through mnemonic architectural sites mirrored the unity of the universe (Gómez de Liaño 1973: 247 and 400; Rossi 1983: 79). In this sense, the poetic painting of *Primero sueño* does not merely illustrate Sor Juana's philosophy. It *is* her philosophy, for it reveals the power of the poet to recreate the universe through images.[22]

In his *De triplici vita* [*Three Books on Life*], Ficino (1989: 342–49) offers three ways of representing the cosmos. The last is a vault painting marked with '*figuris eiusmodi et coloribus*' (which bears resemblance to line 284 of *Primero sueño*: 'colores, las figuras'). The adverb '*eiusmodi*' [of this sort] refers to the previously described heavenly spheres, planets and stars. According to Ficino, his friend Lorenzo della Volpaia should spend not only his waking hours under these mnemonic *imagines* but also his sleeping time. He would then return to daily life carrying the painted image in his mind, noting, not 'the spectacle of individual things' but 'the figure of the universe'. Raphael's *Astrology* in the vault of the Stanza della Segnatura (Figure 5.3) offers a cosmic image of which Ficino approved. Renaissance Hermetism transformed the classical art of memory into a method of imprinting magical mental images; this mystical process aimed at reversing earthly fragmentation and restoring within one's mind a sense of the unity of the cosmos (Yates 1999a: 76 and 191; Quinlan-McGrath 2013: 9).

It is not possible to establish with certainty if Sor Juana had read Ficino. However, her friend Sigüenza y Góngora (1959: 171) quotes him in the *Libra*

---

21   Copenhaver (1992: 2): 'I saw in my mind the light of powers beyond number and a boundless cosmos that had come to be'.
22   To paraphrase Yates (1999b: 289).

FIG. 5.3. Raphael, *Astrology* (c. 1508), Stanza della Segnatura, Musei Vaticani.
Photography © Musei Vaticani.

astronómica y filosófica [*Astronomical and Philosophical Libra*] ('según refiere Marsilio Ficino, *De triplici vita*') [according to Marsilio Ficino's *Three Books on Life*], so the book might have been available in New Spain. In any case, my main theory is that the passage studied from *Primero sueño* fits within the Hermetic tradition. At a time of blurred borders between science and magic, astronomy and astrology, religion and esotericism, Sor Juana's pansophical painting of the cosmos may be seen as the embodiment of a waning belief: that an ancient mnemonic technique might still compete with the scientific method in the epistemological conquest of the world (Rodríguez de la Flor 1988: 212). What mattered most was not that this quest should fail, but that the soul had firstly tried to 'conocer con un acto intuitivo todo lo criado' [grasp in only one intuitive act all of creation] (lines 591–92 in prose, without the hyperbaton) (More 2016: 58).

Sor Juana's evocation of the lighthouse of Alexandria can also be linked with this Hermetic goal. In 1256, Alfonso X of Castile had an Arabic grimoire — the *Ghāyat al-hakīm* — by the Andalusian Pseudo-Majrīṭī, translated into Spanish. Although this version is not extant, the later Latin translation of the work — known in the West as the *Picatrix* — had a considerable circulation in manuscript and became a standard textbook for Renaissance Hermetic magi. Ficino had a copy on his desk while he wrote *De triplici vita*. Pico della Mirandola and Kircher also made use of it (Gatti 2011: 28; Yates 1999a: 50–56; and Gómez de Liaño 2001: 16).

This is particularly relevant because the *Picatrix* (treatise IV, book III) contains a passage that shares common ground with *Primero sueño*. As mentioned, in order to illustrate the fabulous view provided by the cosmographic painting, Sor Juana compares it with the mirror of the lighthouse of Alexandria ('Y del modo | que en tersa superficie, que de Faro | cristalino portento [...] | así ella [i.e. fantasy], sosegada, iba copiando'). Interestingly, both elements (i.e. a lighthouse and the *imagines*) appear in Adocentyn, an Egyptian city, the foundation of which the *Picatrix* credits to Hermes Trismegistus. I will quote Yates' translation from Latin (1999a: 54):

> It was he [i.e. Hermes Trismegistus], too, who in the east of Egypt constructed a City twelve miles (*miliaria*) long within which he constructed a castle which had four gates in each of its four parts. On the eastern gate he placed the form of an Eagle; on the western gate, the form of a Bull; on the southern gate the form of a Lion, and on the northern gate he constructed the form of a Dog. Into these images he introduced spirits which spoke with voices, nor could anyone enter the gates of the City except by their permission. There he planted trees in the midst of which was a great tree which bore the fruit of all generation. On the summit of the castle he caused to be raised a tower thirty cubits high on the top of which he ordered to be placed a light-house (*rotunda*) the colour of which changed every day until the seventh day after which it returned to the first colour, and so the City was illuminated with these colours. Near the City there was abundance of waters in which dwelt many kinds of fish. Around the circumference of the City he placed engraved images and ordered them in such a manner that by their virtue the inhabitants were made virtuous and withdrawn from all wickedness and harm. The name of the City was Adocentyn.

Regardless of whether the *Picatrix* directly influenced *Primero sueño*, much might be learned by reading these texts together. In this respect, I would like to focus on four points: (i) the location of the cities; (ii) the proximity of water; (iii) the talismanic images; and (iv) the lighthouse. According to the *Picatrix*, Adocentyn was placed 'in the east of Egypt'. The original text is more specific, for it calls the magical city al-Asmunain (Ritter and Plessner 1962: 323).[23] This was the Arabic name for Hermopolis Magna, where once stood the most celebrated shrine to Thoth-Hermes Trismegistus (Bauval 2014: 191–92). Sor Juana's choice of Alexandria, a city in the west of Egypt (the Nile delta being the reference point), apparently distances *Primero sueño* from the *Picatrix*. However, her *silva* could also be read in the light of the following prophecy of the *Asclepius*: 'The gods who rule the earth will [withdraw], and they will be stationed in a city founded at Egypt's farthest border toward the setting sun, where the whole race of mortals will hasten by land and sea' (Copenhaver 1992: 83). According to Scott (1985b: 236), 'there cannot be the slightest doubt that Alexandria is meant'. Thus, Sor Juana's choice of this maritime city, in a poem that starts precisely with the setting sun and that emphasises the proximity of nautical activity ('las que distantes lo surcaban naves'), seems consonant with Hermes' prediction. Her Alexandria forms a pendant to Adocentyn: both are Hermetic cities at the west and east of Egypt respectively.

Moreover, like Adocentyn, the island of 'Faro' (opposite Alexandria) is surrounded by water ('del reino casi de Neptuno todo'). There is here a revealing gradation from the *Ghāyat al-hakīm* to the *Picatrix* and from the *Picatrix* to *Primero sueño*. The Arabic original underlines the artificiality of the water around the citadel, for the inhabitants of al-Asmunain breed fish therein (Ritter and Plessner 1962: 323). This last detail disappears in the Latin Adocentyn, where the water is channelled to surround the beacon (Pingree 1986: 189): '*In turris quidem circuitu abundans erat aqua*' [Around the tower, in a circle, water was abundant]. For her part, Sor Juana dismisses both the artificial waterway and the fish breeding. Rather, the wilderness of the sea encircles her lighthouse. In this respect, three cardinal points must be borne in mind.

Firstly, Sor Juana describes neither a historical nor a mythical seascape but a mental one. Later in the poem, when the soul collapses, she is shipwrecked 'en la mental orilla' [on the mental shore] (line 566) (More 2016: 57), which implies that the sea is actually an ocean of knowledge (Méndez Plancarte 1994a: 349). With this allegorical meaning in mind, Sor Juana's choice of a sea instead of an artificial channel is consistent.

Secondly, having introduced the Mediterranean as a setting, Sor Juana elaborates on the ships that one could see from the lighthouse, including details such as 'el número, el tamaño y la fortuna'. This option was not available to the Pseudo-Majrīṭī, for no ships could sail the narrow waterways of Adocentyn. Moreover, Sor Juana's 'naves' are the external avatars of the painted 'figuras' (Beaupied 1997: 49).

---

23   This German edition is the only direct translation from the Arabic available. I have collated it with the Latin text (Pingree 1986), and the modern translations from Latin into French (Bakhouche and others 2003), English (Warnock and Greer 2011) and Spanish (Villegas 1982).

Thus, their inclusion suggests the mental movement of the drawings within the canvas. The mirroring effect of the sea duplicates their visual power.

Thirdly, and linked to the previous point, the fact that the drawings/ships surrounding Alexandria are constantly in motion (unlike the immobile images encircling Adocentyn) could also be significant from a Hermetic viewpoint. As mentioned, Sor Juana was familiar with Kircher's *ars combinatoria*, a mystical system that aimed at a revelation of all knowledge by exhausting every permutational possibility (Osorio 1993: xlii–xlv).[24] In this respect, when the soul breaks down, Sor Juana portrays the cosmic images as a blur ('confusas') because 'cuanto más se implican combinadas | tanto más se disuelven desunidas' [the more they attempt to combine | the more they dissolve apart] (lines 554–55) (More 2016: 57), as if the Llullian wheels had run wild. However, this is not the case with the painting, for the 'figuras'/'naves' navigate through the sea/canvas guided by the lighthouse, which allows them to cover all routes (that is, all possible combinations) while avoiding overlaps. In this respect, the book by Sebastián Izquierdo that linked Kircher's *ars combinatoria* with the pansophical ideal of learning all sciences was titled precisely *Pharus scientiarum* [*The Lighthouse of Sciences*] (1659).[25]

Although the *Picatrix* starts by praising wisdom (Bakhouche and others 2003: 44), its *imagines* do not have this noetic quality. From an epistemological viewpoint, Sor Juana's Alexandria is closer to Campanella's *Città del Sole* [*City of the Sun*] (1623), another utopian city arguably inspired by Adocentyn. The children of the city of the sun 'come to know all the sciences pictorially before they are ten years old' (Campanella 1981: 37). Indeed, the place looks like a gigantic illustrated encyclopaedia, structured as it is by seven circular walls inscribed with didactic images. There is no need to study the external world in order to learn: it suffices to observe their own city. For their part, the *imagines* of the *Picatrix* serve functional purposes of a different sort. The Pseudo-Majrīṭī makes a distinction between two sets of pictures. On the one hand, he introduces the four zoomorphic figures (eagle, bull, lion, dog) on guard duty at the cardinal points of Adocentyn, which prevent people from entering the city without permission. On the other hand, he mentions (but does not describe) the images that make the inhabitants virtuous and protect them from wickedness and harm. The latter seem to be representations of the legendary magical statues of the *Asclepius*, which were not viewed kindly by Christian authors (Armas 1997: 47).

24   She mentions it in her answer to a ballad by Oviedo y Herrera (lines 181–82): 'Pues si la combinatoria, | en que a veces *kirkerizo*' [For if the combinatory | in which I sometimes *Kircherise*]. There is another Kircherian reference in sonnet 193: 'que la combinatoria de Kirkero' [For Kircher's combinatory]. Both poems can be found in Méndez Plancarte (1994a: 158 and 302).

25   Osorio (1993: 61) reproduces a 1665 letter by the Mexican Jesuit Alexandro Favián to Kircher: 'otro autor también he hallado [i.e. Izquierdo] que en un tomo bien grande enseña el modo de aprenderlas brevemente y, al fin, trae las combinaciones de Vuestra Paternidad Reverenda' [I have also found another author who teaches in a very thick volume how to learn all sciences quickly and, in the end, includes Your Reverend Fatherhood's combinations]. Kircher (1669: 4–5) later lauded *Pharus scientiarum*.

Sor Juana could not be so explicit with magical imagery.[26] Perhaps for this reason, all we vaguely know about the content of the painted 'figuras' is that they aim at copying the world. If we compare them with the second set of talismans in the *Picatrix*, we shall conclude that neither text is detailed. This was a typical feature of handbooks on astronomical pictures, which left these choices to the sensitivity of the image maker (Quinlan-McGrath 2013: 165), be it a magus (*Picatrix*) or a mere reader (*Primero sueño*). However, line 265 of *Primero sueño* uses exactly the same words ('imágenes diversas') that the *Picatrix* employs to portray the talismans surrounding Adocentyn (Pingree 1986: 189): '*In circuitu vero civitatis imagines diversas*' [in a circle, around the city, diverse images]. The grimoire also affirms that, for the purposes of making talismans, night is better than daytime (Bakhouche and others 2003: 74). Therefore, since Sor Juana's 'figuras' aim at the esoteric goal of mentally capturing the universe during night-time, they may also have a talismanic significance.[27]

The *Picatrix* presents itself as a general compendium on astral magic. However, most of it is devoted to explaining how to draw celestial spirits down to earth and introduce them into material objects: that is, talismans, which thereupon possess magical powers (Pingree 1980: 4). Adocentyn is the most spectacular creation of this art, for the whole city works as a talisman: all its components have been designed following astronomical and astrological alignments (Bauval 2014: 191). However, the above-mentioned term *imago* — the Latin word for talisman — has multiple meanings throughout the *Picatrix*: it may designate these magical objects but also the process of creating them, the constellations that provide them with power, or even mere images in the ordinary sense of the term (Bakhouche and others 2003: 18).

All four meanings are relevant to Sor Juana's 'imágenes diversas'. These are obviously images, as the noun itself reveals. Furthermore, given that they portray everything in the universe, there is no doubt that planets, galaxies and constellations of stars are present. In fact, as if echoing the content of the cosmographic painting, the soul later measures the immensity of the firmament (line 302: 'la cuantidad inmensa de la Esfera') and examines the rotation of the celestial bodies (lines 303–05: 'ya el curso considera | regular, con que giran desiguales | los cuerpos celestiales') [ponders the predictable orbits of | diverse heavenly bodies] (More 2016: 52). The fact that the nun was a stargazer becomes manifest throughout the *silva* and is confirmed by Diego Calleja's elegy after her death.[28]

26   For the statues of the *Asclepius*, see Copenhaver's translation (1992: 81): 'I mean statues ensouled and conscious, filled with spirit and doing great deeds; statues [...] that make people ill and cure them, bringing them pain and pleasure as each deserves'. Sor Juana's famous line in the *Respuesta* expresses her concerns with religious authority (Salceda 1994: 444; More 2016: 95): 'yo no quiero ruido con el Santo Oficio' [I wish no quarrel with the Holy Office].
27   Magical practices involving talismans also receive much attention throughout Kircher's *Oedipus aegyptiacus*. I refer to Stolzenberg (2004), who studies 'esoteric antiquarianism' as a hallmark of seventeenth-century Neoplatonism.
28   *Fama y obras póstumas* [*Fame and Posthumous Works*] (Cruz 1700): 'Astrónoma, espiaba la techumbre | de los astros' [An astronomer, she spied on the ceiling | of the stars]. In Sor Juana's fifth *Loa a los años del Rey* [*Loa on the King's Birthday*], the sun tells the planets that, setting aside God-given

Moreover, since fantasy is trying to encapsulate the universe in an object, one could argue that the painted 'figuras' of *Primero sueño*, combined with the light of the beacon, work as a *sui generis* talisman. The magical canvas is in the making, of course, for Sor Juana enables us to witness how fantasy crafts it. However, its Hermetic pansophical goal is clear. So is that of the lighthouse of Alexandria, which makes the painting possible. In this respect, although Adocentyn deploys a different kind of magic, the city reveals an Arab belief to which Sor Juana would have subscribed: that the ancient monuments of Egypt (e.g. obelisks, pyramids) were enormous and powerful talismanic constructions (Ritter and Plessner 1962: xliii).[29] In this sense, Sor Juana's *Respuesta* explains the symbolic nature of architecture using an example that was reminiscent of Egyptian sanctuaries: Solomon's temple, a Jewish building where no component was 'solo por el servicio y complemento del Arte, sino simbolizando cosas mayores' [for the service and complement of art alone but rather to symbolise greater things] (Salceda 1994: 448; and More 2016: 99). That could well be the case with her lighthouse of Alexandria, a monument with obelisk-like proportions appearing in the *silva* not merely for the sake of art.

This brings me to the last point of commonality between the *Picatrix* and *Primero sueño*: the lighthouse, which plays different roles in each text. The Pseudo-Majrīṭī presents the beacon and the magical *imagines* as separate entities. However, they are closely connected. The lighthouse sets itself up as a multicoloured brush that daily paints all the hues and shades of Adocentyn — including its surrounding talismans — with the seven planetary colours. In early modern Spain, the protective connotation of beacons led to Catholic forms of allegory. For example, in emblem books, they could represent the pastoral care of the prelate (Olivares 1998: 187). Nevertheless, this religious symbolism seems alien to Sor Juana's Alexandria. Even accepting Catholic readings of the poem (Méndez Plancarte 1994a), the idea that *Primero sueño* conveys is that the pursuit of knowledge is not necessarily different from the search for God, as Kircher taught his correspondents in New Spain (Osorio 1993: xxxix). From a gnostic viewpoint, the pursuit of knowledge *is* the search for God (Beaupied 1997: 88; Martin and Arenal 2009: 38).[30] Christianity and Hermetism were not mutually exclusive, as illustrated by the mosaic pavement of Hermes Trismegistus in Siena Cathedral (Figure 5.4).

Perhaps this is the key to the Hermetic lighthouse: it raises up towards the heavens (God), allows a complete vision of the universe (knowledge), and reflects the achievement in a mirror (art). This mirror and the painted 'figuras' could not be more closely linked, for they form a single conceit. Earlier, we saw how Góngora made the map and the territory indistinct. Similarly, Sor Juana delivers her

free will, 'lo demás todo os compete' [everything else is your domain] (Méndez Plancarte 1994b: 363).

29   In her *Neptuno* (Salceda 1994: 355–56), Sor Juana embraces with uncritical confidence Pierio Valeriano, the author who disseminated Plotinus' esoteric theories on the Egyptian writing system.

30   The description of the centaurs in the *Neptuno* also illustrates the connection between divinity and wisdom (Salceda 1994: 384): 'Claro está que siendo sabios habían de venir de lo alto' [Since they were wise, they obviously had to come from above].

FIG. 5.4. Giovanni di Stefano, *Hermes Trismegistus* (c. 1482), Duomo di Siena.
© Foto LENSINI Siena.

Weltbild as a painting and as a mirror, for both happen to be the same *locus*.[31] Their poetics revolve around the ekphrasis because of this faith in the might of the visual imagination. The 'mapscape' and the mirror-painting embody Benjamin's (1977: 48 and 55) notion of the supreme reality in art: the isolated, self-contained work that contains an image of the world.

31   Her approach brings to mind the chapter 'Come lo specchio è maestro de' pittori' [How the Mirror is a Master of Painters] by Leonardo da Vinci (1817: 205–06). Leiva (1975: 52–55) studied the common ground between Leonardo and Sor Juana.

Mimicry from the 'Margins'

Having delivered the ekphrasis, Sor Juana devotes the next lines of *Primero sueño* (292–96) to the cosmographic canvas' potential to instil beauty and meaning. The soul is absorbed in the vision: 'toda convertida | a su inmaterial ser y esencia bella'. As if she were echoing Góngora's pilgrim on the cliff, the protagonist notes a microcosm within herself, which mirrors the macrocosm that fantasy produced for her. However, unlike the *Soledades*, where spirituality is conspicuous by its absence, *Primero sueño* may be linked to the religious sentiment of forming a bond with the universe and its Creator. Indeed, having glimpsed the spiritual essence of Beauty, the soul notes the 'centella' that the 'alto Ser' placed in her when creating human beings (Sabat de Rivers 1976: 137; Ricard 1975: 26). Hence, the enjoyment lies in her similarity with God ('que con similitud en sí gozaba'), which reveals the divine filiation of humankind. One could argue that these lines fit in with the 'discreet Christianity' of *Primero sueño*. Nevertheless, unlike the protagonist of, say, Saint John of the Cross' *Cántico espiritual* [*Spiritual Canticle*], or Camargo's *San Ignacio*, that of Sor Juana does not seek the mystic union (Volek 2019: 102), or the understanding of Catholic dogmas, but rather complete knowledge through vision. This gnostic component permits one to read the passage from a Hermetic viewpoint.

Earlier, we saw how fantasy represents all things, both visible and invisible. The turn of the screw is that the protagonist is also included among these painted 'figuras'. Thus, by looking at the painting/universe, the soul turns her attention to herself, as line 426 evidences later: 'el alma se miró' [the soul saw herself] (More 2016: 55). Her gaze sees and becomes a reflection, in both senses of the term (Fernández 1996: 53–54). On the one hand, the optical effect explains why *Primero sueño* presents the canvas (the cosmos) as a mirror. As in Velázquez's *Las Meninas* (Foucault 1966: 29 and Figure 5.5), the scene offers a *dédoublement*: the soul reflected in the mirror-painting is also the soul that contemplates it. On the other hand, reflection also means mental self-examination, since the external quest for wisdom ends in an internal search (Beaupied 1997: 4). The protagonist will awaken reborn from the dream (line 975: 'el Mundo iluminado, y yo despierta') [the world illuminated and I, awake] (More 2016: 66) understanding that, despite human limitations, we must persevere in our pursuit of knowledge.[32]

There is an obstacle to this thirst for omniscience. Like Plato's *Phaedo* (82e), Sor Juana's *Primero sueño* introduces the soul as fastened to and thus constrained by the body. However, having been infatuated with the correspondence between the divine and the human, she deems herself 'casi dividida' from the 'corporal cadena' (lines 297–300). The adverb 'casi' is revealing. The link with the physical world has been loosened but not broken: the protagonist is asleep, not dead. Nevertheless, the self-deception of believing that she is a spirit provides her with the courage to pass to other spatio-temporal realms that are usually beyond the human experience (Soriano 1996: 54–55). Indeed, the cosmographic canvas has an irresistible ascensional capacity.

---

32   Robbins (2007: 240): 'Her modernity *vis-à-vis* earlier seventeenth-century writers rests with the clear emphasis in the *Primero sueño* on the fact that the absence, and even the impossibility, of certain knowledge does not itself preclude the search for and pursuit of knowledge'.

FIG. 5.5. Diego de Velázquez, *Las Meninas* (1656),
© Museo Nacional del Prado, Madrid.

In this sense, Álvarez de Velasco and Oviedo y Herrera, two viceregal admirers of Sor Juana, highlighted the uplifting effect of her art. The former affirmed that, after reading her, he started to 'amar a la sabiduría' [love wisdom] (Buxó 1993: 179). For the latter, Sor Juana's works deserved, due to their novelty, a constant rereading: 'hallando tal novedad | en lo propio que he leído, | que me parece otra cosa | aunque me suena a lo mismo' [finding such novelty | in what I have read, | that it appears to me distinct | yet familiar] (Méndez Plancarte 1994a: 150). If read against the background of postcolonial theory, the last two lines almost sound like a Spanish version *avant la lettre* of the discourse of mimicry. Indeed, we can study Sor Juana 'as a subject of a difference that is almost the same, but not quite' (Bhabha 2004: 122). Camargo's self-perceived marginality must have been minimal compared to hers. Sor Juana was not only a woman and Creole but also an illegitimate daughter (Sabat de Rivers 1992: 349). Her life was a constant struggle to prove that, despite these three circumstances, she was as worthy a writer as the peninsular luminaries of the Golden Age. Hence, her erudition, which could compete with that of any highbrow Spanish humanist; hence, her imitation of Góngora, the most respected Iberian model.

Sor Juana wanted her Spanish readership to realise that she, and by extension New Spain, did not flounder in the wilderness of the Americas but arose fully aware of the chief currents of European thought. This could help explain why she exploited the Hermetic potential of the painting. Her *modus operandi* not only reveals a fascination with the occult but also allows for the syncretic combination of literary, artistic and philosophical elements of different traditions. Thus, Sor Juana's poetics are constructed around an ambivalence; as we saw with Camargo, in order to be effective, mimicry must constantly produce its excess, its difference.[33]

In this sense, the ekphrasis shows how Sor Juana explored alternative aspects of the holistic ambition of representing all things in Creation. She conceived of fantasy — that is, the visual or artistic imagination — as the foundation of *inventio*. She stripped down to their essentials both the universal impulse to knowledge and human epistemological limitations, and encapsulated them in a painting. She did not limit herself to the teachings of ancient rhetoric but experimented with the metaphysical dimension of the art of memory. She created a cosmographical, pansophical ekphrasis, an orderly system of spatio-temporal relations that is not a mere image of the world. Rather, it also represents the universe of language, which she breaks into pieces and reconstructs through an inexhaustible permutation of signs, in Góngora's Lucretian manner (or like Kircher's *ars combinatoria*).

These are not marks of submissive imitation. Gongorism in the Americas has often been dismissed as a 'literatura vieja' [outdated literature] that lacks the interest of the works of, say, the Inca Garcilaso, the first 'transatlantic intellectual'.[34] This *mestizo* with multiple cultural competencies was totally alien to Bhabha's notion of mimicry. In his *7 ensayos de interpretación de la realidad peruana* [*7 Essays that Interpret Peruvian Reality*], Mariátegui (1979: 155) mentions Espinosa Medrano's cult of Góngora after lamenting 'la irremediable mediocridad de la literatura de la Colonia'

---

33   The following paragraphs are indebted to Martínez-San Miguel's (2008: 15–16) reading of Sor Juana's mimicry in terms informed by Bhabha (2004: 122). I also draw from Castro-Klarén's (2011: 239 and 492–99) insights on the Inca Garcilaso and Egido's (1996: 174) analysis of Gracián.
34   To borrow Ortega's expression (2010: 43).

[the irredeemable mediocrity of colonial Latin American literature], which he deems a mere continuation or repetition of Spanish models. His condemnation is understandable with minor imitators of Góngora: the poetasters who 'nos quieren vender por extremada | una belleza rota y remendada' [want to sell us the ultimate beauty, | which in fact is torn and patched], in the words of Sor Juana (Méndez Plancarte 1994a: 322). However, *Primero sueño* is not based on the 'metáforas cansadas' [trite metaphors] that the Mexican nun also decried. Like Camargo, Sor Juana is the epitome of the viceregal poet who followed Góngora while innovating. Unlike Camargo, she showed that the 'periphery' can exert a powerful influence upon the 'centre'. His failure contrasts sharply with her success, as any history of Sor Juana's early reception in Spain can attest. Her Baroque rarity and strong poetic voice were unmatchable attractions to her contemporary readership.

In the introductory *loa* to *El divino Narciso* (Cruz 1690a), the *auto sacramental* published two years before *Primero sueño*, Sor Juana even makes explicit the tension between Spain and its Viceroyalty, distance and proximity: '¿Pues no ves la impropiedad | de que en Méjico se escriba | y en Madrid se represente?' [Do you not see the impropriety | that works written in Mexico | are performed in Madrid?]. A few lines earlier, she had described Madrid as 'el Centro, y la Regia Silla | de sus Católicos Reyes' [the royal centre of our faith, | and the most regal seat and throne | of their Catholic Majesties]. According to Benoist (1999: 74–75), the poet might have feared that the *auto* would be received with hostility in Spain, given her personal background.[35] Thus, Sor Juana defends the staging of her work in Spain through the character 'Religión': '¿Pues es cosa nunca vista | que se haga una cosa en una | parte, porque en otra sirva?' [Do you mean you have never seen | a thing created in one place | that is of use in another?] (Méndez Plancarte 1994b: 19; and More 2016: 80).

Indeed, since no one has the monopoly in matters of the intellect, Spanish American literature may also be of use in Spain (Jáuregui 2009: 95–96). The implication of the *loa* is that the European worldview is limited and needs to be completed from the 'margins'. *Primero sueño* is a summa not only of a lifetime of reading and reflection but also of an era. One of the main points of Terry's (1993: 238) chapter on Sor Juana in *Seventeenth-Century Spanish Poetry* is that her oeuvre revived a nearly-exhausted Baroque. Indeed, peninsular Baroque literature would produce no further major works after the death of Calderón (1681). From that date until the death of Sor Juana (1695), Mexico City displaced Madrid as the pivot of Spanish literature. Thus, due to her paradoxical status — canonical as the last landmark of the Golden Age, yet 'marginal' for the three above-mentioned circumstances — Sor Juana transcends conventional demarcations between 'centre' and 'periphery'. The 'margins' are a powerful location, for they can lead to paradigm-shifting reassessments. Perhaps for this reason, in a further displacement after the cosmographic mirror-painting, the poet turned her attention not to Greco-Latin imagery but to the pyramids of Egypt.

---

35 Kirk (2016: 139): 'Scholarly society in Mexico suffered from the stigma of a perceived backwardness which the metropolis had done its best to foster through the restrictions it placed on the importation of books, the lack of prestige accorded to books published in Mexico, and the imputation of intellectual inferiority it levelled at Spain's American colonies.'

A Lo mas profundo del pecho retirò la Naturaleza el corazon humano, ſi bien paraque obraſe conforme a la razon, dejò diſpueſto aquel nativo, i natural color, o aquella llama de ſangre, con que la verguenza encendieſe el roſtro, i le acuſaſe, quando ſe apartaſe de lo honeſto, o ſintieſe vna coſa, i profirieſe otra

FIG. 6.1. Diego de Saavedra Fajardo, *Excaecat candor*, in *Idea de un príncipe político cristiano* [*Idea of a Christian Political Prince*] (1640: 74). Image borrowed from the digital copy of the Herzog August Bibliothek, Wolfenbüttel, Germany.

CHAPTER 6

The Pyramids of Egypt

After the lighthouse of Alexandria, Sor Juana focuses on another ancient wonder: the pyramids of Egypt. The description (lines 340–411) that I shall analyse in this chapter constitutes the most famous digression in *Primero sueño* [*First Dream*]. However, although most scholars agree on its importance, the implications of the ekphrasis remain far from being established. According to the autobiographical *Respuesta a Sor Filotea de la Cruz* [*Reply to Sor Filotea de la Cruz*], after observing the lines formed by the walls and the ceiling of a bedroom, Sor Juana inferred that 'las líneas visuales corren rectas, pero no paralelas, sino que van a formar una figura piramidal' [visual lines run straight, not parallel, but form a pyramidal shape instead] (Salceda 1994: 458; and More 2016: 109). The anecdote of this 'rediscovery' of the laws of perspective, whether apocryphal or not, shows that the pyramid played an important role in the nun's imagination and in her self-fashioning as a person of exceptional vocation and destiny (Luciani 1995: 76).

Primero sueño underlines the relevance of this form from the very first word ('Piramidal'). This beginning demonstrates a conscious attitude toward space that will be key in a poem celebrated for its architectural ekphraseis (Nanfito 2000: 47). Sor Juana imagines a shadow with the form of an infinite truncated cone: its narrowest part rests on the circumference of the earth, while the broadest part opens up as it moves away towards the stars (which brings to mind Saavedra Fajardo's *empresa* XII *Excaecat candor* [*emblem* XII *Its Glow Dazzles*]) (Figure 6.1). In this respect, the nun chose words such as 'Piramidal' and 'obelisco' (lines 1–3) for a reason, namely to prepare the reader from the outset for the later Egyptian digression. The fact that these learned terms are typical of Gongorism must have also influenced her preference.[1]

Sor Juana's interest in Egypt can be explained on two grounds. Firstly, the nun greatly admired the Jesuit Athanasius Kircher, who is a key source for her poetic landscape.[2] Kircher's enthusiasm for everything Egyptian stems from the early modern belief that Egypt was the source of all Western knowledge. I will explore this creed in more detail when referring to the Arab texts that Kircher brought to

---

1   Góngora's ballad *Ojos eran, fugitivos* [*Fleeting eyes*] (1619) contains both elements: 'que, entre pirámides verdes | que ser quieren obeliscos' [which, between green pyramids | that want to be obelisks] (Carreño 1982: 426).

2   Méndez Plancarte (1994a: 594): 'creemos indudable esa fuente [we believe this source is irrefutable]. Kircher's *Oedipus Aegyptiacus* was available in New Spain (Osorio 1993: 97).

FIG. 6.2. Cesare Ripa, 'Filosofia secondo Boetio', in *Nova iconologia* (1618: 191).
Reproduced by permission of the Master and Scholars of Christ's College, Cambridge.
Olivares (1998: 191–92) has studied this image in relation to *Primero sueño*.

the fore, which evidence the link between pyramids and wisdom. This connection
is also present in the iconological representation of philosophy by Ripa (Figure 6.2),
which features a woman dressed as a stepped pyramid. For the moment, suffice it to
add that Sor Juana was as much of an Egyptophile as Kircher was. The literariness
of this Jesuit and other humanists who pioneered the study of hieroglyphs — e.g.
Valeriano — nurtured her imagination.

Secondly, Baroque New Spain saw a surge in appreciation of the indigenous
heritage amongst Creole intellectuals. The nun's penchant for the pyramids may
relate to this trend, for several of her contemporaries (including her friend Sigüenza
y Góngora) believed in the Egyptian origin of Mesoamerican civilisations. This

connection with Egypt endowed New Spain with a transcendent grandeur (Merrim 2010: 181). Having spent most of her life in Mexico City, which is close to the two pyramids of Teotihuacán, Sor Juana was interested in Memphis' ancient monuments. By means of her poetic recreation of these buildings, the nun might have wanted to convey, at least on a symbolic level, that hers was not a 'New World'. Rather, she lived in a densely historical land with an ancestral line that could be traced back to Egypt.

Another possible source for Sor Juana is Bernal Díaz del Castillo. His is an early testimony to the connection between Mesoamerican civilisations and ancient Egypt, as reflected by his account of the first encounter with the pyramids of Yucatan: 'le pusimos por nombre el Gran Cairo' [we named it the Great Cairo]. Bernal also explains how the conquistadores attained knowledge of Tenochtitlán through a teichoscopic perspective from its highest point: 'Y muchos de nuestros soldados subieron en el cu más alto [...] y desde allí vieron la gran ciudad de México y toda la laguna, porque bien se señoreaba todo' [And many of our soldiers climbed the highest pyramidal temple [...] and from there they saw the great city of Mexico and the whole lake, because they could survey everything] (Díaz del Castillo 2011: 21 and 589). The last verb Bernal deploys ('señorear') illustrates the link between vision, power and knowledge. Likewise, Sor Juana describes Egypt from a bird's-eye view. Although the nun lacks Bernal's imperial rhetoric, her 'other' is equally an object of scrutiny.

However, there is an important difference between Bernal's and Sor Juana's pyramids. Those of the conquistador are physical and exist in the real world. Conversely, Sor Juana's constructions are not made of matter. Indeed, the nun introduces the Egyptian pyramids as an ethereal ascending form, which is comparable to an 'ambiciosa llama' [ambitious flame] (line 405). Both images represent the human soul. This lofty symbolism coexists with the portrayal of the pyramids as barbaric monuments. My reading offers an allegoric and stylistic analysis of this passage in *Primero sueño* (lines 340–411), paying attention to its sources. It is my contention that Sor Juana reflects the early modern awareness of its distance from antiquity, which was admired for its greatness and disapproved of for its (pagan) barbarity. Indeed, the gap between the (pre-Christian) ancients and the moderns seemed almost insurmountable, particularly after the Renaissance.[3]

This *décalage* explains the seventeenth-century attempts to moralise pagan literature by means of allegory. The tendency resulted in a doublespeak, which Kluge (2014: 5) studied under the term diglossia: 'Baroque mythological literature [...] oscillates between myth and allegory in its reimagining of the ancient mythical universe, "speaking in two tongues"'. This chapter will deploy the term along the same lines, though not identically. Sor Juana uses Góngora's pejorative lexicon as a starting point to describe the pyramids. Then, she adds a 'twist' (the metaphor of pyramids = soul) that dignifies these monumental structures to an extent that would

---

3   Seznec (1972: 322): 'The notion of antiquity as a distinct historical milieu, as a period that had run its course, did not exist in the Middle Ages; [...] The Renaissance, on the other hand, perceived this historical distance, and had to make a conscious effort to establish harmony between two worlds separated by a lapse of centuries.'

have been unthinkable in Góngora, let alone in Camargo. Therefore, Sor Juana's doublespeak results from her ambivalent approach to Egypt, which comprises both criticism and praise.

If seen from a narratological viewpoint, the description of the pyramids emerges as a hybrid in the Gongorist tradition. Camargo's long ekphraseis often serve non-narrative functions, while Góngora's are shorter and more integrated within the plot. The length of Sor Juana's architectural ekphrasis is halfway between these forerunners. The passage contains enough ramifications to remind us of Camargo's 'diluted' descriptions, yet at the same time it is connected to the plot more explicitly than Góngora's landscape/seascape. Two reasons explain the latter finding. Firstly, the pyramids/flame of *Primero sueño* anticipate the intellectual failure of the soul to apprehend the universe, in fulfilment of a proleptic function. Secondly, and more importantly, the passage closes with the above-mentioned metaphor (pyramids = soul), which is key to the *silva*.

The symbolic nature of the pyramids in *Primero sueño* is revealed by none less than Homer, a protagonist of early modern diglossia. With the advent of Renaissance Neoplatonism, the divinisation of Homer became an established practice: to Ficino and his circle of humanists, the *Iliad* and the *Odyssey* contained truths that were on a par with those of the Old Testament (Ford 2002: 333). However, Sor Juana's approach to Homer is not so clear-cut. In fact, given that the Greek's writings do not mention the pyramids, lines 399–411 of *Primero sueño* puzzled scholars such as Méndez Plancarte, who famously called them an 'intermezzo', as if they constituted an inserted independent passage.[4] Nevertheless, since Kircher (1654: 568) portrayed Greek luminaries as disciples of Egypt, the idea of Homer as a connoisseur of the pyramids ceases to sound so mystifying. According to Sor Juana's perception, this poet represented a receptacle of ancient, revered wisdom that predated Greece (Vossler 1946: 118). In this sense, it is Sor Juana's understanding of Homer, rather than his writings themselves, that is key to my reading of the pyramids in *Primero sueño*.

Condemnation and Praise

The trigger of the oneiric trip to Memphis is the cosmographic canvas. After admiring it, the soul is placed at the peak of a hyperbolically high mountain (lines 309–10). Mount Atlas is a dwarf in comparison, while Mount Olympus 'aun falda suya ser no merecía' [could not be called its foothill] (line 316) (More 2016: 52). The suitability of this mental mountain as an observatory is reinforced by the fact that not even the clouds reach its peak, as they are either scattered by the wind or absorbed by the sun (lines 325–26). Silence therein is undisturbed by a soaring eagle that cannot reach a third of its height (lines 327–39). Then, Sor Juana moves on to the architectural ekphrasis by introducing the pyramids. I will firstly focus on lines 340–53 and 379–82 (Méndez Plancarte 1994a: 343–44):

---

4   Méndez Plancarte (1994a: 608 and footnote about Homer in 593).

Las Pirámides dos — ostentaciones
de Menfis vano, y de la Arquitectura
último esmero, si ya no pendones
fijos, no tremolantes —, cuya altura
coronada de bárbaros trofeos
tumba y bandera fue a los Ptolomeos,
que al viento, que a las nubes publicaba
(si ya también al Cielo no decía)
de su grande, su siempre vencedora
ciudad — ya Cairo ahora —
las que, porque a su copia enmudecía,
la Fama no cantaba
Gitanas glorias, Ménficas proezas,
aun en el viento, aun en el Cielo impresas:
[...]
éstas, que glorias ya sean Gitanas,
o elaciones profanas,
bárbaros jeroglíficos de ciego
error...

[The two pyramids — blazons
of vain Memphis, a masterwork
of hard-wrought architecture, almost like
fixed, unwaving flags —
whose summit crowned with barbaric trophies, tomb
and banner to the Ptolemies, proclaimed to
the wind, to the clouds (if not heaven itself)
Egyptian glories, the great deeds of Memphis,
their proud, ever triumphant
city, called Cairo today,
for fame, struck dumb by the number, did not sing
that glory, those deeds, but they are imprinted
even in the wind, the sky;
[...]
these, whether they be glories
of Egypt or profane pomp,
barbarous hieroglyphs of blind error...][5]

The nun begins her attack in the first line ('ostentaciones'). To begin with, the pyramids are 'barbarian' ('bárbaros trofeos', 'bárbaros jeroglíficos'). She borrows the first of these expressions from Góngora's *Soledad primera*, lines 954–57: 'en cuya orilla [i.e. of the Nile] el viento hereda ahora | pequeños no vacíos | de funerales bárbaros trofeos | que el Egipto erigió a sus Ptolomeos' [on its banks now the wind inherits trophies | deserted and not small | of barbarous funeral rites | erected by Egypt for her Ptolemies] (Góngora 2012: 72–73). As noted by Salcedo Coronel (1636: 183ᵛ), line 956 harks back at least to Martial (1993: I. 12–13), who started his book of *Epigrams* with a famous *incipit*: '*Barbara pyramidum sileat miracula Memphis*' [Let barbarous Memphis speak no more of the wonder of her pyramids].

5   Edith Grossman's translation can be found in More (2016: 53–54). I have introduced adjustments in the first four lines to make it more literal.

However, there is a significant difference between Góngora and Sor Juana. The former betrays the popular belief of the time that most of the pyramids were in ruins; hence his image of air filling the empty space left by their demise (Jammes 2001: I. 392). Góngora overwhelms readers with ruined greatness and an implied reflection of decaying Egyptian civilisation. For her part, Sor Juana offers a typical seventeenth-century vision of an ancient empire, which the Old Testament (in both the *Exodus* and the later books of prophets) describes in terms of a monstrous, impious power that posed a challenge to the God of Israel. Nevertheless, the nun does not make the pyramids vanish. That is not in her interest, for she will deploy their shape as a metaphor for the ascending soul.

According to Serrano de Paz (1673a: 626^v), another commentator of the *Soledades*, the pyramids 'bárbaros son' either 'por vanos' or 'por locos'. Both reasons are relevant to *Primero sueño*. Given their disproportionate height, the pyramids embody these two flaws. First, they represent arrogance and self-assured hubris. This explains why the nun deploys expressions such as 'Menfis vano' and 'elaciones', the latter meaning elevation but also haughtiness. Second, the pyramids reveal the distorted worldview of a civilisation that, despite its military achievements, was rotten to the core ('bárbaros jeroglíficos de ciego | error'). In the Spanish Golden Age, the word 'jeroglífico' was often equated with 'emblema', i.e. an image that, after being deciphered, delivered a moral lesson (Gállego 1984: 24). Sor Juana imagines the pyramids as monuments to the victories, conquests and power of Egypt. Thus, the moral lesson is clear: there is vanity (bordering on insanity) in erecting gigantic constructions to human prowess, as these buildings should only be devoted to God.

All these criticisms could be applied to the protagonist. Her aim of rising to attain complete knowledge is as 'vain' and 'insane' as the pyramids themselves. Even the major censure that underlies every reproach — i.e. Egypt's profaneness ('profanas') — can link pyramids and soul.[6] By condemning the pyramids for their profaneness, the nun is arguably condemning the soul as well (that is, her *alter ego*): both are two sides of the same coin. Indeed, in *Primero sueño*, the emphasis of the oneiric trip is on wisdom, not on God. In this respect, it is inevitable to think of Sor Juana herself, who was the target of criticisms for the pre-eminence that she gave to knowledge and literature. Interestingly, in his 1690 letter to the nun, Manuel Fernández de Santa Cruz (the Bishop of Puebla) drew a parallel between Sor Juana and ancient Egypt that is seldom cited (Salceda 1994: 695; and More 2016: 88):

> Mucho tiempo ha gastado V.md. en el estudio de filósofos y poetas; ya será razón que se perfeccionen los empleos y que se mejoren los libros. ¿Qué pueblo hubo más erudito que Egipto? En él empezaron las primeras letras del mundo, y se admiraron los jeroglíficos [...] Y con todo eso, el Espíritu Santo dice abiertamente que el pueblo de los egipcios es bárbaro: [...] ciencia que no alumbra para salvarse, Dios, que todo lo sabe, la califica por necedad.

---

6   *Diccionario de Autoridades* (1737: 394): 'PROFANO. Se toma regularmente por excesivo en el fausto y lucimiento, con desorden, *que toca en irreligiosidad*, o menos modestia' [PROFANE: it usually means excessively flamboyant and ostentatious, in disarray, *that borders on unreligiousness*, or immodesty] (my emphasis).

[Your Grace has spent a good deal of time studying philosophers and poets; now is the proper moment for you to perfect your pursuits and improve the books you read. Was there ever a nation more erudite than Egypt? The first letters in the world originated there, and their hieroglyphics were a cause of astonishment [...] And yet the Bible states openly that the Egyptian nation is barbaric [...] knowledge that does not light the way to salvation is deemed foolishness by God, who knows all things]

There is common ground between Sor Juana's intermezzo and Fernández de Santa Cruz's letter. Both equate Egypt with a certain grandiosity, all the more pointless for its lack of faith; both other this land by deeming it insurmountably different. For this reason, these texts could be read as early modern forerunners of the Orientalist discourse identified by Said (2003: 20). Orientalism is premised upon exteriority, the principal product of which is representation. Indeed, the dramatic immediacy of the pyramids in *Primero sueño* may make us forget that we are reading a poem where a symbol is singled out to condemn a whole civilisation. Such synecdoche is central to Orientalist images. To paraphrase Foucault (1966: 31), Sor Juana's Egyptian digression constitutes a representation of a representation: that is, the poetic recreation of pyramids, which is based on earlier descriptions that were already infused with myths and factoids. In subsequent centuries, European travellers to Egypt saw what they expected to see, as countless texts preceded experience. Sor Juana did not even have this first-hand knowledge. Hence, her multiple 'mistakes' (Méndez Plancarte 1994a: 592–93; and Méndez 2015: 28–29):

(i) the monumental complex did not have 'Pirámides dos' but three: Cheops, Khafre and Mykerinos. Her misleading source could be Pliny (*Natural History*, book XXXVI, chapter 16);

(ii) the pyramids were not built by the 'Ptolomeos' (as she read in the *Soledad primera*, line 957) but several centuries earlier;

(iii) Memphis does not equate with 'ya Cairo ahora' as she seems to imply. I refer to Pérez-Amador's explanation (2015: 302): 'La información dada por Covarrubias, y aun sus imprecisiones, coinciden con la información dada por Sor Juana, en especial al considerar Cairo la misma ciudad que Menfis. Es probable que Covarrubias fuese la fuente de Sor Juana para estos datos' [Covarrubias' information, including his inaccuracies, coincide with the information given by Sor Juana, especially when identifying Cairo with Memphis. Covarrubias was probably Sor Juana's source for these data];

(iv) the pyramids of *Primero sueño* cast no 'señal de sombra' [vestige of shade] (line 378), which is another ancient legend repeated by likely sources such as Saavedra Fajardo (1659: 77–78): 'Las pirámides de Egipto fueron milagro del mundo, porque en sí mismas tenían la luz, sin manchar con sus sombras las cosas vecinas' [The pyramids of Egypt were a miracle of the world because they held the light within themselves, without covering neighbouring things with their shadow].[7]

---

7   Alatorre (2012: 507–08) gives more examples of this legend.

Two ideas are relevant in this respect. Firstly, Sor Juana did not approach Egypt as a historian or an archaeologist but as a poet. Nevertheless, even though she was writing a fictional work, her relationship with this subject matter was conditioned by a horizon of expectations. The prominent place that the nun gives to the fantastic, borrowing myths such as the pyramids' lack of shadow serves as an authorising frame for her Egyptian digression. By including this imaginary but conventional content, Sor Juana hoped to meet the demands of her European/Creole audience, who expected marvels of this sort from Egypt.

Secondly, Sor Juana's engagement with what Said (2003: 94) calls a 'dialectic of reinforcement' necessarily entails imposing Western patterns on the East. This *modus operandi* has ideological consequences: namely, it increases the distance between 'us' (Catholics) and 'them' (ancient Egyptians). No wonder the apparent outcome (that is, ancient Egyptians were barbarians) is the confirmation/reinforcement of Martial and Góngora. They all represent the Western tradition of approaching Egypt as an alien object that can be named, analysed and explained — in a word: represented — to European readers.

Sor Juana herself was not European but a Creole of Spanish descent, which complicates consideration of this issue. What then is the reason for *Primero sueño*'s 'mixture of interest and watchfulness' (to borrow Kluge's expression) towards Egypt? We must take a step back to answer this question. The diglossia of seventeenth-century mythological literature was the consequence of the pressure of hegemonic Baroque culture (Maravall 2011: 131–73 and 266–304) on ideas that could challenge it. This pressure and the authors' literary strategies to circumvent it produced a tension, which Benjamin (1977: 177) defined as the synthesis that arises 'in allegorical writing as a result of the conflict between theological and artistic intentions, a synthesis not so much in the sense of a peace as a *treuga dei* [i.e. truce of God] between the conflicting opinions'. Kluge deems this conflict more marked in Spain than elsewhere.[8] Setting aside this claim, it is my contention that diglossia was prevalent not only in early modern Europe but also in the Americas. In fact, Creoles produced texts where this doublespeak is even more pronounced than in Iberian models.

Sor Juana is a good example of this phenomenon, as the ideological pressure experienced by Spanish peninsular authors must have been minimal compared to that which she suffered. Indeed, gaining a place in the intellectual circles of patriarchal New Spain was not an easy task for a nun. Neither was impressing Spanish readers for a Creole. Despite her success, Sor Juana was perceived as an 'exotic oddity' (in Spain) and criticised for devoting too much time to secular writing (in New Spain). Conversely, Góngora wrote almost without hindrance, even though he also combined a career in the Church with nonspiritual verse (Paz 2015).

In this respect, the nun had good reasons to believe that certain attacks were motivated by her gender. Other criticisms were motivated by her religious condition, which implied — for some — that she had to devote her entire life and work to God. See the *Respuesta*: 'ni ajenas represiones — que he tenido muchas —,

---

8   This paragraph is indebted to the book *Diglossia* (Kluge 2014: 21, 99 and 295).

ni propias reflejas [...] han bastado a que deje de seguir este natural impulso que Dios puso en mí' [neither the reprimands of others — I have had many — nor my own reflections [...] have sufficed to make me abandon this natural impulse that God placed in me] (Salceda 1994: 444; and More 2016: 95). The above-mentioned letter by the Bishop of Puebla (1690) proves that her concerns were justified. Thus, *Primero sueño* stems not only from an emphasis on human limitations when competing with God (e.g. pyramids, Babel), but also from a certain insecurity and Sor Juana's subsequent willingness to conform to hegemonic Baroque culture.

Having said that, the nun's watchfulness may seek to counterbalance her actual fascination with the pyramids. This tension explains the poem's ambiguous address to ancient Egypt (that is, its profound diglossia). In the West, ambivalent attitudes towards Egypt hark back to Herodotus: the Greek imaginary construction of the Orient evoked the idea of masses enslaved by a tyrant with unlimited power. Herodotus' attention to the living conditions of the slaves can be read along these lines. However, his concern coexists with wonderment at Egyptian achievements.[9] Likewise, Sor Juana combines criticism with praise of the pyramids. For instance, in the reference to their architectural magnificence ('de la Arquitectura | último esmero'), as well as to their loftiness ('altura | coronada'), in which the adjective 'crowned' suggests a majestic pre-eminence. In fact, the wondrous dimension of these constructions is heightened further by allusions to wind, clouds and sky (Nanfito 2000: 52): 'que al viento, que a las nubes publicaba', 'aun en el viento, aun en el Cielo impresas'. Even the Spanish term 'bárbaro' examined above can be read as a sign of admiration.[10]

Sor Juana summarises the historical functions of pyramids in three words: 'tumba y bandera'. The nun does not elaborate further on their funereal nature, which was known to Góngora and his contemporaries (Salcedo Coronel 1636: 183^v). She characterises these constructs as memorials to Egypt's greatness and glory to an extent ('siempre vencedora'), and with an enthusiasm ('Gitanas glorias, Ménficas proezas') that exceeds that of her Hispanic predecessors. Moreover, the assimilation of the pyramids with the 'jeroglíficos' emphasises the visual-iconic quality of these buildings. In Baroque Europe, the word 'jeroglífico' not only meant emblem but also the actual Egyptian script. The hieroglyph was believed to be the sacred Egyptian writing designed to state hidden truths. Hieroglyphs were immensely popular among humanists: Ficino, Valeriano and Kircher shared the conviction that they were images of divine ideas, containing ancient wisdom the decipherment of which would illuminate every obscurity of nature (Gállego 1984: 24; Yates 1999a: 163–64; and Benjamin 1977: 169–70).

---

9   Herodotus (2013: 172): 'It is a wonder beyond description [...]. Certainly, there can be no doubting that the Labyrinth would have cost more in terms of sweat and gold than all the walls and public monuments built by the Greeks put together'. Paz (1982: 236) popularised the study of Sor Juana's enthusiasm for Egypt.

10   Solís (1684: 22): 'Bárbara resolución, que si la hubiera favorecido el suceso, pudiera merecer el nombre de hazaña' [Extraordinary resolution: had it been favoured by fortune, it would have qualified as a feat].

In fact, Sor Juana opens her *Neptuno alegórico* [*Allegorical Neptune*] (1680) with an approach to the hieroglyphs: the passage that contains her first ever references to Egypt (Merrim 2010: 186). Judging from this text, the poet believed that the 'jeroglíficos' stood for everything invisible, or even at the limits of the thinkable. In other words, hieroglyphs hide content that poses an intellectual, hermeneutical challenge, no matter how obvious they may deceitfully appear before our eyes. She gives several examples of things that this script could represent (Salceda 1994: 355–56): 'los días, meses y semanas [...] los elementos' [the days, months and weeks [...] the elements]. However, the nun also affirms that the hieroglyphs were developed 'por reverencia de las deidades, por no vulgarizar sus misterios a la gente común e ignorante' [out of reverence to their deities, in order not to disseminate their mysteries to the common and ignorant people].

This assertion reflects the early modern connotations of the term. Both when understood as images with symbolic/moral value (hieroglyphs *lato sensu*) or as Egyptian ideograms (hieroglyphs *sensu stricto*), the 'jeroglíficos' were often linked with the occult (Blanco 2012c: 281–82). For this reason, her allusion to religious mysteries, combined with the emphasis on the discordance between picture and object represented ('fue necesario buscarles jeroglíficos, que por similitud, ya que no por perfecta imagen, las representasen') [it became necessary to look for hieroglyphics, which being similar, yet not perfectly identical, would represent them], suggests that Sor Juana did not presuppose the hieroglyphs' translatability in all cases.

In this respect, the poet's hyperbolic admiration is similar to Kircher's. The Jesuit believed that ancient Egyptian writing was so sublime that it was impossible to decode scientifically. Not that Kircher did not attempt to translate hieroglyphs, but he trusted that their lofty symbolism was closer to abstractions than a script composed of letters: hence, the practical difficulties of an accurate translation. In fact, since 'jeroglíficos' is a synecdoche, Sor Juana's appreciation extends to the buildings that contained them — which she ends up calling 'maravillas' and 'milagros' (line 413) — and even to Egyptian civilisation *in toto*.

What is the reason for such enthusiasm? Kircher (1654: 568) had developed a theory — already present in Herodotus and the Neoplatonic tradition — that led to Egypt as the origin of knowledge. In *Oedipus Aegyptiacus*, he argued that Hermes Trismegistus not only created the hieroglyphs ('*primus hieroglyphicorum institutor*') but also all Egyptian philosophy and theology ('*totius theologiae et philosophiae aegyptiacae princeps et parens*'). Ancient philosophers — even Homer and Plato — merely followed Trismegistus ('*deinde reliqui philosophi secuti sunt*'). Ergo: Egypt is the point of departure for understanding all nations and faiths, including those of Meso-America, as we shall see later. The belief in Egypt as the fountainhead of the *prisca theologia* [ancient theology], reinforced by the tradition that Greek luminaries visited that land and learned from their priests, harks back to the second century. The pro-Egyptian mood of the Greco-Latin world imbued Renaissance Neoplatonism from Ficino onwards (Yates 1999a: 5). Sor Juana is heir to this tradition: hence, her spirited portrayal of Egypt.

In *Obeliscus pamphilius*, Kircher took various Arab legends as primary models in order to tell the story of Hermes Trismegistus and the origins of the *prisca theologia*. These sources — notably the history of Egypt by Al-Suyuti (whom Kircher calls 'Gelaldinus') — emphasised the role of an earlier Hermes who had preserved wisdom from the Flood by building the pyramids (Stolzenberg 2013: 161–62). This myth combined two motifs: the Jewish Flood story and the hiding of knowledge. The outcome was a new Flood myth in which Hermes plays the role of the ark-builder, and the pyramids take on the role of the ark (Fodor 1970: 342).[11] There are three reasons why this legend may be relevant to *Primero sueño*. First, in the Bible, the *Genesis* Flood narrative (6–9) comes shortly before the tower of Babel (11). In this respect, at the end of the intermezzo, Sor Juana juxtaposes the pyramids (the counterpart to the ark) with that very same tower (lines 412–14). Second, the logic of wrongdoing followed by punishment of the Biblical Flood story is key to the *silva*, which portrays the soul's quest for knowledge — represented by the pyramids — as transgression (Beaupied 1997: 41). Third, Kircher's sources on Egypt fit in with the key metaphor (pyramids = soul) of the intermezzo. I shall explore this analogy further in the next section. For the moment, suffice it to add that the *silva* shares with these sources the focus on the link between pyramids and wisdom: in *Primero sueño*, these constructions ascend towards a gnostic goal; in Al-Suyuti's Flood legend, they already contain the sum total of knowledge.

Whereas this tradition emphasised the role of the first Hermes Trismegistus, the pyramid builder, Kircher underlined the role of the second Hermes, who revived that knowledge after the Flood and carved it on obelisks using hieroglyphs. Note the difference between the two: the former hid wisdom in pyramids to prevent its destruction by the Flood, while the latter hid wisdom in obelisks to prevent the uninitiated from having access to it (Stolzenberg 2013: 162; Fodor 1970: 339).[12] In this respect, Sor Juana's aesthetic reflects a similar kind of belief in the virtues of concealment. It is thus unsurprising that she approved of the elitist nature of hieroglyphs. This writing system was reserved for very few high-ranking officials of the divinised pharaoh and priests. Thus, it was associated with dignity and solemnity, yet not necessarily with the occult. The Baroque mind did not value knowledge easily presented and acquired. The esoteric qualities with which early modern ignorance endowed hieroglyphs became their main appeal (Iversen 1993: 45).

Therefore, concealment is the corollary of Sor Juana's hyperbolic admiration for Egypt: the loftier the poetic subject matter, the lower the number of intended readers. Gongorism fits into this logic. No wonder Francisco Fernández de Córdoba

---

11   Kircher (1650: 45): '*dicitur quoque quod Hermes Trismegistus* [...] *cum praecognouisset diluuium, eas aedificauit, in eas que coniecit omnes suas diuitias, et libros, et quidquid habebat pretiosum, et dignum conseruatione*' [it is also said that Hermes Trismegistus [...] since he had foreseen the Flood, built the pyramids, in them he threw together all his riches, and books, and whatever valuables he had that were worthy of conservation].

12   Kircher (1650: 45): '*donec uenit secundus Hermes, qui primus pyramides in obeliscos mutasse dicitur, tanquam aptiores ad, in his, sapientiae suae monumenta consignanda*' [until the second Hermes came who, it is said, was the first who replaced the pyramids with obelisks, as if these were better suited to the purpose of sealing the monuments of his wisdom].

(the Abbot of Rute) resorted to hieroglyphs when defending the style of his friend Góngora.[13] In fact, the above-mentioned quotation from the *Neptuno*, with its emphasis on preventing the ignorant from accessing mysterious content, seems redolent of the attributed *Carta en respuesta* [*Letter in Response*] (1613). Indeed, after highlighting 'lo misterioso que encubren' [the mysterious quality concealed in] his *Soledades*, Góngora allegedly added: 'Demás, que honra me ha causado hacerme obscuro a los ignorantes, que esa es la distinción de los hombres doctos' [Moreover, being beyond the understanding of the ignorant has brought me honour, for that is what distinguishes learned men] (Carreira 1999: 2).

In *Primero sueño*, the image of the Egyptian God of Silence (lines 74–76: 'uno y otro sellando labio obscuro | con indicante dedo, | Harpócrates, la noche, silencioso') [silent dark Harpocrates, the night, seals | lips, one after the other | with an indicant finger] embodies a similar need for exclusivity (More 2016: 47). Bonasone's study for *Harpocrates* (Figure 6.3) offers a visual representation of Sor Juana's poetic image. No doubt, the nun could have expressed the venture of the soul in a more accessible way. However, it would be unfair to reproach her for the apparent inscrutability of the *silva*. Elitist poetry for courtly and ecclesiastical consumption was the order of the day in the Baroque. Sor Juana followed the available models of high literary culture.

In this respect, there is a towering figure in Western literature whose all-encompassing wisdom mirrors that of the Egyptian pyramids. Ancient Greeks hailed Homer as the most comprehensive source. Several centuries later, in the circle of Ficino, we encounter the notion that the Greek poet was divinely inspired. Not surprisingly, Homer appears as 'divino' [divine] in Sor Juana's *romance* [ballad] 38 (Méndez Plancarte 1994a: 108). His role in *Primero sueño* is crucial, for he will render explicit the metaphor that justifies the intermezzo of the pyramids, thereby breaking the apparent balance between condemnation and praise.

Homer in Egypt

'It is said that Homer visited Egypt; and it has excited some surprise that he did not consider the pyramids worthy of being celebrated in his verses' (Lane 2000: 196). This myth, mentioned by a nineteenth-century British Orientalist, harks back at least to Diodorus Siculus (first century BC). According to this Greek historian, Homer shaped certain events in his poems following religious practices he had witnessed in Egypt. It is uncertain where Diodorus took this reference from: unlike Herodotus' *History*, Homer's works betray only a vague notion of this land

---

13   Artigas (1925: 421): 'Pasemos pues, a probar, y a comprobar con ejemplo el estilo de las *Soledades* dado caso, que sea (como V. m. nos le pinta) oscuro [...] ¿De los egipcios quién ignora el cuidado en ocultar al vulgo los misterios de su teología, y ciencia, pues teniendo letras comunes todos, las tenían propias, y particulares los sacerdotes solos, enseñados por tradición de padres a hijos? [Let us now examine, using examples, the style of the *Soledades* to see whether (as Your Honour portrays it) it is obscure [...] Who is not aware of the care with which the Egyptians hid from the commoners the mysteries of their theology, and science, for though they all shared an alphabet, their priests also had their own particular writing system, passed on from father to son?].

FIG. 6.3. Giulio Bonasone (c. 1498–1580), *Harpocrates*, National Gallery of Art, Washington, D.C.

(Murphy 1990: 126; and Gilbert 1939). As far as I know, no other ancient source contains this legend. Sor Juana quotes Diodorus three times in the *Neptuno*.[14] She refers to the Greek poet in lines 399–411 of *Primero sueño* (Méndez Plancarte 1994a: 345):

> según de Homero, digo, la sentencia,
> las Pirámides fueron materiales
> tipos solos, señales exteriores
> de las que, dimensiones interiores,
> especies son del alma intencionales:
> que como sube en piramidal punta
> al Cielo la ambiciosa llama ardiente,
> así la humana mente
> su figura trasunta,
> y a la Causa Primera siempre aspira
> —céntrico punto donde recta tira
> la línea, si ya no circunferencia,
> que contiene, infinita, toda esencia—.

> [Following the maxim, I say, of Homer,
> pyramids were mere material models,
> exterior signs of those which,
> in their inner dimensions, are the
> intentional species of the soul:
> for as the ambitious flame burns upward in a
> pyramidal tip toward heaven,
> so does the human mind,
> miming that form,
> ever aspire to the First Cause,
> the center toward which all straight lines extend, if
> not the circumference that holds,
> infinite, all essences.][15]

In fact, the excursus on Homer had already started in line 382 ('según el Griego') [according to the Greek], which up to line 411 makes thirty lines devoted either to this poet or to his alleged insight into the soul. Inserted in the intermezzo of the pyramids, the passage constitutes a sub-digression. I will start by explaining what Homer meant to Sor Juana. Then, I will explore the key metaphor (pyramids = soul), the meaning of which he discloses. Although the *Iliad* was available in New Spain, it is not possible to establish with certainty if Sor Juana had read any Homer. Her references to him in *Primero sueño* and other works seem second-hand.[16] Nevertheless, for the purposes of the *silva*, it was probably his reputation rather than his actual work that mattered most to her. Homer served to consolidate the authority of Sor Juana, i.e. her 'Egyptian expertise' vis-à-vis her audience, part of which was as ill-informed on Greek literature as herself (Méndez 2015: 29).

---

14   Salceda (1994: 361, 365 and 367).
15   Edith Grossman's translation can be found in More (2016: 54). I have introduced adjustments to make it more literal.
16   I refer to the five Homer quotations in the *Neptuno* (Salceda 1994: 368, 380, 390, 391, 395). According to Martin and Arenal (2009: 99, 130, 158, 160, 173), Sor Juana borrows all these references from the Italian mythographer Natale Conti.

It is worth taking a step back in order to assess the meaning of this passage in *Primero sueño*. In his essay 'Of the most outstanding men', Montaigne (1958: 569) included two reasons from the past to praise Homer. Both will help understand his role in Sor Juana's intermezzo. Firstly, Montaigne was astonished that the Greek poet, 'who by his authority created and brought into credit in the world many deities, has not himself gained the rank of a god'. Secondly, those living after Homer 'have used him as a master very perfect in the knowledge of all things, and his books as a nursery of every kind of ability'.[17]

Let us start with the first of these compliments: veneration turned into a cult surrounding Homer. During the Renaissance, humanists made efforts to bring their admired pagan poets into line with Christianity. In this context, a syncretist theory appeared: Homer was divinely inspired and his works conveyed Christian truths in mythical form (Ford 2002: 343, and 2007: 214–15).[18] Sor Juana could have used Homer in this way. Nevertheless, her approach is different. In *Primero sueño*, the 'deification' of Homer does not arise from any mystical revelation but rather from his literary achievements. Poetic excellence and divinity are two sides of the same coin: readers admire a verbal power, which is indistinguishable from that of (re)creating, ordering or reconstructing the cosmos. Hence, the 'triple impossibility' topos of lines 391–98: it is easier to take away (i) Jupiter's lightning, or (ii) Hercules' club, than (iii) a single hemistich from the countless lines 'de los que le dictó propicio Apolo' [a well-disposed Apollo dictated to Homer] (More 2016: 54).

Although Homer appears as divinely inspired, there is more to these lines than hyperbolic praise. Interestingly, none of Sor Juana's likely sources conveys a literal belief in the 'triple impossibility'. Macrobius (2011: II. 243–44) makes his character Avienus add, after presenting the list: 'yet by choosing just the right spot in his own work [i.e. the *Aeneid*] to take over the earlier bard's words [i.e. the *Iliad* and the *Odyssey*] he caused them to be thought his own'. Ergo: Virgil succeeded in his wise selection and arrangement of Homeric source material.

For his part, Espinosa Medrano (2017: section III, paragraph 30) gives a turn to the screw. His initial formulation is almost a verbatim account of Macrobius: 'Por tan imposible como quitarle el rayo a Júpiter y a Hércules la clava, juzgó la antigüedad el usurpar los versos a Homero' [Antiquity considered that passing Homer's lines off as yours was as impossible as taking Jupiter's lightning or Hercules' club]. Then, he adds two exceptions to this rule. The first is obviously Virgil. The second, Góngora: 'el usurpar la inversión latina no ha sido sino grandeza: *Clavam Herculi extorquere*' [to borrow hyperbaton from Latin has resulted in nothing but greatness: to wrest the club from Hercules]. Thus, Góngora triumphed equally with his Latinised Spanish.

Yet the most compelling text on this subject is Sor Juana's own *Carta atenagórica* [*Letter Worthy of Athena*], which mentions a woman as the exception to the ancient

---

17 I owe the references to Diodorus and Montaigne to Alatorre (2012: 508).
18 Homer was deemed either a prophet (Seznec 1972: 98), or even '*par superis ipsique Iovi*' [equal to the gods and to Jupiter himself] (Poliziano 2004: 98–99). Sor Juana quotes Poliziano in the *Neptuno* (Salceda 1994: 361).

belief (Salceda 1994: 434): 'A vista del elevado ingenio del autor aun los muy gigantes parecen enanos. ¿Pues qué hará una pobre mujer? Aunque ya se vio que una quitó la clava de las manos a Alcides, siendo uno de los tres imposibles que veneró la antigüedad' [Given the towering wit of the author, even the giants seem to be dwarves by his side. What is a poor woman to do? However, it was a woman who removed the club from the hands of Alcides, one of the three impossibilities that antiquity venerated]. Indeed, Omphale appropriated not only Hercules' club but also Thespian Lion's skin, both emblems of masculine prowess. The nun's allusion to this role reversal, while criticising the sermon of a celebrated Jesuit (the Portuguese António Vieira), is indicative of her opinion of gender stereotypes (Scott 1985: 514).

At the end of Chapter 4, I presented the corollary of Espinosa Medrano's praise of Góngora: if his *Polifemo* surpassed its Greco-Latin predecessors, a Creole could outdo Europeans. Sor Juana's *Carta atenagórica* adds a 'gender twist' to this reasoning: if Omphale seized Hercules' club, why could a woman not beat a man in the field of ideas? *Primero sueño* is far from being that explicit. However, thanks to this letter (1690), which was written just a few years after the *silva* (c. 1685), we know that Sor Juana was as sceptical as her predecessors about the 'triple impossibility' topos. When read in conjunction with the *Carta atenagórica*, the reference of the intermezzo to Homer seems to imply less of an unattainable model than a challenge to outdo the greatest human minds, regardless of gender.[19]

Nevertheless, Homer is not just the paragon of Western poetry. Montaigne's second compliment highlighted his pansophical knowledge. Indeed, many scholars considered the Greek not only a divinely inspired poet but also a savant who laid the foundations of all the sciences and philosophies developed since his death (Ford 2007: 1).[20] If we read *Primero sueño* through this lens, Homer takes on a greater stature, and the intermezzo connects with the preceding lines (i.e. the cosmographic painting-mirror of the lighthouse of Alexandria, lines 266–301) with unexpected consistency. Three ideas are key in this respect.

Firstly, Sor Juana's lines 385–86 ('Aquileyas proezas | o marciales de Ulises sutilezas') [heroic feats of Achilles | or the martial subtleties of Ulysses] (More 2016: 54) fit in well with deeming Homer's works a nursery of every kind of ability. Indeed, the reference to Achilles and Ulysses, the respective protagonists of the *Iliad* and the *Odyssey*, seems a tribute to the physical and intellectual achievements of ancient Greece, which established the foundations of Western civilisation. Petrarch famously ended his letter to Homer with a confession: 'I realise how far from me you are' (Greene 1982: 29). *Primero sueño* reveals a similar sense of distance. However, Sor Juana does not emphasise the pathos of belatedness but rather the vast lore of the source.

---

19   I refer to the chronology in Arenal and Powell (2009: xxvi). Sor Juana's irreverent *romance* [ballad] 50 is also relevant, for she mentions 'los traspieses que dió Ovidio, | los tropezones de Homero, | los vaguidos de Virgilio' [Ovid's blunders | Homer's stumbles | Virgil's blackouts] (Méndez Plancarte 1994a: 155 and 445).

20   Poliziano (2004: 104–05): '*Omnis ab hoc doctas sapientia fonte papyros | irrigat*' [All philosophy waters its learned pages from this font].

Secondly, Homer's pivotal role as the origin of all knowledge and the guardian of the past explains his inclusion in the guild of historians (lines 388–90): '...lo acepta | (cuando entre su catálogo lo cuente) | que gloria más que número le aumente' [it accepts him (when it counts him in its records) | to swell these more by glory than by number] (More 2016: 54). By proposing the idea of Homer as a historian, Sor Juana suggests that, besides being a 'dulcísimo Poeta' [very sweet poet] (line 383), the Greek tells the unvarnished truth. Thus, his works should not only be read for the sake of entertainment but also revered as a fount of wisdom.

Thirdly, the appearance of Homer can also reflect a desire to underline the inner nature of the vision, since that kind of 'seeing' was the only one that the Greek, 'ciego también' [also blind] (line 383), could enjoy (Beaupied 1997: 57). By looking inside himself, Homer depicted a shield (*Iliad*, XVIII. 478–608) that is as comprehensive a representation of the universe as the cosmographic painting-mirror of *Primero sueño*, which contains 'las imágenes todas de las cosas' [images of all things] (line 281) (More 2016: 51). Both descriptions contribute to making the world aesthetically intelligible: the former, by encapsulating in an artefact the link between knowledge and empire; the latter, by presenting knowledge freed from that bond, in a purely artistic form.

Moreover, Sor Juana's portrayal of Homer as an educator is even clearer in his disclosure of a key metaphor. According to the Greek poet, the nun affirms, the pyramids' outer layout stands for the soul's 'dimensiones interiores'. Alatorre (1995: 394) identified Celio Agostino Curione (quoted in the *Neptuno* as 'el que añadió jeroglíficos' [the one who added hieroglyphics] to Valeriano's works) as a source of this symbolic interpretation of the pyramids: '*qui etiam hoc ipsum id est, animam nostram Pyramidis formam habere mihi testari videtur, in Timaeo cum ait [...]*' [He [i.e. Plato] seems to me to testify also to this very thing, that is, that our soul has the form of a pyramid, when he says in the *Timaeus* that...] (Valeriano 1604: 640).[21] The reason why Sor Juana attributed this analogy to Homer remains unknown. Having examined the *Odyssey*, the *Iliad*, the *Homeric Hymns* and works by Philo Judaeus, Alexandrian Homer scholars and Plutarch, I have not found any evidence to sustain this attribution.

In any case, there are two sides to the metaphor of pyramids = soul. As we saw earlier, both the soul's aspirations and the pyramids' height can be read as symbols of human vanity. However, this moral reading is absent in the final part of the intermezzo. Rather, Homer traces this parallel as praise, for these constructions represent the longing for ascension in human nature. The inference is that the soul, like the pyramids, is an object of wonder (Nanfito 2000: 49; Lowe 1976: 411–12).

Later in *Primero sueño*, Sor Juana introduces the topos '*Magnum miraculum est homo*' [Man is a great miracle] more explicitly. As mentioned, Camargo's approach to this motif was an unquestioning encomium. At first, the nun expresses a similar enthusiasm: 'última perfección de lo criado | y último de su Eterno Autor agrado' [ultimate perfection of creation | and ultimate delight of the Eternal Creator] (lines

---

21   *Timaeus* (34c–36b). I owe this reference to Alatorre (2012: 509–10). The quotation from the *Neptuno* can be found in Salceda (1994: 355).

673–74) (More 2016: 60). This assessment is in tune with Pico della Mirandola's humanistic ideal (1956: 7): 'I have placed you [i.e. man] at the very centre of the world, so that from that vantage point you may with greater ease glance round about you on all that the world contains'.[22]

Nevertheless, the ambivalent portrayal of the pyramids seems to prefigure that of the human condition. Unlike Camargo, Sor Juana does not call man the 'emperador' [emperor] of all creatures. Rather, to her the source of wonder is his chameleonic nature. Man has free will, thus, he can explore the universe and gain knowledge in order to touch the sky ('al Cielo toca', line 678), or he can degrade himself to the level of the ground ('sella el polvo la boca', line 679). We are a mixture of stellar qualities and dust — something like stardust (Nava 2013: 160). The oxymoron 'altiva bajeza' [exalted lowliness] (line 694) summarises this balanced approach.[23]

Thus, Homer's account of the pyramids marks a turning point. The intermezzo is no longer describing their historical functions. Having given us a taste of Egypt, Sor Juana transforms matter into spirit (Soriano 2000: 169). Given the general obscurity of the *silva*, the straightforwardness of this passage is striking. The nun did not have qualms about confronting her readers with a *tour de force*. However, she made sure that they would understand what the pyramids stand for. It is not rare for ekphraseis to herald hermeneutical keys for a poem (Lizcano 2003: 66). What is more unusual is that a Baroque author is so unequivocal about their meaning. Sor Juana's approach has two important consequences. On an ideological level, with the hindsight provided by this explicit metaphor, her previous lines of condemnation sound less imposing. She would not have chosen the pyramids as symbols for the soul if she had not regarded them highly. From a narratological viewpoint, any concern as to the apparent lack of connection between the intermezzo and the rest of *Primero sueño* is now out of the question. This is not a disjointed digression in the manner of Marino.

Thus, Sor Juana's Egyptian intermezzo appears as a hybrid within the ekphrastic tradition of Gongorism. The passage is almost as long as, say, Camargo's still life of Manresa. In fact, the number of lines that Sor Juana devotes to this excursus (seventy-two) constitutes some 7% of the work's total extension (975 lines). Camargo would have had to write a 625-line ekphrasis to reach this level. He never did. Relatively speaking, Sor Juana spends more lines digressing than Camargo.[24] However, setting aside these comparisons, the intermezzo, with its ramifications in every possible direction from Homer to his heroes, resembles the meandering structure that we encountered in the *San Ignacio*.

---

22   I also refer to the *Asclepius*, which Pico quotes: 'a human being is a great wonder, a living thing to be worshipped and honoured' (Copenhaver 1992: 69).

23   Lines 692–93 of *Primero sueño* are also important: 'compendio que absoluto | parece al Ángel, a la planta, al bruto' [absolute compendium | that resembles the angels, the plants, the brutes] (More 2016: 60). Sor Juana's balanced vision of humanity is comparable to that of Pico della Mirandola (1956: 9).

24   The comparison might seem unfair, for the *San Ignacio*, unlike *Primero sueño*, is an epic poem of thousands of lines. But so is Marino's *Adone*, which still devotes more verse to digressions than to the plot (Chapelain 1988: 28).

Moreover, the pyramids represent no less than the protagonist of *Primero sueño*. We can take other images, such as the eagle of lines 327–39, as doppelgängers for the soul. Nevertheless, these constructs are her manifest embodiment. Thus, the identification of the ekphrasis with the narrative is more direct than in Góngora. Sor Juana's metaphoric explicitness swerves from the Cordovan poet, who did not believe in laying bare the secret meaning of the loftiest poetry, as evidenced by the above-mentioned *Carta en respuesta* (Carreira 1999: 2).

Despite this departure from Gongorism, Sor Juana embraces this style throughout *Primero sueño*. As noted by Blanco (2012c: 393), the repetition of certain verbal constellations or *paradigms* is essential to the invention of a poetic language. From this perspective, Sor Juana's insistence on certain terms (e.g. pyramids, obelisks) is consistent. In fact, the nun enriches this imagery with another element of Gongorist flavour: the 'ambiciosa llama' that, due to its 'piramidal punta', offers a new representation of the soul.[25] This is yet another example of a metaphor that combines clarity with multivalent symbolism. Its pertinence was beyond dispute for readers of the time, as evidenced by Álvarez de Lugo's explanation: 'Porque *pyr* en lengua griega es lo mismo que fuego, y la forma que guarda una pirámide [...] es parecida a una llama' [For *pyr* in Greek means fire, and the shape of a pyramid [...] is similar to that of a flame] (Sánchez Robayna 1991: 62).

Catalá (1987: 195–96) noticed that Torquemada's *Monarquía indiana* [*Indian Monarchy*] had merged both aspects of Sor Juana's metaphor (the pyramid and the flame) in one single image. Indeed, according to the Franciscan friar, the first ominous sign that announced the collapse of the Aztecs was 'una llama de fuego, notablemente grande y resplandeciente, hecha en figura piramidal, a la manera de una grande hoguera, la cual parecía estar clavada en medio del cielo teniendo su principio en el suelo' [a flame, remarkably large and resplendent, in the shape of a pyramid, as if it were a big bonfire, which seemed to be pinned to the middle of the sky with its base on the ground] (Figure 6.4). The book specifies that the vision took place at night. The analogy between the shape of the pyramid and that of the flame is a Platonic topos (*Timaeus* 56b). However, Torquemada is quoted explicitly in the *Neptuno* (Salceda 1994: 385). Sor Juana knew his work and perhaps used it as a source of her image.[26]

Although the poet's 'llama ardiente' (line 405) does not have any threatening connotations *per se*, that of Torquemada forms a haunting subtext that strengthens the bond between the intermezzo and the plot. From a narratological viewpoint, both images fulfil a proleptic function. The friar introduces fire as the herald

---

25 Góngora's song *Nenias en la muerte del señor Rey Don Felipe III* [*Funeral Song on the Death of the King Philip III*] (1621) offers a similar image (Micó 1990: 176): 'su forma de la más sublime llama | que a egipcio construyó bárbara fama' [the shape of the most sublime flame | that brought to the Egyptians barbarian fame]. Kircher (1654: 534) is another likely source: '*Hinc pyramides, ignis pariter symbolum*' [Hence the pyramids, equally a symbol of fire].
26 I refer to Torquemada (1975: 320). In the same page, the friar adds that 'así parece por los libros de pintura de estos indios que yo tengo en mi poder [...] y el padre fray Bernardino de Sahagún en sus *Memoriales* así lo testifica' [so it seems from the Indians' painting books that I possess [...] and the father fray Bernardino de Sahagún in his *Memoranda* attests to it]. Blanco (2012c: 443) offers more examples of the analogy between pyramids and flames.

FIG. 6.4. Bernardino de Sahagún, Pyramid of Fire, in *Florentine Codex* (c. 1575–1577). Source: Biblioteca Medicea Laurenziana, Florence, Ms. Med. Palat. 220, f. 408r. By permission of the Ministry of Cultural Heritage and Activities (MiBAC), Italy.

FIG. 6.5. Athanasius Kircher, Temple of Mexican God, volume I of *Oedipus Aegyptiacus* (1652). Source: Cornell University Library, Digital Collections.

of approaching conflict and ultimately as the bringer of downfall. Similarly, the pyramidal flame of the *silva*, which ascends but never enough to reach its target, may be interpreted as a warning. The adjective 'ambitious' is also indicative of the impending denouement. The higher the aspiration level ('al Cielo la ambiciosa') (line 405), the greater the failure.

In fact, the juxtaposition of Homer with the pyramid/flame metaphor may be read from yet another perspective. Sor Juana's friend Sigüenza y Góngora (1928: 33–34) believed that the ancestors of the native Mexicans left Egypt shortly after the erection of the tower of Babel. He based his theory on parallelisms such as the Egyptians' 'modo de explicar sus conceptos por jeroglíficos, y por símbolos, fábrica de sus templos, gobierno político, y otras cosas de que quiso apuntar algo el P. Athanasio Kirchero en el *Oedipo Egypciaco*' [their way of explaining concepts with hieroglyphics and symbols, construction of their temples, political government, and other things that Father Athanasius Kircher pointed out in his *Oedipus Aegyptiacus*].

Kircher (1654: 422) illustrated the comparison with a pyramidal Mexican temple (Figure 6.5).

Moreover, Sigüenza y Góngora never missed a chance to praise pre-Columbian civilisations vis-à-vis the Greco-Latin world (Leonard 1929: 100; Keen 1971: 190). Although one cannot find such 'competition' between cultures in Sor Juana, the poet also engaged in the syncretisation of the classics. In her *Neptuno*, the Egyptian goddess Isis, presented as Neptune's mother, so dominates the 'Razón de la fábrica' [Rationale of the Triumphal Arch] as to pervade the whole text with an Egyptianised, Kircherian tone (Salceda 1994: 365; Merrim 2010: 186). As for the reference to Homer in *Primero sueño*, the passage places the pyramids/flame side by side with him, thereby showing that the 'antiquity' of New Spain (assuming its Egyptian origin) was as honourable as that of Europe (González Echevarría 2016: 290).

As if this movement towards the past were not enough, Sor Juana directs the pyramidal flame to a vanishing point where all metaphors for the soul converge like projections of parallel lines: 'y a la Causa Primera siempre aspira'. Indeed, the apex of the 'piramidal punta' is the centre to which the soul aspires: the 'circunferencia' that Sor Juana also mentions in the *Respuesta* (Nanfito 2000: 53). However, there is a difference between both texts. In the *Respuesta*, Sor Juana emphasises that the infinite circumference is both the departure and the arrival point for all radii (that is, beings) in Creation.[27] This information is missing in *Primero sueño*, which instead specifies that a straight line forms the infinite circumference: 'recta tira | la línea, si ya no circunferencia'. Paz (1982: 427 and 492) argues that Nicholas of Cusa is the source of this notion. As evidenced by the figure attached to his proof — Cusa (1997: 103) and Figure 6.6 — 'in the maximum line [i.e. that of the infinite circle] curvature is straightness'. Kircher (1654: 89) reproduces a similar figure. Both texts confirm that Sor Juana's circular 'recta' is oxymoronic but mathematically rigorous.

Setting aside geometrical considerations, Catholic scholars have tended to interpret the passage as the soul's desire to find refuge in God. Indeed, there are reasons to sustain a fideistic reading of the *silva* such as that of Méndez Plancarte (1951: xxxiv): 'el Dios de la revelación Cristológica, este en el que culmina su ascensión del *Primero sueño*' [the God of the Christological revelation, in which her ascension in *Primero sueño* culminates]. In the *Respuesta*, Sor Juana fashions herself as an autodidact whose ultimate goal was to arrive at 'la cumbre de la Sagrada Teología; pareciéndome preciso, para llegar a ella, subir por los escalones de las ciencias y artes humanas' [the summit of sacred theology; [...] and to reach it, I thought it necessary to ascend by the steps of human sciences and arts] (Salceda 1994: 447; and More 2016: 98).[28] Following this logic, the protagonist of *Primero sueño* would incline

---

27   Salceda (1994: 450) and More (2016: 101): 'Así lo demuestra el R. P. Atanasio Quirquerio en su curioso libro *De Magnete*. Todas las cosas salen de Dios, que es el centro a un tiempo y la circunferencia de donde salen y donde paran todas las líneas criadas' [Reverend Father Athanasius Kircher demonstrates this in his curious book *On the Magnet*. All things emanate from God, who is at once the centre and circumference from which all created lines emerge and where they end]. One can find this ancient idea in Ebreo (2009: 269), who attributes it to the Arabs (Salstad 1979: 600).

28   Francomano (2008: 115): 'Sor Juana takes special care in spelling out the relationship between

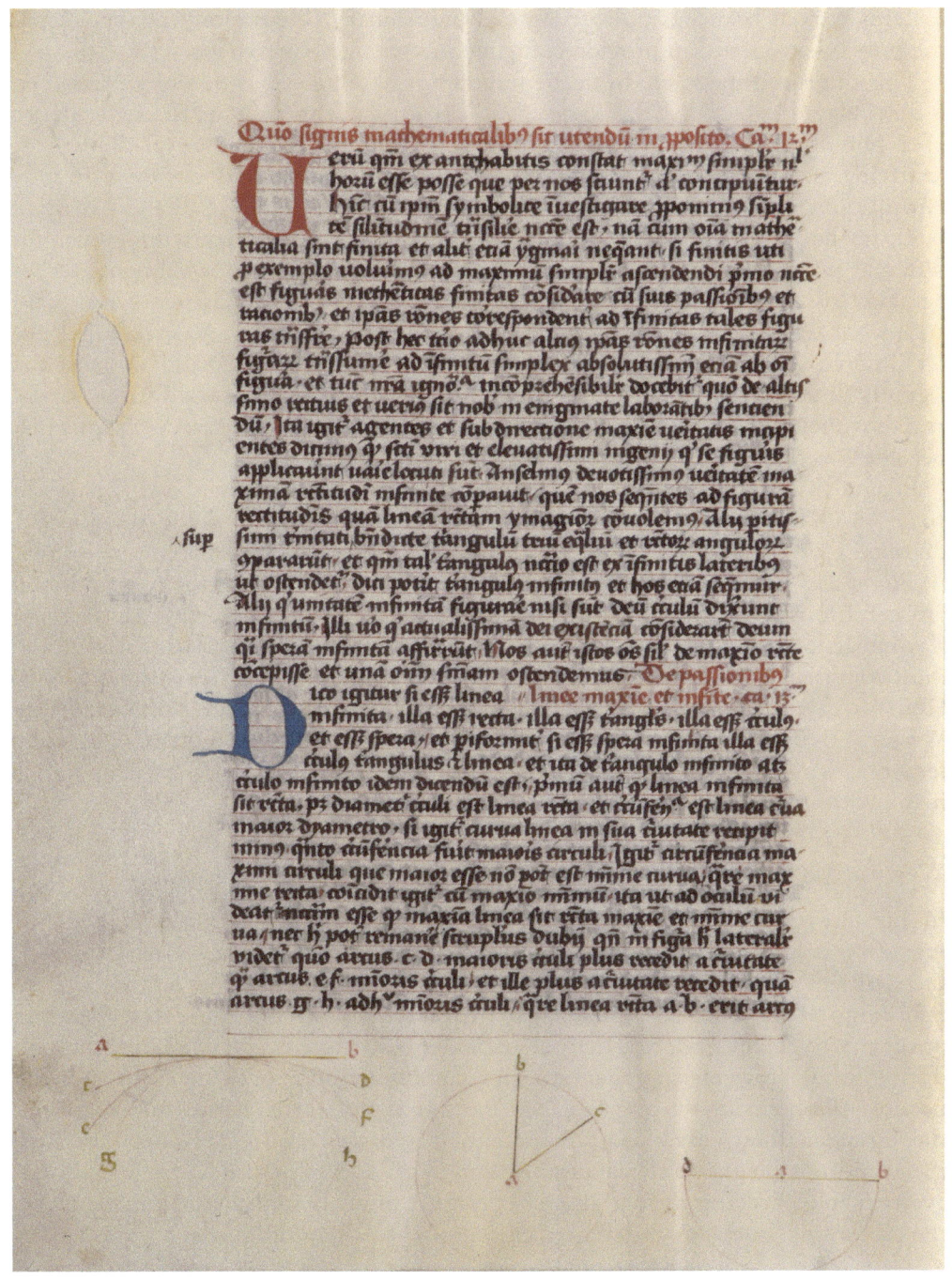

FIG. 6.6. Nicholas of Cusa, Infinite Line, in *On Learned Ignorance* (1440). Source: Cod. Cus. 218, Bl. 6ᵛ. Photograph by Erich Gutberlet / © St. Nikolaus-Hospital, Bernkastel-Kues, Germany. The infinite line is at the bottom left hand corner of the page.

towards various branches of learning as a preliminary preparation, for theology is the only science that can provide complete knowledge (Buxó 1996: 17).

This thesis is impeccable from the standpoint of scholastic orthodoxy. However, it downplays the fact that the *Respuesta* is a rhetorical exercise, i.e. the self-defence of a nun for a life devoted to literature (Perelmuter 1983: 151–52). This self-justifying goal is lacking in *Primero sueño*: hence, its more ambiguous tone. In fact, Grossi (2007: 100) questioned the idea that Sor Juana is alluding to the Christian God. In the *Neptuno*, she had used the metaphor of the infinite circumference for different purposes: 'Costumbre fue de la antigüedad, y muy especialmente de los egipcios, adorar sus deidades debajo de diferentes jeroglíficos y formas varias: y así a Dios solían representar en un círculo, como lo escribe Pierio Valeriano [...] por ser símbolo de lo infinito' [It was customary in antiquity, especially amongst the Egyptians, to worship their deities using different hieroglyphics and various forms: and thus they used to represent God with a circle, as Pierio Valeriano explains [...], because it is the symbol of infinity] (Salceda 1994: 355).[29]

Images that seem disparate may be linked as elements in a synthesis (Benjamin 1977: 58). The 'Causa Primera' that the soul/flame points to could well be the divinity. However, a more abstract call to return to the inception of culture — that is, Egypt and Greece — proves a stronger common ground with the pyramids and Homer. From an epistemological viewpoint, this approach has a genuinely Platonic flavour. Knowledge in *Primero sueño* appears as a return to the origin as if even the most comprehensive learning were a form of remembrance.[30] From this viewpoint, Homer's dignified gloss is crucial, as ancient Egypt was deemed the cradle of Western civilisation. The passage also illustrates knowledge's potential to cross temporal as well as spatial boundaries, a feature central to the understanding of Sor Juana within the Hispanic Baroque.

Westward Knowledge

In his foreword to *Primero sueño*, Méndez Plancarte (1951: xxxix) praised Sor Juana for encapsulating Creation within a 'breve círculo' [pithy circle]. In fact, the soul sees more than she can understand (lines 448–50): 'aunque a la vista quiso manifiesto | dar señas de posible, | a la comprehensión no...' [appeared clear and possible | to the eye but not the understanding...] (More 2016: 55). Thus, the nun distinguishes between apprehension and comprehension, only the former being possible (Robbins 2007: 238; Sánchez Robayna 1991: 216). Earlier in the poem, the Egyptian intermezzo had already anticipated this *décalage*. Having described the wondrous height of the pyramids, Sor Juana adds that the 'vista' [eye] is not even capable of seeing their peaks: 'sin permitir mirar la sutil punta' [unable to see the subtle tip] (line 360). After attempting to reach them, it falls, as a punishment:

her drive for learning and the soul's drive for knowledge of divinity; she [...] must first understand the seven liberal arts before she can dare to study theology, the "Queen of the Sciences." '

29   Sor Juana is referring to Valeriano (1604: 399).

30   *Meno*, 81d: 'research and learning are wholly recollection' (Lamb 1977: 303). This paragraph is also indebted to Franco (1989: 32).

'no descendida, sino despeñada' [it did not descend but plunged] (line 363) (More 2016: 53). The proleptic content of these lines is clear: like the 'ambiciosa llama', the pyramids anticipate the collapse of the soul (Sabat de Rivers 1976: 138).

Sor Juana might have learned this approach from Góngora, whose ekphraseis often fulfil proleptic functions. In fact, the *Soledades* had an impact not only on the motifs and the style of *Primero sueño*, but also on its meandering structure. As reflected in the summary of Diego Calleja, Sor Juana's first biographer, her *silva* has a (minimal, but existent) storyline. The summary can be found in the 'Aprobación' [Approval] of her *Fama y obras póstumas* [*Fame and Posthumous Works*] (1700): 'Siendo de noche, me dormí; soñé, que de una vez quería comprender todas las cosas de que el Universo se compone; no pude, ni aun divisas por sus categorías, ni aun solo un individuo. Desengañada, amaneció, y desperté' [After nightfall, I fell asleep; I dreamed that I wanted to grasp at once all the things of which the Universe is composed; I could not, not even after dividing them into categories, not even after focusing on one single item. Dawn came, and I woke up disillusioned].

Despite its departure from this plot, the Egyptian intermezzo is not alien to the discourse of *Primero sueño*. On the contrary: like Camargo's ekphraseis, Sor Juana's digression constitutes a meta-aesthetic tool that permits the best visualisation of the fissures of the poem. That is, the doublespeak the nun developed given the tension between her intellectual/artistic interests and her religious orthodoxy.[31] Indeed, the excursus reflects the conflict between a fascination with Egypt (source of all Western knowledge) and a certain watchfulness (given its profaneness).

Homer resolves the diglossia by revealing the symbolic meaning of the pyramids, which are metaphors for the soul. However, to reach a full understanding of the Homeric reference, we must take a step back. Interestingly, Góngora's first edition, which was published posthumously as *Obras en verso del Homero español* [*Poetry by the Spanish Homer*] (1627), reached New Spain and Peru (Sabena and Stein 2016: 9).[32] This popular epithet may have influenced Sor Juana's preference. His contemporaries named Góngora the Spanish Homer for at least four reasons. All of them are relevant to *Primero sueño*.

Firstly, the analogy stems from the fact that both poets cultivated, to a certain extent, the epic genre. I refer to Villar's *Fragmentos del Compendio poético* [*Fragments of the Compendium on Poetry*] (2016: 31–32), written c. 1635–1636: 'Todas estas leyes guardó nuestro poeta don Luis en las *Soledades*, *Polifemo*, *Panegírico* y otras obras donde cumplió exactamente las obligaciones de lo heroico [...] y así Pedro Díaz de Rivas en la edición de Madrid le intitula el *Homero español*' [Our poet Góngora followed all these rules in the *Soledades*, *Polifemo*, *Panegírico* and in other works where he met the requirements of the epic genre [...] for this reason, Pedro Díaz de Rivas entitles his Madrid edition: *Works of the Spanish Homer*]. *Stricto sensu*, it is debatable whether the *Soledades* belongs to the 'heroico' genre. However, there is no doubt

---

31   These lines are indebted to Benjamin (1977: 177) and Kluge (2014: 99 and 242).
32   I refer to Rovira (2004) and Guibovich (2003: 183). Espinosa Medrano (2017: section XI, paragraph 120) exonerated Góngora from responsibility for his epithet: 'Llámanle Homero algunos: Él no tiene la culpa' [Some people call him Homer: it is not Góngora's fault].

that it has epic components, notably in the second part.[33] Similarly, *Primero sueño* is not strictly 'heroico' but also has epic features. The towering stature of Homer, Góngora's Greek 'avatar', emphasises the enormous dimensions of the pyramids (that is, the soul) on which he will discourse (Nanfito 2000: 132). By doing so, he endows the venture with a heroic quality.

Secondly, Homer and Góngora had the reputation of being poets with wild, untameable creativity. Scaliger (1994: 62) described the Greek with Ovid's line on chaos before Creation (2014: I. 2–3): *'rudis indigestaque moles'* (i.e. 'a rough, unordered mass', *Metamorphoses*, book I, line 7). This line could be compared to Jáuregui's closure of his *Discurso poético* [*Discourse on Poetry*] (2016: 40ᵛ), which related Gongorism to pre-Creation darkness: 'Dios no crió tinieblas ni las tinieblas requerían creación. Bastaba no criar luz para que las hubiese' [God did not create darkness, and darkness did not need to be created. It was enough not to create light for darkness to exist]. Hence, Homer fits into *Primero sueño*, a cosmographic poem that deploys Gongorism in order to poeticise the exuberant 'cúmulo incomprehensible' [incomprehensible accumulation] (line 447) of the cosmos.

Thirdly, in the *Soledades*, Góngora employed various Homeric techniques to achieve the Greek ideal of *enargeia*: to deliver vivid descriptions that set objects right before the readers' eyes (Blanco 2012b: 262–63). Carducho praised this aspect of his poetry (1865: 146): 'en su *Polifemo* y *Soledades* parece que vence lo que pinta, y que no es posible que ejecute otro pincel lo que dibuja su pluma' [in his *Polifemo* and the *Soledades* it seems that he masters the skill of painting, and that it is impossible for another brush to match what his quill draws]. Since Sor Juana shared this poetic goal, the Homeric reference, framed within Gongorism, serves to sanction doubly the *pittoricità* or pictorial character of *Primero sueño*.

Finally, Góngora's Homeric greatness derives from his influence on other poets. Lope had criticised his style, which he deemed a cul-de-sac that could not lead the way to new poetic forms.[34] The impact of Gongorism in Spain and viceregal America proved him wrong. It also strengthened the analogy between Góngora and Homer. Both were beacons of their respective periods (Bonilla 2010: 210); both lit new paths for poetry that Sor Juana followed.

Said (1985: 94) deployed the term 'Westering' to explain the European tradition of seeing 'the Orient as ceding its historical preeminence and importance to the world spirit moving westwards away from Asia and towards Europe'. Given that Sor Juana's 'barbarian' East is anchored in the past, as opposed to the 'civilised' West from which she writes, this worldview is relevant to *Primero sueño*. In fact, Creoles never thought that the *translatio studii* had stopped in Europe. Quite the contrary: from a viceregal perspective, Sor Juana showed how knowledge was transmitted from Greece (through Rome) to Spain, and then to the Americas: Góngora, like a second Columbus, culminated the process.[35]

33   According to Góngora's friend Francisco Fernández de Córdoba (the Abbot of Rute), 'es necesario confesar que es poema, que los admite y abraza a todos' [we must confess that the *Soledades* encompasses all genres] (Artigas 1925: 424).
34   I refer to Conde's introduction in Vega (2015).
35   Villar (2016: 15–16): 'Engolfose don Luis en el océano abundante y provechoso de la lección antigua y tomando alturas de seguros polos, halló nuevos y no conocidos rumbos, Colón de no

The *translatio studii* is a useful notion with which to frame the nun within the Hispanic Baroque. The idea of belatedness coexisted with the thesis of the perfectibility of poetry that Scaliger had promoted in the Renaissance by praising Virgil at the expense of Homer (Ford 2007: 282). Almost a century later, even Gracián (2003: 161), the epitome of the Baroque epigone, still allowed for the possibility of improvement: 'Todo está ya en su punto, y el ser persona en el mayor. Más se requiere hoy para un sabio que antiguamente para siete' [Everything is at its pinnacle, particularly the art of being human. A sage must know more today than seven sages in former times]. Needless to say, such advancement would take place within the male, Iberian, author(itative) class (Mayers 2012: 127).[36]

Every historical period produces the art that best fits its worldview. Therefore, teleological statements about any poet representing a 'progression' with respect to previous authors are arbitrary. For our purposes, what matters is not the validity of the argument or lack thereof, but rather the impact that it may have had on Sor Juana. In this respect, her sceptical approach to the 'triple impossibility' topos in *Primero sueño*, read in combination with the rebuttal of gender stereotypes in the *Carta atenagórica*, suggests that she absorbed the rationale behind Scaliger's claim. Sor Juana overcame her anxiety of influence[37] by refusing to accept that the Western canon was a *numerus clausus*.

The episteme that placed European man at the pinnacle of humankind made possible the supremacist discourse that undervalued Sor Juana as a woman and as a Creole. In the *Carta atenagórica*, the nun affirms that her gender is 'tan desacreditado en materia de letras con la común acepción de todo el mundo' [so discredited in intellectual matters, to general acceptance] (Salceda 1994: 412). Creole contemporaries expressed their resentment at metropolitan prejudice.[38] Nonetheless, given the gulf between her status and her empowerment by writing, the nun could not accept male or Iberian superiority (see Franco 1989: xv). *Primero sueño* attests that she paid no heed to these constructs and, indeed, rose above them by emulating the classics. Unlike her admired Phaethon, she would not fall — at least not as a poet.

menos preciosas Indias' [Góngora embarked on the abundant and profitable ocean of the classics, and following safe poles, he found new and unknown routes, like a Columbus of no less precious Indies].
36   Cervantes (1615: 97ʳ): 'Los tiempos mudan las cosas | y perfeccionan las artes | y añadir a lo inventado | no es dificultad notable' [The passage of time changes things | and perfects the arts | and improving on that which has already been invented | is not particularly difficult]. Lope (Vega 2006) would have agreed with him, as evidenced by lines 174–80 of his *Arte nuevo de hacer comedias* [*New Art of Writing Plays*] (1609).
37   To borrow Bloom's title (1973).
38   Espinosa Medrano: 'los europeos sospechan seriamente que los estudios de los hombres del Nuevo Mundo son bárbaros' [Europeans truly suspect that research undertaken by New World Creoles is barbaric] (Tamayo 1982: 325). Similar reproaches can be found in Sigüenza y Góngora (1959: 85).

EPILOGUE: BEYOND EKPHRASIS

Although not every early modern work gave to Phaethon the allegorical significance that he has in *Primero sueño* [*First Dream*], the myth was recurrent in Baroque poetry. For instance, Bernardo de Balbuena (1562–1627), a Spanish-born viceregal poet who was Góngora's exact contemporary, mentions 'Faetón' seven times in *El Bernardo* (1624), usually in the context of mythological sunrises/sunsets or in ekphraseis of works of art.[1] The poem sometimes appears in anthologies of Latin American Gongorism. This seems hardly justifiable since Balbuena wrote the bulk of his epic during the late sixteenth century, before Góngora developed his *nuevo estilo* [new style] (Van Horne 1927: 163).[2] However, although Balbuena was not a Gongorist writer, the *Bernardo* shares four commonalities with the corpus examined in this monograph: (i) it shows a fascination with the 'pictorial' power of language, as evidenced by the fact that 1,550 of the 5,000 octaves of the poem are descriptive (Zulaica 2016: 178); (ii) it lacks any close unity: the digressions and intercalated stories are so tangled, so varied, and so lengthy, that the reader often loses track of the main plot; (iii) it betrays a diglossia between its rich, sensuous imagery and its Counter-Reformation spiritual/devotional ideas (Pierce 1945: 6–8, 12); and (iv) it has an encyclopaedic nature: the poem includes, in a *totum revolutum*, chivalric, mythological, nationalist, religious, romantic, allegorical, philosophical and genealogical themes (Van Horne 1927: 168–73).[3]

In this respect, book XXI has a scene that combines some of the above-mentioned elements. At the castle of Carpio, a mysterious lady (we shall learn later that she is the niece of Orontes, Bernardo's tutor) takes the hero to a mirror that reflects both the past and the future. The scene serves two main purposes. Firstly, it strengthens the link between the *Bernardo* and the chivalric tradition, where magic mirrors are a common device. Secondly, it serves a nationalist goal, for the protagonist sees both

---

1   Lines I, 215.7; VI, 17.5; VI, 104.5; VII, 3.6; VII, 53.3; XVI, 32.3; and XXIII, 109.8.
2   Carilla (1946: 29) started his chapter on Góngora's influence in New Spain with Balbuena, although he himself conceded that 'difícil parece encontrar en él reminiscencias gongorinas' [it seems difficult to find Gongorist traces in his work]. Chevalier (1966: 394–95) proved that stylistic similarities between Góngora and Balbuena are superficial and inconclusive.
3   The subtitle gives a sense of the book's contents (Balbuena 1624): 'Obra toda tejida de una admirable variedad de cosas, antigüedades de España, casas y linajes nobles de ella, costumbres de gentes, geográficas descripciones de las más floridas partes del mundo, fábricas de edificios y suntuosos palacios, jardines, cazas y frescuras, transformaciones y encantamientos de nuevo y peregrino artificio, llenos de sentencias y moralidades' [Work entirely woven of an admirable variety of things, the history of Spain, houses and noble lineages, people's customs, geographical descriptions of the most beautiful parts of the world, construction of buildings and sumptuous palaces, gardens, hunting and pure nature, transformations and enchantments of new and rare artfulness, full of maxims and moralities].

his lineage and the future glory of his offspring (and of Spain) in the 'artificioso espejo' [artful mirror] (Triviños 1980: 318).[4] I refer to Vilà (2014: 469–70) for an exploration of the role of magic in the poem, since a detailed analysis of its book XXI is beyond the scope of this Epilogue. However, I will deploy two of its stanzas (30–31) to sum up my arguments on Gongorism, its relationship with painting and its significance to viceregal poetry. These are the lines where Bernardo sees moving forms in the mirror before the 'dama' [lady] explains their meaning to him (Balbuena 2017: II. 1019–20):

> Ahora el techo y distancias de la sala
> en tal aspecto y reflexión tuviese,
> que cuanto en ella por adorno y gala
> el pincel puso en su cristal se viese;
> o el arte allí a lo natural iguala,
> o con cercos su artífice fingiese
> bullirse tras la clara vidrïera
> encantadas figuras de oro y cera.

> En él se vían notables hermosuras,
> gusto a los ojos y al sentido espanto,
> y por su limpio seno las figuras,
> aunque muertas moverse por encanto;
> y en bellos ademanes y posturas
> dar deleite a la vista y entre tanto
> que Bernardo lo goza desde afuera,
> la dama prosiguió de esta manera.

> [Now the ceiling and the far spaces of the room
> had such an appearance and reflection,
> that the brush included everything that was there for
> ornamentation, so that it would be visible in the glass,
> either art is the equal of nature,
> or its maker simulated with magic forms
> circling behind the clear glass
> enchanted figures of gold and wax.

> Remarkably beautiful things could be seen in it
> a pleasure for the eyes, and a fright for the senses,
> and the figures, although dead,
> moved around its clean surface by enchantment
> and in graceful gestures and postures
> gave delight to the eye, and while
> Bernardo enjoys it from outside
> the lady resumes her explanation.]

Let us unpack this passage in five parts. Firstly, as pointed out by Fernández (2006: 19), the mirror of the *Bernardo* is the product of an art that matches nature in its creative might ('o el arte allí a lo natural iguala'). Shortly thereafter, Balbuena

---

4   Ariosto's (1992: I. 49–74) genealogical exaltation of the d'Este family in the *Orlando furioso* is a clear source (Chevalier 1966: 371). Balbuena's passage also brings to mind the magic mirror of the second book of *Clarián de Landanís* (Neri 2007: 159).

describes the marvels 'que este cristal en su artificio encierra' [that this glass contains behind its artfulness]. The lines may be linked to one of the leitmotifs of this monograph. In the Introduction, I noted the imitation of reality as the goal of both painting and poetry.[5] Subsequently, I suggested that the *Soledades* underlines its own *artificio* [artfulness] by representing nature as art. This feature can be read in light of the foreword to Marino's *Adone*, where Chapelain (1988: 34) affirms that 'la vertu de tout artisan, au rang desquels se met le poète, ne se remarque pas par la richesse de la matière, mais par la rareté de son artifice à la traiter' [the virtue of every craftsman, among which I include the poet, does not lie in the richness of the subject, but in the oddity of his artfulness when treating it]. Góngora, Camargo and Sor Juana shared this belief in varying degrees.

In this respect, the verbally sophisticated descriptions of these authors can be linked to what Blanco (1992: 376) terms the 'formalism' of *conceptismo*. According to this scholar, the seventeenth-century theorist Tesauro (1664: 648–50) deployed subjects of little substance (e.g. a dead bee in amber) to show that any topic, no matter how minor, can serve to develop every form of wit. This aesthetic helps explain the Baroque trend to put more emphasis on the folding and unfolding of connections between objects than on the objects in themselves (Deleuze 1988: 5, 1993: 3). Jáuregui's *Antídoto* [*Antidote*] censored the *Soledad primera* for focusing on 'raterías' [trifles] and 'vilezas vulgarísimas' [the most vile vulgarities], i.e. rustic subject-matter with — to his mind — no interest whatsoever (Joiner Gates 1960: 96 and 121). However, Góngora's point was precisely to present a new poetic code that linked objects with mathematical precision, regardless of their inherent nature. At the end of Chapter 2, I illustrated this finding with two concentric spheres, which could be used to understand Gracián's conceptualisation of the *agudeza compuesta* [compound conceit].

If, to paraphrase Wittgenstein (2001: 5), language has as its job the depiction of everything that is the case, then Camargo and Sor Juana also sought this goal with their respective 'worldscapes' (Chapters 4 and 5), which echo the Gracianesque spheres. These figures embody the highest ambition of a *conceptista* writer: to represent the cosmos in a poem as if the whole universe could fit in a conceit. With this comes a tension between the authors' audacity in challenging the cosmic hierarchy and their 'inevitable failure to create anything but a deceptive mirror image', as Plato argued in the *Republic* (book X) (Bergmann 1979: 71). Sor Juana dealt with this strain by facing steadfastly the themes of failure (Phaethon) and the mirror in the lighthouse (Chapter 5). Góngora and Camargo left their poems unfinished and thus invited readers to complement them with their imagination.[6]

5   Balbuena (2011: 274–75): 'Y así dijo muy bien fray Luis de León [...] como la poesía no sea otra cosa que una pintura que habla y todo el estudio y perfección suya consista y esté en imitar la naturaleza' [And so Fray Luis de León very rightly said [...] that poetry is nothing but painting that speaks, and studying and perfecting it consists of imitating nature].
6   Plato (2013: II. 397): ' "take a mirror, if you like, and carry it round with you everywhere. In no time you will make a sun and the heavenly bodies, the earth, yourself, and all the other living creatures, objects and plants that we've just been talking about." "Things we can perceive, yes," he said, "but not, I think, the things that are real in the true sense." '

In a 1647 letter to his patron Paul Fréart de Chantelou, the artist Poussin (1824: 278) linked the poet's 'merveilleux artifice' [wonderful artfulness] with his ability to 'mettre devant les yeux les choses qu'il décrit' [set before the eyes the things he describes], which he also calls 'des objets à peindre' [the objects to be painted]. This connection between *artificio* and visual suggestiveness takes me to the second point from Balbuena's *Bernardo*: the magic mirror deploys tools from painting ('pincel') in order to bring pleasure to the eyes of the beholder ('gusto a los ojos', 'dar deleite a la vista'). From the viewpoint of the Greek ideal of *enargeia*, in which vivid descriptions make the reader feel like an eyewitness, the Lucretian attention to detail of these Hispanic authors, who deem no subject unworthy of treatment, could not be more apt.[7] Hence, their focus on digressive ekphraseis at the expense of plot-based narratives. This is particularly the case with Sor Juana, who chose an 'unpoetic' philosophical subject that she then coloured with abundant descriptions. While possibly less so with Camargo given his sacred topic, the comparison with his Ignatian predecessors revealed that his most remarkable contributions arose at the margins of his meandering discourse. This also holds true for Góngora, as we saw when studying the juxtaposition of ekphrasis and teichoscopy as a new lens through which to read the *Soledades*' union of the epic and the bucolic, the poetic and the pictorial (Chapters 1 and 2).

Thirdly, Balbuena's paintbrush decorates the magic mirror with 'adorno y gala'. In this respect, all of these poets are virtuosos in linguistic adornment. For Góngora, Camargo and Sor Juana, the world of sensory delights encompasses everything from the simplest forms of nature (ekphrasis *lato sensu*) to the visual arts (ekphrasis *sensu stricto*). Their concept of beauty, like that of the Baroque generally, is one of elaborate and rich decoration at the service of grandeur (Priest 1967: xxiii–xxvii). It was on this basis that the seventeenth century assessed the virtues of an author, as is evidenced by the enthusiasm of Góngora's early reader Villar (2016: 37), who admired the *Soledades* for 'la valentía y viveza con que logra en floreadas pinturas las mayores alusiones que presumió formar la idea' [the boldness and liveliness with which Góngora delivers, in flowery paintings, the greatest allusions that the Idea could produce]. He does not just praise the *enargeia* of the poem but also its flowery Idea of beauty. Camargo and Sor Juana would have approved of this poetic standard, which they complemented with an ideological 'twist'.

As we saw, the exuberance of its descriptions becomes one of the main reasons for writing, and even for reading, the *San Ignacio* (Mayers 2009: 6). Indeed, given their length and Marinist cult of *préciosité*, Camargo's 'diluted' ekphrases make us lose sight of the gist of the epic (theoretically, the life of Ignatius of Loyola), disclosing an unexpected potential. Literary hedonism, art for art's sake *avant la lettre*, threatens to take over the Counter-Reformation trenches. Camargo's diglossia anticipates that of Sor Juana. After lifting *Primero sueño*'s veil of euphuism, we found a similar 'venting' function in her ekphrases, which is comparable to Méndez Plancarte's (1951: xxxi) 'válvula desahogante'. Moreover, the nun uses the motif as a

---

7   Chapelain (1988: 41): 'pour mettre les choses devant les yeux, il faut descendre aux particularités' [to set things before the readers' eyes, one must descend to particularities].

meta-aesthetic instrument to reveal inner tensions in her life (patriarchy vs. proto-feminism), time (Baroque vs. Enlightenment) and space (Spain vs. New Spain). The result is no small achievement and attests to the Gongorist ideal of reaching the maximum verbal and semantic condensation, offering multiple and often opposing meanings in few lines (*multum in parvo*) [less is more].

Given the ornate style, abundant Latinisms and imitation of Latin syntax (hyperbaton) typical of Gongorism, the *Soledades*, *San Ignacio* and *Primero sueño* pose a challenge to readers.[8] This takes me to the fourth point from the *Bernardo* to which I want to draw attention: the fact that the 'notables hermosuras' of the mirror do not only produce pleasure but also aversion ('y al sentido espanto'). In the preaching manual *Retórica cristiana...* [*Christian Rhetoric...*] (1647), the Jesuit Joan Baptista Escardó summarised his opposition to the *nuevo estilo* in these terms: 'nuestra era en que está más en su punto poner mucho cuidado en predicar pensamientos encarecidos y agudezas muy sutiles, acompañadas de un lenguaje tan culto o, por mejor decir, oculto, que casi se pierde de vista' [our era in which one must be very careful when preaching valuable thoughts and very subtle conceits, using a language so cultured or, I should rather say, occult, that it becomes almost incomprehensible] (Solervicens 2012: 186). The pun between euphuism ('culto') and inscrutability ('oculto') points out the risk of leaving readers behind. The *Carta en respuesta* addressed these concerns directly. Góngora allegedly approved of Ovid's difficulty because it sharpened the wit, and he claimed the same merit for his own complexity (Jones 1963: 1).

The texture of these Gongorist works is dense indeed. However, their intricacy is different from the private elusiveness of, say, surrealist poetry, which is alien to the *conceptista* consistency of meaning. The language of Góngora, Camargo and Sor Juana retains the strict forthrightness and determination to articulate a discourse that was typical of classic and Baroque literature's self-imposed Horatian duty to instruct (*prodesse*) as well as to entertain (*delectare*). This fact finds its counterpart in the early modern commentators' trust in the text's determinacy of meaning. Gongorist scholars such as Pellicer, Salcedo Coronel and Serrano de Paz were convinced that there is always a correct explanation, a key to the sense of every line in the *Soledades*, if only it can be discerned. Poets and readers alike shared this cultural attitude as part of a broader *Weltanschauung* where the notion of mimesis affected not only their approach to texts, but also their whole way of perceiving reality (Lawrance 2013: 113).[9]

---

8   Góngora's attributed *Carta en respuesta* [*Letter in Response*] is relevant in this respect: 'siendo lance forzoso venerar que nuestra lengua a costa de mi trabajo haya llegado a la perfección y alteza de la latina' [one must admit that Spanish has reached the perfection and height of Latin thanks to my work] (Carreira 1999: 2). Sabena and Stein (2016: 10) suggest that Góngora's difficulty may have delayed the acceptance of his *nuevo estilo* in viceregal America.

9   I refer to Álvarez de Lugo's commentary on *Primero sueño*: 'Las tinieblas más obscuras con que quiso sor Juana Inés de la Cruz (ingenio bien conocido) dar a conocer a todos la claridad de su ingenio (en un sueño que finge), ya menos tenebrosas con la luz de algún comento' [The most obscure darkness with which Sor Juana Inés de la Cruz (well-known author) wanted to convey the clarity of her wit (in a dream that she crafts), already less obscure with the light of some commentary] (Sánchez Robayna 1991: 158).

Fifthly, the arts of perception, to borrow Robbins' title (2007), are also essential to Balbuena's passage and its significance to Gongorism. The magic mirror employs the expressive power and illusionism of painting in order to produce painstaking images where none existed before ('encantadas figuras de oro y cera', 'aunque muertas moverse por encanto'). This is the bedrock from which Sor Juana created the 'linterna mágica' (line 873) of *Primero sueño*, although there is a significant difference between both artefacts: Balbuena's mirror is a product of magic, whereas Sor Juana's lantern is an invention based on the interplay of light, shade, and various types of lenses and mirrors. Sor Juana emphasises the still underdeveloped nature of the technology that projects the 'fingidas' [feigned] figures onto the wall. The magic lantern does not produce a stable light (line 877: 'trémulos reflejos') [tremulous reflections] and requires beholders to keep a distance in order to preserve the illusion (lines 878–79: 'los competentes lejos | guardando de la docta perspectiva') [the distance mandated by | a learned perspective] (More 2016: 64). Despite these limitations, the invention is yet another example of art matching nature, as the lantern represents images by rationalising space (Fernández 2006: 19–21). In the words of Balbuena (1624: 249ᵛ): 'a toda la materia vence el arte' [art can portray any subject].

In the last volume of a novel that starts with a magic lantern representing chivalric scenes, *In Search of Lost Time*, Proust (1981: III. 931) argued that 'style for the writer, no less than colour for the painter, is a question not of technique but of vision'. Language does not give names to pre-existing things: it articulates our experience of the world. Thus, if Gongorism is understood not only as a way of writing but also as a way of seeing, then this style could be compared with the figures reflected upon the walls of a dark chamber. When Camargo and Sor Juana left the *camera obscura* of the *Soledades*, their Spanish American surroundings may have appeared transformed and transfigured. Having read so much Góngora in terms of the world, they could then see the world in terms of Góngora. Indeed, they both succeeded at looking at things with the mindset of their poetic mentor, scanning motifs to find artistic and conceitful 'bricks' in order to erect their own poems.[10]

Both Camargo and Sor Juana aimed to produce poetry 'newly formed from the familiar', to paraphrase Horace (2011: 112).[11] To this end, the imitation of one model, no matter how authoritative, would not have sufficed. Instead of the *imitatio simplex*, the *imitatio multiplex* is more suitable to describe their poetics. A wealth of classic and modern European works was crucial to the formation of viceregal poetry. In his 'Isagoge a los lectores' [Foreword to my Readers] to the hagiographic epic *Thomasíada* [*Thomasiad*] (Guatemala, 1667), which was thus entitled 'imitando a Homero' [imitating Homer], Sáenz Ovecuri affirmed that 'siempre me precié de imitar a los otros, y en especial, a los antiguos' [I was always proud of imitating others, and especially, the ancients]. His canon of the best poets includes, among

10   For more information on the *camera obscura* and its importance for seventeenth-century theories of the visual, I refer to Bergmann (2013a: 147–48, and 2013b: 115–18), whose essays include references to Góngora and Sor Juana. This paragraph also follows Gombrich (1978: 78 and 258).

11   *Ars poetica*, line 240: '*ex noto fictum carmen sequar*'. The next paragraphs on *imitatio* are indebted to Ponce Cárdenas (2016).

others, Virgil, Ovid, Garcilaso, Camões, Lope, Quevedo and 'todo Don Luis de Góngora' [everything Góngora]. This quotation illustrates explicitly what I have showed in Chapters 3–6: viceregal authors were engaged in a dialogue that was not limited to the Spanish context. Rather, it included the whole European tradition, particularly the legacy of the Renaissance (Cacho 2015: 207). In the case of Sor Juana, the melting pot also welcomed components of native American cultures. The literary strategies of these viceregal poets secured them a place within the Western canon, while emphasising their sense of cultural distinctness, and distance from Europe.

Moreover, as we concluded after examining Espinosa Medrano's reference to the 'papagayo' [parrot] in the *Apologético en favor de Don Luis de Góngora [Defence of Góngora]* (Chapter 3), Creoles did not limit themselves to mirroring what they received from Europe.[12] Instead, they combined creatively their multiple sources in order to produce something new. In his *Compendio apologético en alabanza de la poesía [Apologetic Compendium in Praise of Poetry]*, following friar Jerónimo Román, Balbuena (2011: 275) explained the *imitatio multiplex* with a classic bee metaphor: 'los tales poetas fueron alabados en lo antiguo y siempre lo merecieron ser, y comparados en las figuras jeroglíficas a la abeja: que de la misma manera que ella pone cuidado y solicitud en hacer sus panales de miel, así los poetas dan la dulzura de su decir, con grande invención y artificio' [these poets were praised in antiquity and always deserved to be, and were also compared in their hieroglyphic figures to the bee: for, in the same way that the bee makes honeycombs, carefully and meticulously, so poets offer their sweet sayings, with great invention and artfulness].[13]

Traditionally, the main point of the topos was that, just as bees sip the nectar of different flowers to produce honey, poets read and absorb various models in order to write their works. However, Balbuena takes this notion for granted and emphasises the artfulness of the whole process. Sor Juana would have approved of his comparison of poetry with hieroglyphs. In any case, the bee metaphor fits my argument on *imitatio* perfectly. Creoles produced a Baroque corpus that rethought and renewed the European heritage in all its complexity. On certain occasions, this was done boldly (*Primero sueño*), or even extravagantly (*San Ignacio*). Nevertheless, Sor Juana and Camargo did not place themselves against or outside the Western tradition. Instead, they enriched it by developing new hybrid forms.

Furthermore, Balbuena's 'figuras jeroglíficas' are in line with the above-mentioned *Carta en respuesta*, which revealed an understanding of poetic artefacts as intricate spaces of signification that, following Beverley (1980: 15), could even

---

12   Arguably, they would have endorsed Poliziano's letter (c. 1485–1488) to Paolo Cortese: 'In my view, anyone who composes by imitation alone is like a parrot or a magpie, seeming to voice what he does not understand' (DellaNeva 2007: 3). Footnote 240 in Espinosa Medrano (2017) contains more information on the parrot topos.

13   The topos harks back to Seneca's epistle LXXXIV (1920: II. 276–85). Petrarch used it in a letter to Boccaccio. So did Erasmus in his *Ciceronianus* (Reiss 2002: 349). The bee image is a leitmotif in Góngora (Ponce Cárdenas 2016: 47), and can also be found in Espinosa Medrano (2017: section XII, paragraph 122) and Sigüenza y Góngora (1984: 193–94). I refer to García Galiano (1992) for a study of the poetic *imitatio* in the Renaissance.

be compared to labyrinths.[14] As we saw in Chapter 1, and to paraphrase Gombrich (2002: 323–24), there must always be two sides to poetic innovations: the writer who introduces them and the readership that accepts the challenge. Readers are more willing to make this effort when a *nuevo estilo* has already acquired prestige. There is no doubt that Camargo and Sor Juana lived in such a period. By embracing Gongorism, they implicitly appealed to the reputation of Góngora to justify their poetic experimentation and even their rebelliousness. Early readers found the *Soledades* hard to understand. They had not yet been trained to interpret poetry as the exploration of language's combinatory possibilities (Chapter 2). However, the *Soledades* formed, fashioned and enlarged a public for Gongorism throughout the seventeenth century. When the *San Ignacio* (Camargo 1666) and *Primero sueño* (Cruz 1692) were published, the Hispanic world benefited from something not to be found, to the same extent, when Góngora circulated manuscript copies of his *silva* (c. 1613): namely, an appreciative audience. From this viewpoint, the *Soledades* created its own posterity.

As is well known, this interest ended with the dawn of the Enlightenment. Neoclassical tastemakers introduced a *cordon sanitaire* around Gongorism. For more than two centuries, readers ignored this corpus. It seemed that Gracián's (2001a: I. 63) architecture of wit had not given rise to an artful mechanism of conceits admired by acolytes, but to unvisited obelisks in a desert. In this respect, Proust (1981: I. 572), who once compared his *Recherche* to a cathedral, wrote the following reflection: 'since one's contemporaries are incapable of the necessary detachment, works written for posterity should be read by posterity alone, like certain pictures which one cannot appreciate when one stands too close to them'.[15] The allusion to the Horatian *ut pictura poesis* [poetry is like painting] insightfully illustrates how the distance required to appreciate Gongorism in all its depth was primordially temporal.

Today, unencumbered by anti-Baroque prejudices, we can understand what Gongorism offered to Spanish American poets: an instrument to think and to create with liberty. Camargo and Sor Juana followed the *nuevo estilo* while exploiting creatively the *Soledades*' panorama of illusions. Their poetic achievements were so remarkable that Góngora's findings seem even more relevant in retrospect. In the ruins of great unfinished constructions, the Idea of the blueprint speaks more impressively than in lesser buildings, no matter how well preserved they may be (Benjamin 1977: 235). The writer's right to incompletion does not prevent others continuing the task. Perhaps for this reason, Góngora may have been pleased 'de haber dado principio a algo' [to have started something] (Carreira 1999: 2). Initially, he nurtured the poetry of his followers. Afterwards, it was in their hands that

---

14   Vázquez Siruela: 'cuánta necesidad tienen los poetas de este hilo de oro, que guíe sin error a los demás por sus laberintos' [poets have a great need for this golden thread of exegetes, which guides readers unerringly through their labyrinths] (Cerdan and Vitse 1995: 104). Camargo's line 'arquitecto gentil de laberintos' [gentle architect of labyrinths] (*San Ignacio*, book I, canto I, XXXIII.8) could be read as his portrait of a poet.

15   Proust's reflection can be compared to the distance required to appreciate the Venetian *pittura a macchia* (Chapter 1) and to the figures of Sor Juana's magic lantern (Chapter 5).

Gongorism grew. From the fragments of the *Soledades* to the fragments of the *San Ignacio* and *Primero sueño*, these poems were milestones in an unending process: the reshuffling and rebuilding of the universe of signs.

~

BIBLIOGRAPHY

ACOSTA, JOSÉ DE. 1590. *Historia natural y moral de las Indias* (Sevilla: Juan de León)

ACUÑA, LUIS ALBERTO. 1964. *Diccionario biográfico de artistas que trabajaron en el Nuevo Reino de Granada* (Bogotá: Instituto Colombiano de Cultura Hispánica)

ADORNO, ROLENA. 1993. 'Reconsidering Colonial Discourse for Sixteenth- and Seventeenth-Century Spanish America', *Latin American Research Review*, 28: 135–45

ALATORRE, ANTONIO. 1993. 'Lectura del *Primero sueño*', in *Y diversa de mí misma entre vuestras plumas ando. Homenaje internacional a sor Juana Inés de la Cruz*, ed. by Sara Poot Herrera (México, D.F.: El Colegio de México), pp. 101–26

——. 1995. 'Notas al *Primero sueño* de Sor Juana', *Nueva Revista de Filología Hispánica*, 43: 379–407

—— (ed.). 2012. *Obras completas de Sor Juana Inés de la Cruz. I. Lírica personal* (México, D.F.: Fondo de Cultura Económica)

ALONSO, DÁMASO. 1955. *Estudios y ensayos gongorinos* (Madrid: Gredos)

ALPERS, SVETLANA. 1983. *The Art of Describing: Dutch Art of the Seventeenth Century* (London: Penguin)

ÁLVAREZ, MARÍA CECILIA. 2008. 'Un repinte con historia: *La Trinidad* de Gregorio Vásquez', in *El oficio del pintor: Nuevas miradas a la obra de Gregorio Vásquez*, ed. by Constanza Toquica (Bogotá: Ministerio de Cultura de Colombia), pp. 91–92

ANASTÁCIO, VANDA. 2013. 'Literary Exchange in the Portuguese-Brazilian Atlantic before 1822', in *Theorising the Ibero-American Atlantic*, ed. by Harald Braun and Lisa Vollendorf (Leiden/Boston: Brill), pp. 159–71

ANDREWS, MALCOLM. 1999. *Landscape and Western Art* (Oxford: Oxford University Press)

AQUINAS, THOMAS. 1505. *Tertia pars summe sancti Thome* (Venice: Boneto Locatelli)

ARELLANO, IGNACIO. 2016. 'Para la edición del *Poema heroico de San Ignacio* de Domínguez Camargo, hipergongorino indiano', *Revista de crítica literaria latinoamericana*, 42: 119–42

ARENAL, ELECTA, and AMANDA POWELL (eds.). 2009. *The Answer / La Respuesta: Including Sor Filotea's Letter and New Selected Poems / Sor Juana Inés de La Cruz* (New York: Feminist Press at the City University of New York)

ARIOSTO, LUDOVICO. 1992. *Orlando furioso*, 2 vols, ed. by Lanfranco Caretti (Torino: Einaudi)

ARMAS, FREDERICK DE. 1997. 'The Art of Making Gods: Hermeticism and Spectacle in Calderón's *La fiera, el rayo y la piedra*', in *The Calderonian Stage: Body and Soul*, ed. by Manuel Delgado (Lewisburg/London: Bucknell University Press), pp. 45–54

——. 2006. 'Isis y el silencio hermético en *El vergonzoso en palacio* de Tirso de Molina', in *Tirso, escuela de discreción: actas del Congreso Internacional organizado por el GRISO, de la Universidad de Navarra, y el Departamento de Anglística, Germanística y Romanística de la Universidad de Copenhague (Copenhague, 10–11 de mayo de 2006)*, ed. by Eva Galar and Blanca Oteiza (Madrid/Pamplona: GRISO, Universidad de Navarra), pp. 9–26

ARROM, JOSÉ JUAN, and JOSÉ MANUEL RIVAS SACCONI. 1959. 'La *Laurea crítica* de Fernando Fernández de Valenzuela, primera obra teatral colombiana', *Thesaurus*, 14: 161–85

ARTIGAS, MIGUEL. 1925. *Don Luis de Góngora y Argote: biografía y estudio crítico* (Madrid: Tipografía de la Revista de Archivos)

AUGUSTINE OF HIPPO. 1958. *On Christian Doctrine*, ed. by Durant Waite Robertson (Indianapolis: Bobbs–Merrill)

BAKHOUCHE, BÉATRICE, FRÉDÉRIC FAUQUIER, and BRIGITTE PÉREZ-JEAN (eds.). 2003. *Picatrix: un traité de magie médiéval* (Turnhout, Belgium: Brepols)

BALBUENA, BERNARDO DE. 1624. *El Bernardo, o victoria de Roncesvalles. Poema heroico* (Madrid: Diego Flamenco)

——. 2011. *Grandeza mexicana*, ed. by Asima F. X. Saad Maura (Madrid: Cátedra)

——. 2017. *El Bernardo*, 2 vols, ed. by Martín Zulaica (Siero: Ars Poetica)

BALDI, BERNARDINO. 1992. *Egloghe miste*, ed. by Domenico Chiodo (Torino: Edizioni RES)

BARASCH, MOSHE. 1978. *Light and Color in the Italian Renaissance Theory of Art* (New York: New York University Press)

BASS, LAURA. 2009. 'Imitación e ingenio: *El amar su propia muerte* de Juan de Espinosa Medrano y la comedia nueva', *Lexis*, 33: 5–31

BAUVAL, ROBERT. 2014. *Secret Chamber Revisited: The Quest for the Lost Knowledge of Ancient Egypt* (Rochester, Vermont: Bear & Company)

BEAUPIED, AÍDA. 1997. *Narciso hermético. Sor Juana Inés de la Cruz y José Lezama Lima* (Liverpool: Liverpool University Press)

BÉHAR, ROLAND. 2009. 'Visualidad y Barroco: Góngora', in *Congreso Internacional Andalucía Barroca: actas*, 4 vols, ed. by Alfredo J. Morales, III, pp. 17–30

BELLINI, GIUSEPPE. 1991. 'Presencia de la literatura italiana en la América hispana de los siglos XVI y XVII', in *España e Italia: un encuentro de culturas en el nuevo mundo. Atti del colloquio italo–spagnolo (Barcellona, 20–22 aprile 1989)* (Roma: Bulzoni), pp. 37–57

BELMONTE BERMÚDEZ, LUIS DE. 1609. *Vida del padre maestro Ignacio de Loyola, fundador de la Compañía de Jesús* (México: Imprenta de Gerónimo Balli)

BENÍTEZ I RIERA, JOSEP M. 1996. *Jesuïtes i Catalunya: Fets i figures* (Barcelona: Publicacions de l'Abadia de Montserrat)

BENJAMIN, WALTER. 1977. *The Origin of German Tragic Drama*, trans. by John Osborne (London: NLB)

BENOIST, VALÉRIE. 1999. ' "El escribirlo no parte de la osadía": tradición y mímica en la loa para *El divino Narciso* de Sor Juana Inés de la Cruz', *Latin American Theatre Review*, 33: 73–84

BERGMANN, EMILIE. 1979. *Art Inscribed: Essays on Ekphrasis in Spanish Golden Age Poetry* (Cambridge, Massachusetts: Harvard University Press)

——. 2013A. 'Embodying the Visual, Visualizing Sound in Sor Juana Inés de la Cruz's *Primero sueño*', in *Objects of Culture in the Literature of Imperial Spain*, ed. by Mary Barnard and Frederick de Armas (Toronto: University of Toronto Press)

——. 2013B. 'Sor Juana, Góngora and Ideologies of Perception', *Calíope*, 18: 113–35

BERGMANN, EMILIE, and STACEY SCHLAU (eds.). 2017. *The Routledge Research Companion to the Works of Sor Juana Inés de La Cruz* (New York: Routledge)

BERNUCCI, LEOPOLDO M. 1998. 'Unfulfilled Promises: Epic and Hagiography in Hernando Domínguez Camargo's *Poema heroico*', *Calíope*, 4: 270–82

BEVERLEY, JOHN. 1980. *Aspects of Góngora's Soledades* (Amsterdam: John Benjamins Publishing Company)

——. 2008. *Essays on the Literary Baroque in Spain and Spanish America* (Woodbridge: Tamesis)

BHABHA, HOMI K. 2004. *The Location of Culture* (London/New York: Routledge)

BLANCO, MERCEDES. 1988. 'El mecanismo de la ocultación. Análisis de un ejemplo de agudeza', *Criticón*, 43: 13–36

——. 1992. *Les rhétoriques de la pointe: Baltasar Gracián et le conceptisme en Europe* (Geneva: Slatkine)

——. 1996. 'Lienzo de Flandes: las *Soledades* y el paisaje pictórico', in *Actas del IV Congreso Internacional de la Asociación Internacional Siglo de Oro*, 2 vols, ed. by María Cruz García de Enterría and Alicia Cordón Mesa (Alcalá de Henares: Universidad de Alcalá), i, pp. 263–74

——. 2006. 'Les *Solitudes* de Góngora: une poétique du paysage?', in *Nature et paysages: l'émergence d'une nouvelle subjectivité à la Renaissance*, ed. by Dominique de Courcelles and Jean-Pierre Bat (Paris: École nationale des chartes), pp. 117–38

——. 2012A. 'El paisaje erótico entre poesía y pintura', *Criticón*, 114: 101–37

——. 2012B. *Góngora heroico: las Soledades y la tradición épica* (Madrid: Centro de Estudios Europa Hispánica)

——. 2012C. *Góngora o la invención de una lengua* (León: Universidad de León)

BLECUA, JOSÉ MANUEL (ed.). 1945. *Cancionero de 1628* (Madrid: Consejo Superior de Investigaciones Científicas)

BLOOM, HAROLD. 1973. *The Anxiety of Influence: A Theory of Poetry* (New York: Oxford University Press)

BLUMENBERG, HANS. 1995. *Naufragio con espectador*, trans. by Jorge Vigil (Madrid: Visor)

BOLLANDUS, JOHANNES, and JAN TOLLENAER (eds.). 1640. *Imago primi saeculi Societatis Jesu a provincia Flandro-Belgica eiusdem Societatis repraesentata* (Antwerp: Balthasar Moretus)

BONILLA, RAFAEL. 2010. 'Góngora: ¿Homero español?', in *Cuenca Capta: los libros griegos del s. XVI en el Seminario Conciliar de San Julián*, ed. by Israel Muñoz, Rafael Bonilla, and Rafael Fernández (Cuenca: Servicio de Publicaciones de la Diputación de Cuenca), pp. 207–48

BORGES, JORGE LUIS. 1989. *Obras completas*, 2 vols, ed. by Carlos V. Frías (Buenos Aires: Emecé)

BOSTEELS, BRUNO. 1998. 'From Text to Territory: Félix Guattari's Cartographies of the Unconscious', in *Deleuze & Guattari: New Mappings in Politics, Philosophy, and Culture*, ed. by Eleanor Kaufman and Kevin Jon Heller (Minneapolis/London: University of Minnesota Press), pp. 145–74

BOTELHO DE OLIVEIRA, MANUEL. 2005. *Música do Parnaso*, ed. by Ivan Teixeira (Cotia, São Paulo: Ateliê Editorial)

BRAUN, HARALD, and JESÚS PÉREZ MAGALLÓN. 2016. 'Introduction', in *The Transatlantic Hispanic Baroque: Complex Identities in the Atlantic World*, ed. by Harald Braun and Jesús Pérez Magallón (London/New York: Routledge), pp. 1–14

BROOKE, ALICE. 2012. 'Between Two Worlds: Baroque Spectacle and Enlightenment Thought in the *autos sacramentales* by Sor Juana Inés de la Cruz (1648–1695)' (unpublished doctoral thesis: University of Oxford)

——. 2018. *The Autos Sacramentales of Sor Juana Inés de La Cruz: Natural Philosophy and Sacramental Theology* (Oxford: Oxford University Press)

BROWN, JONATHAN. 1991. *The Golden Age of Painting in Spain* (New Haven/London: Yale University Press)

BROWN, RAYMOND EDWARD. 1998. *The Death of the Messiah*, 2 vols (New York/London: Doubleday)

BUTRÓN, JUAN DE. 1626. *Discursos apologéticos, en que se defiende la ingenuidad del arte de la pintura* (Madrid: Luis Sánchez)

BUXÓ, JOSÉ PASCUAL. 1960. *Góngora en la poesía novohispana* (México, D.F.: Universidad Nacional Autónoma de México)

——. 1993. *El enamorado de Sor Juana: Francisco Álvarez de Velasco Zorrilla y su Carta laudatoria (1698) a Sor Juana Inés de la Cruz* (México, D.F.: Universidad Nacional Autónoma de México)

——. 1996. 'Prólogo', in *Premio nacional de ensayo Sor Juana Inés de la Cruz (1995)* (Toluca: Instituto Mexiquense de Cultura), pp. 1–17

——. 2004A. 'El *Sueño* de Sor Juana: reflexión y espectáculo', in *Memoria de la palabra: Actas del VI Congreso de la Asociación Internacional Siglo de Oro*, ed. by María-Luisa Lobato and

Francisco Domínguez Matito (Madrid/Frankfurt am Main: Iberoamericana/Vervuert), pp. 89–110

——. 2004B. 'Góngora y Sor Juana: *ut pictura poesis*', *Prolija Memoria: Estudios de Cultura Virreinal*, 1: 29–54

——. 2006A. 'Combates de la luz y de la sombra en el *Sueño* de sor Juana', *Revista de la Universidad de México*, 30: 12–17

——. 2006B. *Sor Juana Inés de la Cruz. Lectura barroca de la poesía* (Sevilla: Renacimiento)

CABANI, MARIA CRISTINA. 2005. *L'occhio di Polifemo: studi su Pulci, Tasso e Marino* (Pisa: ETS)

CACHO, RODRIGO. 2007. 'Góngora in Arcadia: Sannazaro and the Pastoral Mode of the *Soledades*', *The Romanic Review*, 98: 435–55

——. 2012A. *La esfera del ingenio: las silvas de Quevedo y la tradición europea* (Madrid: Biblioteca Nueva)

——. 2012B. 'Quevedo y la filología de autor: edición de la silva *El pincel*', *Criticón*, 114: 179–212

——. 2015. 'Balbuena's *Grandeza mexicana* and the American Georgic', *Colonial Latin American Review*, 24: 190–214

CALDERÓN DE LA BARCA, PEDRO. 2009. *La hija del aire*, ed. by Francisco Ruiz Ramón (Madrid: Cátedra)

CALLEJO, ALFONSO. 1986. 'Tradición pastoril-piscatoria y menosprecio de corte en las *Soledades* de Góngora', in *Cervantes and the Pastoral*, ed. by José J. Labrador Herraiz and Juan Fernández Jiménez (Cleveland: Cleveland State University), pp. 37–50

CAMARGO, HERNANDO DOMÍNGUEZ. 1666. *San Ignacio de Loyola, fundador de la Compañía de Jesús. Poema heroico* (Madrid: José Fernández de Buendía)

CAMÕES, LUIS DE. 1834. *Obras completas*, 2 vols, ed. by J. D. Barreto and J. G. Monteiro (Hamburg: Langhoff)

CAMPANELLA, TOMMASO. 1981. *La Città Del Sole: Dialogo Poetico / The City of the Sun: A Poetical Dialogue*, ed. by Daniel John Donno (Berkeley: University of California Press)

CAMPO, ROBERTO E. 1998. *Ronsard's Contentious Sisters: The Paragone between Poetry and Painting in the Works of Pierre de Ronsard* (Chapel Hill: U.N.C. Department of Romance Languages)

CANCELLIER, ANTONELLA. 2000. 'Un banchetto italiano nell'epica barocca ispanoamericana: l'esempio di Hernando Domínguez Camargo in *San Ignacio de Loyola. Poema heroico*', in *Soavi sapori della cultura italiana*, ed. by Bart Van den Bossche, Michel Bastiaensen, and Corinna Salvadori Lonergan (Firenze: Franco Cesati Editore), pp. 27–35

CARDUCHO, VICENTE. 1865. *Diálogos de la pintura* (Madrid: Imprenta de M. Galiano)

CARILLA, EMILIO. 1946. *El gongorismo en América* (Buenos Aires: Universidad de Buenos Aires)

——. 1948. *Hernando Domínguez Camargo* (Buenos Aires: R. Medina)

CARREIRA, ANTONIO (ed.). 1999. *Luis de Góngora. Epistolario completo* (Zaragoza: Libros Pórtico)

——. 2018. 'Góngora en los orígenes de la poesía brasileña: el caso de Gregorio de Matos', *Bulletin hispanique*, 120: 1–17

CARREÑO, ANTONIO (ed.). 1982. *Romances / Luis de Góngora* (Madrid: Cátedra)

CARRUTHERS, MARY J. 2008. *The Book of Memory: A Study of Memory in Medieval Culture* (Cambridge/New York: Cambridge University Press)

CARVAJAL Y ROBLES, RODRIGO DE. 1950. *Fiestas de Lima por el nacimiento del príncipe Baltasar Carlos*, ed. by Francisco López Estrada (Sevilla: Escuela de Estudios Hispano-Americanos)

——. 2000. *Poema heroico del asalto y conquista de Antequera*, ed. by Bautista Martínez Iniesta (Málaga: Servicio de Publicaciones de la Universidad de Málaga)

CASCALES, FRANCISCO DE. 1975. *Tablas poéticas*, ed. by Benito Brancaforte (Madrid: Espasa-Calpe)

CASTELLANOS, JUAN DE. 1857. *Elegías de varones ilustres de Indias*, ed. by Buenaventura Carlos Aribau (Madrid: M. Rivadeneyra)

CASTELLVÍ LAUKAMP, LUIS. 2015A. 'Food for Thought: The Fruit Still Life in Góngora's *Polifemo*', *Bulletin of Hispanic Studies*, 92: 629–44

——. 2015B. 'Presentación', in *Poema heroico y otras flores poéticas. Hernando Domínguez Camargo* (Bogotá: Ministerio de Cultura, Biblioteca Nacional de Colombia), pp. 9–16

——. 2016. 'Ekphrasis Meets Teichoscopy: The Panoramic Landscape in Góngora's *Soledad Primera*', *Hispanic Research Journal*, 17: 473–88

——. 2019. 'Sor Juana's Diglossia: The Pyramids of *Primero sueño*', *Bulletin of Spanish Studies*, 96: 1195–1219

CASTRO-KLARÉN, SARA. 2011. *The Narrow Pass of Our Nerves. Writing, Coloniality and Postcolonial Theory* (Madrid/Frankfurt am Main: Iberoamericana/Vervuert)

CATALÁ, RAFAEL. 1987. *Para una lectura americana del barroco mexicano: Sor Juana Inés de la Cruz & Sigüenza y Góngora* (Minneapolis: Prisma Institute)

CERDAN, FRANCIS, and MARC VITSE (eds.). 1995. *Autour des Solitudes / En torno a las Soledades de don Luis de Góngora: actes de la journée d'études tenue à Toulouse, le 25 novembre 1994, à l'occasion de la parution de l'Hommage à Robert Jammes* (Toulouse: Presses Universitaires du Mirail)

CERVANTES, MIGUEL DE. 1615. *Ocho comedias y ocho entremeses nuevos, nunca representados* (Madrid: Viuda de Alonso Martín)

CHANG-RODRÍGUEZ, RAQUEL (ed.). 2009. *Discurso en loor de la poesía / Epístola a Belardo* (Lima: Pontificia Universidad Católica del Peru)

CHAPELAIN, JEAN. 1988. 'Lettre ou discours de M. Chapelain a Monsieur Favereau', in *L'Adone*, 2 vols (Milano: Adelphi), I, pp. 11–45

CHÂTILLON, WALTER OF. 2007. *The Alexandreis: A Twelfth-Century Epic*, trans. by David Townsend (Peterborough, Ontario: Broadview Press)

CHEMRIS, CRYSTAL ANNE. 2008. *Góngora's Soledades and the Problem of Modernity* (Woodbridge: Tamesis)

CHEVALIER, MAXIME. 1966. *L'Arioste en Espagne, 1530–1650: recherches sur l'influence du Roland furieux* (Bordeaux: Féret)

CICERO. 2001. *On the Ideal Orator (De Oratore)*, ed. by James M. May and Jakob Wisse (New York: Oxford University Press)

CIOCCHINI, HÉCTOR. 1960. *Góngora y la tradición de los emblemas* (Bahía Blanca: Instituto de Humanidades, Universidad Nacional del Sur)

CIORAN, E. M. 1995. *Tears and Saints*, trans. by Ilinca Zarifopol-Johnston (Chicago: University of Chicago Press)

CIPLIJAUSKAITÉ, BIRUTÉ (ed.). 1975. *Sonetos completos / Luis de Góngora* (Madrid: Castalia)

CLUNIES, MARGARET. 2010. *The Cambridge Introduction to the Old Norse-Icelandic Saga* (Cambridge: Cambridge University Press)

COLLINS, MARSHA S. 2002A. 'Mastering the Maze in Góngora's *Soledades*', *Calíope*, 8: 87–102

——. 2002B. *The Soledades, Góngora's Masque of the Imagination* (Columbia/London: University of Missouri Press)

COLOMBÍ-MONGUIÓ, ALICIA DE. 1985. *Petrarquismo peruano: Diego Dávalos y Figueroa y la poesía de la Miscelánea austral* (London: Tamesis)

——. 1986. 'Piélagos de voz: Sobre la poesía de Domínguez Camargo', *Revista de Filología Española*, LXVI: 273–96

COPENHAVER, BRIAN P. (ed.). 1992. *Hermetica: The Greek Corpus Hermeticum and the Latin Asclepius in a New English Translation* (Cambridge/New York: Cambridge University Press)

COVARRUBIAS, SEBASTIÁN DE. 1943. *Tesoro de la lengua castellana o española*, ed. by Martín de Riquer (Barcelona: Horta)

CREIXELL, JUAN. 1914. *San Ignacio en Manresa. Reseña histórica de la vida del santo (1522–1523)* (Barcelona: Tipografía de la viuda de P. Patau)

———. 1946. *San Ignacio de Loyola. Ascética y mística* (Manresa: Imprenta y encuadernaciones de San José)

CRISTINA, MARÍA TERESA. 1989. 'La literatura en la conquista y la colonia', in *Nueva historia de Colombia*, 8 vols, ed. by Jaime Jaramillo Uribe (Bogotá: Planeta), I, pp. 253–99

CRUZ, SOR JUANA INÉS DE LA. 1689. *Inundación castálida de la única poetisa, musa décima, Sor Juana Inés de la Cruz* (Madrid: Juan García Infanzón)

———. 1690A. *Auto sacramental del Divino Narciso* (México: Imprenta de la viuda de Bernardo Calderón)

———. 1690B. *Poemas de la única poetisa americana, musa décima, Sor Juana Inés de la Cruz* (Madrid: Juan García Infanzón)

———. 1692. *Segundo volumen de las obras de Sor Juana Inés de la Cruz* (Sevilla: Tomás López de Haro)

———. 1700. *Fama y obras póstumas del fénix de México, décima musa, poetisa americana, Sor Juana Inés de la Cruz* (Madrid: Imprenta de Manuel Ruiz de Murga)

CURTIUS, ERNST ROBERT. 1990. *European Literature and the Latin Middle Ages*, trans. by Willard R. Trask (Princeton: Princeton University Press)

CUSA, NICHOLAS OF. 1997. *Selected Spiritual Writings*, ed. by H. Lawrence Bond (New York: Paulist Press)

DARST, DAVID H. 1998. *Converting Fiction: Counter Reformational Closure in the Secular Literature of Golden Age Spain* (Chapel Hill: University of North Carolina at Chapel Hill)

DELEUZE, GILLES. 1988. *Le pli: Leibniz et le Baroque* (Paris: Minuit)

———. 1993. *The Fold: Leibniz and the Baroque*, trans. by Tom Conley (Minneapolis: University of Minnesota Press)

DELLANEVA, JOANN (ed.). 2007. *Ciceronian controversies*, trans. by Brian Duvick (Cambridge, Massachusetts: Harvard University Press)

DÍAZ DE RIVAS, PEDRO. 1624. 'Anotaciones y defensas a la primera *Soledad*', Biblioteca Nacional de Madrid, ms. 3726

DÍAZ DEL CASTILLO, BERNAL. 2011. *Historia verdadera de la conquista de la Nueva España*, ed. by Guillermo Serés (Barcelona/Madrid: Galaxia Gutenberg/Círculo de Lectores/Real Academia Española)

DIEGO, GERARDO. 1961. 'La poesía de Hernando Domínguez Camargo en nuevas vísperas', *Thesaurus. Boletín del Instituto Caro y Cuervo*, XVI: 281–310

EBREO, LEONE. 2009. *Dialogues of Love*, ed. by Rossella Pescatori, trans. by Damian Bacich and Rossella Pescatori (Toronto: University of Toronto Press)

ECHAVARREN, ARTURO. 2012. '"Babilonias rebeldes de cristales": el tópico épico de la tempestad en el *Poema heroico* (1666) de Domínguez Camargo', *Bulletin of Spanish Studies*, 89: 33–59

ECHEVERRÍA, BOLÍVAR. 1996. 'El ethos barroco', *Debate Feminista*, 13: 67–87

———. 2008. 'El ethos barroco y los indios', *Revista de Filosofía "Sophia"*, 2: 1–11

EGIDO, AURORA. 1990. *Fronteras de la poesía en el Barroco* (Barcelona: Crítica)

———. 1996. *La rosa del silencio: estudios sobre Gracián* (Madrid: Alianza Editorial)

ELLIOTT, BRIDGET, and ANTHONY PURDY. 2006. 'A Walk Through Heterotopia. Peter Greenaway's Landscape by Numbers', in *Landscape and Film*, ed. by Martin Lefebvre (New York: Routledge), pp. 267–90

ELLIOTT, J. H. 1977. 'Self-Perception and Decline in Early Seventeenth-Century Spain', *Past & Present*, 74: 41–61

——. 2002. *Imperial Spain (1469–1716)* (London: Penguin)

——. 2007. *Empires of the Atlantic World: Britain and Spain in America 1492–1830* (New Haven/ London: Yale University Press)

ESCOBAR Y MENDOZA, ANTONIO DE. 1613. *San Ignacio. Poema heroico* (Valladolid: Francisco Fernandez de Córdoba)

ESPINOSA MEDRANO, JUAN DE. 2017. *Apologético en favor de Don Luis de Góngora*, ed. by Héctor Ruiz (OBVIL) <http://obvil.sorbonne-universite.site/corpus/gongora/1662_apologetico> [accessed 5 October 2019]

ESPINOSA PÓLIT, AURELIO, and GONZALO ZALDUMBIDE (eds.). 1960. *Los dos primeros poetas coloniales ecuatorianos, siglos XVII y XVIII: Antonio de Bastidas y Juan Bautista Aguirre* (Puebla: J. M. Cajica)

EVIA, JACINTO DE (ed.). 1676. *Ramillete de varias flores poéticas* (Madrid: Imprenta de Nicolás de Xamares)

FAJARDO, MARTA. 2011. 'Del grabado europeo a la pintura americana. La serie *El Credo* del pintor quiteño Miguel de Santiago', *Revista de Historia Regional y Local*, 3: 193–213

FERNÁNDEZ, CRISTINA BEATRIZ. 1996. 'El primado del ojo (sobre el *Primero sueño* de Sor Juana Inés de la Cruz)', *Quaderni ibero americani*, 80: 49–60

FERNÁNDEZ, LUIS MIGUEL. 2006. *Tecnología, espectáculo, literatura: dispositivos ópticos en las letras españolas de los siglos XVIII y XIX* (Santiago de Compostela: Universidade de Santiago de Compostela)

FEUILLET, MICHEL. 2008. 'Le bestiaire de l'*Annonciation*: l'hirondelle, l'escargot, l'écureuil et le chat', *Italies*, 12: 231–42

FICINO, MARSILIO. 1989. *Three Books on Life*, ed. by Carol V. Kaske and John R. Clark (Binghamton, New York: Medieval & Renaissance Texts & Studies / The Renaissance Society of America)

FIGUEROA, CRISTO RAFAEL. 1991. 'El Barroco de Hernando Domínguez Camargo. Afirmación de una conciencia criolla en el lenguaje', *Texto y Contexto*, 17: 98–112

FINDLEN, PAULA. 2004. 'Introduction. The Last Man Who Knew Everything... or Did He? Athanasius Kircher, S.J. (1602–80) and His World', in *Athanasius Kircher: The Last Man Who Knew Everything*, ed. by Paula Findlen (New York: Routledge), pp. 1–48

FODOR, A. 1970. 'The Origins of the Arabic Legends of the Pyramids', *Acta Orientalia Academiae Scientiarum Hungaricae*, 23: 335–63

FORD, PHILIP. 1997. *Ronsard's Hymns: A Literary and Iconographical Study* (Binghamton, New York: Medieval & Renaissance Texts & Studies)

——. 2002. 'Classical Myth and Its Interpretation in Sixteenth-Century France', in *The Classical Heritage in France*, ed. by Gerald N. Sandy (Leiden/Boston: Brill), pp. 331–49

——. 2007. *De Troie à Ithaque: réception des épopées homériques à la Renaissance* (Genève: Droz)

FOUCAULT, MICHEL. 1966. *Les mots et les choses: une archéologie des sciences humaines* (Paris: Gallimard)

FRANCO, JEAN. 1989. *Plotting Women: Gender and Representation in Mexico* (New York: Columbia University Press)

FRANCOMANO, EMILY. 2008. *Wisdom and Her Lovers in Medieval and Early Modern Hispanic Literature* (New York: Palgrave Macmillan)

FRIEDMAN, EDWARD H. 2002. 'Realities and Poets: Góngora, Cervantes, and the Nature of Art', *Calíope*, 8: 55–68

GÁLLEGO, JULIÁN. 1984. *Visión y símbolos en la pintura española del Siglo de Oro* (Madrid: Cátedra)

GARCÍA GALIANO, ÁNGEL. 1992. *La imitación poética en el Renacimiento* (Kassel: Deusto/ Reichenberger)

GATTI, HILARY. 2011. *Essays on Giordano Bruno* (Princeton: Princeton University Press)

GAUNA, CHIARA. 1998. 'Giudizi e polemiche intorno a Caravaggio e Tiziano nei trattati d'arte spagnoli del XVII secolo: Carducho, Pacheco e la tradizione artistica italiana', *Ricerche di storia dell'arte*, 64: 57–78

GENETTE, GÉRARD. 1980. *Narrative Discourse*, trans. by Jane E. Lewin (Oxford: Blackwell)

GENTIC, TANIA, and FRANCISCO LaRUBIA-PRADO. 2017. 'Introduction', in *Imperialism and the Wider Atlantic: Essays on the Aesthetics, Literature, and Politics of Transatlantic Cultures*, ed. by Tania Gentic and Francisco LaRubia-Prado (Cham, Switzerland: Palgrave Macmillan), pp. 1–18

GERLI, MICHAEL. 1984. '*El castillo interior* y el arte de la memoria', *Bulletin Hispanique*, 86: 154–63

GIL TOVAR, FRANCISCO. 1989. 'Las artes plásticas durante el período colonial', in *Nueva historia de Colombia*, 8 vols, ed. by Jaime Jaramillo Uribe (Bogotá: Planeta), I, pp. 239–52

GILBERT, PIERRE. 1939. 'Homère et l'Égypte', *Chronique d'Egypte*, 14: 47–61

GIMBERNAT DE GONZÁLEZ, ESTER. 1987. 'Apeles de la reinscripción: a propósito del *Poema heroico* de Hernando Domínguez Camargo', *Revista Iberoamericana*, 53: 569–79

GLANTZ, MARGO. 2005. *La desnudez como naufragio: borrones y borradores* (Madrid/Frankfurt am Main: Iberoamericana/Vervuert)

GOMBRICH, E. H. 1978. *Norm and Form* (London: Phaidon)

——. 2002. *Art and Illusion: A Study in the Psychology of Pictorial Representation* (London: Phaidon)

GÓMEZ DE LIAÑO, IGNACIO (ed.). 1973. *Giordano Bruno. Mundo, magia, memoria: selección de textos* (Madrid: Taurus)

——. 2001. *Itinerario del éxtasis o las imágenes de un saber universal* (Madrid: Siruela)

GÓNGORA, LUIS DE. 1627. *Obras en verso del Homero español* (Madrid: Viuda de Luis Sánchez)

——. 2012. *The Solitudes*, trans. by Edith Grossman (New York: Penguin Books)

GONZÁLEZ, ANA MARÍA. 2002. '*La Cristiada*. Edición crítica y anotada' (unpublished doctoral thesis: University Massachusetts Amherst)

GONZÁLEZ ECHEVARRÍA, ROBERTO. 1993. *Celestina's Brood: Continuities of the Baroque in Spanish and Latin American Literatures* (Durham/London: Duke University Press)

——. 1996. 'Colonial Lyric', in *The Cambridge History of Latin American Literature*, 3 vols, ed. by Roberto González Echevarría and Enrique Pupo-Walker (Cambridge: Cambridge University Press), I, pp. 191–230

——. 2016. 'Sor Juana y la cosmología barroca: *Primero sueño*', *Anales de Literatura Hispanoamericana*, 45: 287–300

GRACIÁN, BALTASAR. 1938. *El Criticón*, 3 vols, ed. by Miguel Romera-Navarro (Philadelphia: University of Pennsylvania Press)

——. 2001A. *Agudeza y arte de ingenio*, 2 vols, ed. by Evaristo Correa Calderón (Madrid: Castalia)

——. 2001B. *El discreto*, ed. by Aurora Egido (Zaragoza: Gobierno de Aragón, Departamento de Cultura y Turismo/Institución 'Fernando el Católico'/Diputación de Zaragoza)

——. 2003. *El héroe. Oráculo manual y el arte de prudencia*, ed. by Antonio Bernat (Madrid: Castalia)

GRANT, WILLIAM LEONARD. 1965. *Neo-Latin Literature and The Pastoral* (Chapel Hill: University of North Carolina Press)

GREENE, THOMAS M. 1982. *The Light in Troy: Imitation and Discovery in Renaissance Poetry* (New Haven/London: Yale University Press)

GROSSI, VERÓNICA. 2007. *Sigilosos v(u)elos epistemológicos en Sor Juana Inés de la Cruz* (Madrid/Frankfurt am Main: Iberoamericana/Vervuert)

GUIBOVICH, PEDRO. 2003. *Censura, libros e inquisición en el Perú colonial, 1570–1754* (Sevilla: Consejo Superior de Investigaciones Científicas/Universidad de Sevilla)

GUILLÉN, CLAUDIO. 1998. *Múltiples moradas: ensayo de literatura comparada* (Barcelona: Tusquets)

HADOT, PIERRE. 1993. *Plotinus or the Simplicity of Vision* (Chicago/London: University of Chicago Press)

HALL, HENRY MARION. 1912. *Idylls of Fishermen. A History of The Literary Species* (New York: Columbia University Press)

HALL, MARCIA B. 1992. *Color and Meaning: Practice and Theory in Renaissance Painting* (Cambridge: Cambridge University Press)

HEFFERNAN, JAMES A. W. 1991. 'Ekphrasis and Representation', *New Literary History*, 22: 297–316

HERODOTUS. 2013. *The Histories*, ed. by Paul Cartledge, trans. by Tom Holland (New York: Viking)

HILL, RUTH. 2000. *Sceptres and Sciences in the Spains: Four Humanists and the New Philosophy (ca. 1680–1740)* (Liverpool: Liverpool University Press)

HOLLANDER, JOHN. 1995. *The Gazer's Spirit: Poems Speaking to Silent Works of Art* (Chicago: University of Chicago Press)

HOLLOWAY, ANNE. 2013. '*Sonoro cristal*: Pedro Soto de Rojas and the Eloquent Galatea', *Bulletin of Spanish Studies*, 90: 19–40

——. 2017. *The Potency of Pastoral in the Hispanic Baroque* (Woodbridge: Tamesis)

HORACE. 1989. *Epistles, Book II; and Epistle to the Pisones (Ars Poetica)*, ed. by Niall Rudd (Cambridge: Cambridge University Press)

——. 2004. *Odes and Epodes*, ed. by Niall Rudd (Cambridge, Massachusetts/London: Harvard University Press)

——. 2011. *Satires and Epistles*, ed. by Robert Cowan (Oxford: Oxford University Press)

HOUELLEBECQ, MICHEL. 2010. *La carte et le territoire* (Paris: Flammarion)

HUARD-BAUDRY, EMMANUELLE. 2012. 'En torno a las *Soledades*: el abad de Rute y los lienzos de Flandes', *Criticón*, 114: 139–78

HUARTE DE SAN JUAN, JUAN. 1989. *Examen de ingenios para las ciencias*, ed. by Guillermo Serés (Madrid: Cátedra)

HUERGO, HUMBERTO. 2001. 'Las *Soledades* de Góngora ¿"lienço" de Flandes o "pintura valiente"?', *La Torre: Revista de la Universidad de Puerto Rico*, 6: 193–232

——. 2017. 'Góngora y la estética del borrón. Otra vez el soneto al Greco', *Creneida: Anuario de Literaturas Hispánicas*, 5: 280–332

HUGHES, JENNIFER. 2010. *Biography of a Mexican Crucifix: Lived Religion and Local Faith from the Conquest to the Present* (New York/Oxford: Oxford University Press)

HUNT, KATHLEEN. 1988. 'Figures of Disclosure: Pictorial Space in Marvell and Góngora', *Comparative Literature*, 40: 245–58

HUYSMANS, JORIS-KARL. 1908. *Trois églises et trois primitifs* (Paris: Librairie Plon)

HYMAN, AARON. 2017. 'Inventing Painting: Cristóbal de Villalpando, Juan Correo, and New Spain's Transatlantic Canon', *The Art Bulletin*, 99: 102–35

INGRAM, DAVID. 2008. *Green Screen. Environmentalism and Hollywood Cinema* (Exeter: University of Exeter Press)

IVERSEN, ERIK. 1993. *The Myth of Egypt and its Hieroglyphs in European Tradition* (Princeton: Princeton University Press)

JAMMES, ROBERT (ed.). 2001. *Soledades / Luis de Góngora*, 2 vols (Madrid: Castalia)

JÁUREGUI, CARLOS. 2009. 'Cannibalism, the Eucharist, and Criollo Subjects', in *Creole Subjects in the Colonial Americas: Empires, Texts, Identities*, ed. by Ralph Bauer and José Antonio Mazzotti (Chapel Hill: University of North Carolina Press), pp. 61–100

JÁUREGUI, JUAN DE. 2016. *Discurso poético*, ed. by Mercedes Blanco (OBVIL) <http://obvil. paris-sorbonne.fr/corpus/gongora/1624_discurso-poetico/> [accessed 5 October 2019]

JAY, MARTIN. 1988. 'Scopic Regimes of Modernity', in *Vision and Visuality*, ed. by Hal Foster (Seattle: Bay Press), pp. 3–23

JOINER GATES, E. (ed.). 1960. *Los Discursos apologéticos de Pedro Díaz de Rivas / El Antídoto de Juan de Jáuregui* (México, D.F.: El Colegio de México)

JONES, R. O. 1963. 'Neoplatonism and the *Soledades*', *Bulletin of Hispanic Studies*, 40: 1–16

KALKAVAGE, PETER (ed.). 2001. *Plato's Timaeus* (Newburyport, Massachusetts: Focus Publishing/R. Pullins Company)

KAMARALLI, ANNA (ed.). 2018. *Much Ado About Nothing / William Shakespeare* (London: Bloomsbury)

KAUFMAN, ELEANOR. 1998. 'Introduction', in *Deleuze & Guattari: New Mappings in Politics, Philosophy, and Culture*, ed. by Eleanor Kaufman and Kevin Jon Heller (Minneapolis/ London: University of Minnesota Press), pp. 3–13

KEEN, BENJAMIN. 1971. *The Aztec Image in Western Thought* (New Brunswick, New Jersey: Rutgers University Press)

KIRCHER, ATHANASIUS. 1650. *Obeliscus pamphilius* (Rome: Typis Ludovici Grignani)

——. 1654. *Oedipus Aegyptiacus*, 3 vols (Rome: Vitalis Mascardi), III

——. 1669. *Ars magna sciendi* (Amsterdam: Apud Joannem Janssonium à Waesberge, & Viduam Elizei Weyerstraet)

KIRK, STEPHANIE. 2016. *Sor Juana Inés de La Cruz and the Gender Politics of Knowledge in Colonial Mexico* (New York: Routledge)

KLOR DE ALVA, J. JORGE. 1992. 'Colonialism and Postcolonialism as (Latin) American Mirages', *Colonial Latin American Review*, 1: 3–23

KLUGE, SOFIE. 2002. 'Góngoras *Soledades*. Der Barocke Traum von Der Enzyklopädischen Beherrschung Der Welt', *Orbis Litterarum*, 57: 161–80

——. 2010. *Baroque, Allegory, Comedia: The Transfiguration of Tragedy in Seventeenth-Century Spain* (Kassel: Reichenberger)

——. 2013. 'Un epilio barroco: el *Polifemo* y su género', in *Los géneros poéticos del Siglo de Oro: centros y periferias*, ed. by Rodrigo Cacho and Anne Holloway (Woodbridge: Tamesis), pp. 153–70

——. 2014. *Diglossia: The Early Modern Reinvention of Mythological Discourse* (Kassel: Reichenberger)

KOOPMAN, NIELS. 2018. *Ancient Greek Ekphrasis: Between Description and Narration* (Leiden/ Boston: Brill)

KRIEGER, MURRAY. 1992. *Ekphrasis: The Illusion of the Natural Sign* (Baltimore/London: Johns Hopkins University Press)

LAMB, W. R. M. (ed.). 1977. *Plato's Laches. Protagoras. Meno. Euthydemus* (Cambridge, Massachusetts/London: Harvard University/W. Heinemann)

LANE, EDWARD WILLIAM. 2000. *Description of Egypt*, ed. by Jason Thompson (Cairo: American University in Cairo Press)

LAS CASAS, BARTOLOMÉ DE. 1984. *Brevísima relación de la destrucción de las Indias*, ed. by André Saint-Lu (Madrid: Cátedra)

LASKI, MARGHANITA. 1961. *Ecstasy. A Study of Some Secular and Religious Experiences.* (London: Cresset Press)

LATCHMAN, RICARDO A. 1956. 'San Ignacio de Loyola en los poemas mayores de inspiración jesuítica', *Finis Terrae*, 3: 3–13

LAWRANCE, JEREMY. 2013. '"El yugo de ambos sexos sacudido" (*Soledad* I: 237–83): Góngora's Serranas and Nympholepsy', in *A Poet for All Seasons: Eight Commentaries on Góngora*, ed. by Oliver Noble Wood and Nigel Griffin (New York: Hispanic Seminary of Medieval Studies), pp. 111–36

LEFEBVRE, MARTIN. 2006A. 'Between Setting and Landscape in the Cinema', in *Landscape and Film*, ed. by Martin Lefebvre (New York: Routledge), pp. 19–59

——. 2006B. 'Introduction', in *Landscape and Film*, ed. by Martin Lefebvre (New York: Routledge), pp. xi–xxviii

LEIVA, RAÚL. 1975. *Introducción a Sor Juana: sueño y realidad* (Ciudad de México: Universidad Nacional Autónoma de México)

LEONARD, IRVING A. 1929. *Don Carlos de Sigüenza y Góngora, a Mexican Savant of the Seventeenth Century* (Berkeley: University of California Press)

——. 1971. *Baroque Times in Old Mexico: Seventeenth-Century Persons, Places, and Practices* (Michigan: University of Michigan Press)

——. 1992. *Books of the Brave: Being an Account of Books and of Men in the Spanish Conquest and Settlement of the Sixteenth-Century New World* (Berkeley: University of California Press)

LEONARDO DA VINCI. 1817. *Trattato della pittura* (Roma: Stamperia de Romanis)

LEONE, MASSIMO. 2010. *Saints and Signs: A Semiotic Reading of Conversion in Early Modern Catholicism* (Berlin: De Gruyter)

LESSING, GOTTHOLD EPHRAIM. 1984. *Laocoön: An Essay on the Limits of Painting and Poetry*, trans. by Edward Allen McCormick (Baltimore: Johns Hopkins University Press)

LEZAMA LIMA, JOSÉ. 2001. *La expresión americana*, ed. by Irlemar Chiampi (México, D.F.: Fondo de Cultura Económica)

LISI, FRANCESCO LEONARDO (ed.). 1990. *El tercer concilio limense y la aculturación de los indígenas sudamericanos: estudio crítico con edición, traducción y comentario de las actas del concilio provincial celebrado en Lima entre 1582 y 1583* (Salamanca: Universidad de Salamanca)

LIZCANO, SUSANA. 2003. '*Pictura et poesis*: narración mítica, imagen y descripción iconográfica en las *Imagines* de Filóstrato el Viejo' (unpublished doctoral thesis: Universidad Complutense de Madrid)

LOCKHART, JAMES, and STUART SCHWARTZ. 1983. *Early Latin America: A History of Colonial Spanish America and Brazil* (Cambridge: Cambridge University Press)

LÓPEZ TORRIJOS, ROSA. 1990. 'Los temas de Góngora en la pintura española de su tiempo', in *Góngora en su siglo y en el nuestro*, 2 vols (München: Spanisches Kulturinstitut), II, pp. 35–50

LOVATT, HELEN. 2013. *The Epic Gaze: Vision, Gender and Narrative in Ancient Epic* (Cambridge: Cambridge University Press)

LOWE, ELIZABETH. 1976. 'The Gongorist Model in *El primero sueño*', *Revista de Estudios Hispánicos*, X: 409–27

LOYOLA, IGNACIO DE. 2013. *Obras*, ed. by Manuel Ruiz Jurado (Madrid: Biblioteca de Autores Cristianos)

LUCENA, MANUEL. 2016. 'The Creole Metropolis', in *The Transatlantic Hispanic Baroque: Complex Identities in the Atlantic World*, ed. by Harald E. Braun and Jesús Pérez Magallón (London/New York: Routledge), pp. 171–86

LUCIANI, FREDERICK. 1995. 'Anecdotal Self-Invention in Sor Juana's *Respuesta a Sor Filotea*', *Colonial Latin American Review*, 4: 73–83

LUCRETIUS. 2001. *On the Nature of Things*, ed. by Martin Ferguson (Indianapolis/Cambridge: Hackett Publishing Company)

LUISELLI, ALESSANDRA. 1993. *El sueño manierista de sor Juana Inés de la Cruz* (Toluca: Gobierno del Estado de México/Universidad Autónoma del Estado de México)

——. 2017. '*Primero sueño*. Heresy and Knowledge', in *The Routledge Research Companion to the Works of Sor Juana Inés de la Cruz*, ed. by Emilie Bergmann and Stacey Schlau (New York: Routledge), pp. 176–88

MACROBIUS. 2011. *Saturnalia*, 3 vols, ed. by Robert A. Kaster (Cambridge, Massachusetts: Harvard University Press)

MAFFEI, JOHANNES PETRUS. 1837. *De vita et moribus sancti Ignatii Loiolae qui Societatem Jesu fundavit*, 3 vols (Verona: Testori), I

MAGRIS, CLAUDIO. 1986. *Danubio* (Milano: Garzanti)

MALCOLM, NOEL. 2004. 'Private and Public Knowledge. Kircher, Esotericism, and the Republic of Letters', in *Athanasius Kircher: The Last Man Who Knew Everything*, ed. by Paula Findlen (New York: Routledge), pp. 297–308

MARAVALL, JOSÉ ANTONIO. 2011. *La cultura del Barroco. Análisis de una estructura histórica* (Barcelona: Ariel)

MARCAIDA, JOSÉ RAMÓN. 2014. *Arte y ciencia en el barroco español: historia natural, coleccionismo y cultura visual* (Sevilla: Fundación Focus-Abengoe)

MARIÁTEGUI, JOSÉ CARLOS. 1979. *7 ensayos de interpretación de la realidad peruana* (Caracas: Biblioteca Ayacucho)

MARINO, GIAMBATTISTA. 1988. *L'Adone*, 2 vols, ed. by Giovanni Pozzi (Milano: Adelphi)

MARTIAL. 1993. *Epigrams*, 3 vols, ed. by D. R. Shackleton Bailey (Cambridge, Massachusetts: Harvard University Press)

MARTIN, VINCENT, and ELECTA ARENAL (eds.). 2009. *Neptuno alegórico / Sor Juana Inés de la Cruz* (Madrid: Cátedra)

MARTÍNEZ, MIGUEL. 2016. *Front Lines: Soldiers' Writing in the Early Modern Hispanic World* (Philadelphia: University of Pennsylvania Press)

MARTÍNEZ-OSORIO, EMIRO. 2016. *Authority, Piracy, and Captivity in Colonial Spanish American Writing: Juan de Castellano's Elegies of Illustrious Men of the Indies* (Lewisburg: Bucknell University Press)

MARTÍNEZ-SAN MIGUEL, YOLANDA. 2008. *From Lack to Excess: 'Minor' Readings of Latin American Colonial Discourse* (Lewisburg: Bucknell University Press)

MATOS, GREGÓRIO DE. 1990. *Obra poética*, 2 vols, ed. by James Amado and Emanuel Araújo (Rio de Janeiro: Editora Record)

MAYERS, KATHRYN M. 2009. 'American Artifice: Ideology and Ekphrasis in the *Poema heroico a San Ignacio de Loyola*', *Hispanofila*, 155: 1–19

———. 2012. *Visions of Empire in Colonial Spanish American Ekphrastic Writing* (Lewisburg: Bucknell University Press)

MAYO, ARANTZA. 2007. *La lírica sacra de Lope de Vega y José de Valdivielso* (Pamplona/Madrid/Frankfurt am Main: Universidad de Navarra/Iberoamericana/Vervuert)

———. 2013. 'La crucifixión como materia poética en la América colonial: Hernando Domínguez Camargo y su romance *A la pasión de Cristo*', in *Los géneros poéticos del Siglo de Oro: centros y periferias*, ed. by Rodrigo Cacho and Anne Holloway (Woodbridge: Tamesis), pp. 253–70

———. 2014. 'Seeing the Old World from the New: Hernando Domínguez Camargo's *Poema heroico*', in *Artifice and Invention in the Spanish Golden Age*, ed. by Terence O'Reilly and Stephen Boyd (Leeds: Legenda), pp. 161–72

MÉNDEZ PLANCARTE, ALFONSO (ed.). 1951. *Sor Juana Inés de la Cruz. El sueño* (México, D.F.: Imprenta universitaria)

—— (ed.). 1994a. *Obras completas de Sor Juana Inés de la Cruz. Lírica personal*, 4 vols (México, D.F.: Fondo de Cultura Económica), I

—— (ed.). 1994b. *Obras completas de Sor Juana Inés de la Cruz. Autos y loas*, 4 vols (México, D.F.: Fondo de Cultura Económica), III

MÉNDEZ, SIGMUND. 2015. 'El sueño, la fantasía y sus alegorías en el *Primero sueño* de sor Juana Inés de la Cruz', *Bulletin of Spanish Studies*, 93: 1–37

MENDOZA, EDUARDO. 1969. *Hernando Domínguez Camargo. Antología poética* (Medellín: Bedout)

MEO ZILIO, GIOVANNI. 1967. *Estudio sobre Hernando Domínguez Camargo y su S. Ignacio de Loyola. Poema heroico* (Firenze: Casa Editrice G. D'Anna)

———. 1986. 'Prólogo', in *Hernando Domínguez Camargo. Obras* (Caracas: Biblioteca Ayacucho), pp. IX–XCV

MERRIM, STEPHANIE. 1999. *Early Modern Women's Writing and Sor Juana Inés de La Cruz* (Nashville: Vanderbilt University Press)

——. 2010. *The Spectacular City, Mexico, and Colonial Hispanic Literary Culture* (Austin: University of Texas Press)

MICÓ, JOSÉ MARÍA (ed.). 1990. *Canciones y otros poemas en arte mayor / Luis de Góngora* (Madrid: Espasa Calpe)

MITCHELL, W. J. T. 1994. *Picture Theory: Essays on Verbal and Visual Representation* (Chicago/London: University of Chicago Press)

MOLTMANN, JURGEN. 1974. *The Crucified God: The Cross of Christ as the Foundation and Criticism of Christian Theology*, trans. by John Bowden and R. A. Wilson (London: SCM Press)

MONTAIGNE, MICHEL DE. 1958. *Complete Essays*, trans. by Donald M. Frame (Stanford: Stanford University Press)

MORA, CARMEN DE. 1983. 'Naturaleza y Barroco en Hernando Domínguez Camargo', *Thesaurus*, 38: 59–81

MORÁN, MIGUEL, and FERNANDO CHECA. 1985. *El coleccionismo en España. De la cámara de maravillas a la galería de pinturas* (Madrid: Cátedra)

MORAÑA, MABEL. 1988. 'Barroco y conciencia criolla en Hispanoamérica', *Revista de Crítica Literaria Latinoamericana*, 28: 229–51

MORE, ANNA (ed.). 2016. *Sor Juana Inés de La Cruz. Selected Works*, trans. by Edith Grossman (New York/London: W. W. Norton & Company)

MORPURGO-TAGLIABUE, GUIDO. 1987. *Anatomia del Barocco* (Palermo: Aesthetica Edizioni)

MOTTET, JEAN. 2006. 'Toward a Genealogy of the American Landscape. Notes on Landscapes in D. W. Griffith (1908–1912)', in *Landscape and Film*, ed. by Martin Lefebvre (New York: Routledge), pp. 61–90

MUNDY, BARBARA E. 2015. *The Death of Aztec Tenochtitlan, the Life of Mexico City* (Austin, Texas: University of Texas Press)

MURPHY, EDWIN (ed.). 1990. *The Antiquities of Egypt: A Translation with Notes of Book I of the Library of History, of Diodorus Siculus* (New Brunswick, New Jersey: Transaction Publishers)

NANFITO, JACQUELINE C. 2000. *El Sueño: Cartographies of Knowledge and the Self* (New York: Peter Lang)

NAVA, ALEXANDER. 2013. *Wonder and Exile in the New World* (University Park, Pennsylvania: Pennsylvania State University Press)

NERI, STEFANO. 2007. *Antología de las arquitecturas maravillosas en los libros de caballerías* (Alcalá de Henares: Centro de Estudios Cervantinos)

NEWLYN, LUCY. 2000. *Reading, Writing, and Romanticism: The Anxiety of Reception* (Oxford/New York: Oxford University Press)

NIEREMBERG, JUAN EUSEBIO. 1645. *Vida de San Ignacio de Loyola* (Madrid: María de Quiñones)

NOWAKOWSKI, DENISE. 1994. *Julian of Norwich's Showings: From Vision to Book* (Princeton: Princeton University Press)

OLIVARES, ROCÍO. 1998. 'La figura del mundo en el *Sueño*, de Sor Juana Inés de la Cruz' (unpublished doctoral thesis: Universidad Nacional Autónoma de México)

——. 2014. 'De la *tristitia salutifera* a la elocuencia circunspecta: texturas de la simbólica espiritual en el *Primero sueño*', in *IX Colóquio de Estudos Barrocos. O eterno retorno do Barroco*, ed. by Francisco Ivan and Samuel Lima (Natal: Universidade Federal do Rio Grande do Norte), pp. 119–66

ONGARO, ANTONIO. 1998. 'Alceo', in *Favole*, ed. by Domenico Chiodo (Torino: Edizioni RES), pp. 1–130

OÑA, PEDRO DE. 1941. *El Vasauro. Poema heroico*, ed. by Rodolfo Oroz (Santiago: Prensas de la Universidad de Chile)

——. 1992. *El Ignacio de Cantabria*, ed. by Mario Ferreccio, Gloria Muñoz, and Mario Rodríguez (Santiago de Chile: Universidad de Concepción)

ORLANDINI, NICOLÒ. 1614. *Historiæ Societatis Iesv. Prima Pars* (Roma: Bartholomaeum Zannettum)

OROZCO, EMILIO. 1947. *Temas del Barroco de poesía y pintura* (Granada: Universidad de Granada)

ORTEGA, JULIO. 2003. 'Post-teoría y estudios transatlánticos', *Iberoamericana*, 3: 109–17

——. 2010. 'Transatlantic Representations', *Literal. Latin American Voices*, 21: 42–44

——. 2012. 'Crítica transatlántica a comienzos del siglo XXI', in *Viajeros, diplomáticos y exiliados: escritores hispanoamericanos en España (1914–1939)*, 3 vols, ed. by Carmen de Mora Valcárcel and Alfonso García Morales (Bruxelles: P. I. E. Peter Lang), I, pp. 23–38

OSORIO, IGNACIO (ed.). 1993. *La luz imaginaria: epistolario de Atanasio Kircher con los novohispanos* (México, D.F.: Universidad Nacional Autónoma de México)

OSUNA, RAFAEL. 1969. 'La fuente de dos pasajes del *San Ignacio de Loyola* de Domínguez Camargo', *Thesaurus*, 24: 12–22

OVID. 2014. *Metamorphoses*, 2 vols, ed. by G. P. Goold, trans. by Frank Justus Miller (Cambridge, Massachusetts: Harvard University Press)

OVIEDO Y HERRERA, LUIS ANTONIO DE. 1867. *Santa Rosa de Lima. Poema heroico* (Lima: Administración del Perú católico)

PABST, WALTER. 1966. *La creación gongorina en los poemas Polifemo y Soledades*, trans. by Nicolás Marín (Madrid: Consejo Superior de Investigaciones Científicas)

PACHECO, FRANCISCO. 1956. *Arte de la pintura*, 2 vols (Madrid: Instituto de Valencia de Don Juan)

PADRÓN, RICARDO. 2004. *The Spacious Word: Cartography, Literature, and Empire in Early Modern Spain* (Chicago/London: University of Chicago Press)

——. 2007. 'Against Apollo: Góngora's *Soledad primera* and the Mapping of Empire', *Modern Language Quarterly*, 68: 363–93

PALEOTTI, GABRIELE. 2002. *Discorso intorno alle immagini sacre e profane (1582)* (Città del Vaticano: Libreria editrice vaticana)

PALME, PER. 1959. 'Ut Architectura Poesis', in *Idea and Form. Studies in the History of Art*, ed. by Nils Gösta Sandblad (Stockholm: Almqvist & Wiksell), pp. 95–107

PANOFSKY, ERWIN. 1968. *Idea: A Concept in Art Theory* (New York: Harper and Row)

PAZ, AMELIA DE. 2015. 'Góngora en la visita del obispo Pacheco (Elogio y nostalgia de Dámaso Alonso)', *Criticón*, 123: 5–38

PAZ, OCTAVIO. 1982. *Sor Juana Inés de la Cruz o las trampas de la fe* (Barcelona: Editorial Seix Barral)

PELLICER, JOSÉ. 1630. *Lecciones solemnes a las obras de Don Luis de Góngora y Argote, Píndaro Andaluz, Príncipe de los Poetas Líricos de España* (Madrid: Imprenta del Reino)

PEREDA, FELIPE. 2017. *Crimen e ilusión: el arte de la verdad en el Siglo de Oro* (Madrid: Marcial Pons)

PERELMUTER, ROSA. 1983. 'La estructura retórica de la *Respuesta a Sor Filotea*', *Hispanic Review*, 51: 147–58

——. 2004. *Los límites de la femineidad en Sor Juana Inés de la Cruz: estrategias retóricas y recepción literaria* (Pamplona/Madrid/Frankfurt am Main: Universidad de Navarra/Iberoamericana/Vervuert)

PÉREZ DE OLIVA, FERNANDO. 1995. *Diálogo de la dignidad del hombre. Razonamientos. Ejercicios*, ed. by María Luisa Cerrón Puga (Madrid: Cátedra)

PÉREZ-AMADOR, ALBERTO (ed.). 2015. *El precipicio de Faetón: edición y comento de 'Primero sueño' de Sor Juana Inés de la Cruz* (Madrid/Frankfurt am Main/Ciudad de México: Iberoamericana Editorial/Vervuert/Universidad Autónoma Metropolitana)

PERRY, ELIZABETH. 2012. 'Sor Juana *Fecit*: Sor Juana Inés de La Cruz and the Art of Miniature Painting', *Early Modern Women*, 7: 3–32

PETRARCA, FRANCESCO. 1999. *Canzoniere*, ed. by Marco Santagata (Milano: Mondadori)

PEZZINI, SARA (ed.). 2018. *Décimas / Luis de Góngora* (Alessandria: Edizioni dell'Orso)

PFANDL, LUDWIG. 1963. *Sor Juana Inés de la Cruz. La décima musa de México. Su vida, su poesía, su psique*, ed. by Francisco de la Maza (México, D.F.: Universidad Nacional Autónoma de México)

PHILLIPS, ADAM. 2006. *Side Effects* (London: Penguin)

PHILOSTRATUS THE ATHENIAN. 2005. *The Life of Apollonius of Tyana*, 3 vols, ed. by Christopher P. Jones (Cambridge, Massachusetts: Harvard University Press)

PHILOSTRATUS THE ELDER. 2014. 'Imagines', in *Elder Philostratus. Younger Philostratus. Callistratus*, ed. by Jeffrey Henderson, trans. by Arthur Fairbanks (Cambridge, Massachusetts: Harvard University Press)

PICO DELLA MIRANDOLA, GIOVANNI. 1956. *Oration on the Dignity of Man*, trans. by A. Robert Caponigri (Washington, D.C.: Regnery)

PICÓN-SALAS, MARIANO. 1944. *De la conquista a la independencia. Tres siglos de historia cultural hispanoamericana* (México, D.F.: Fondo de Cultura Económica)

PIERCE, DONNA, ROGELIO RUIZ GOMAR, and CLARA BARGELLINI. 2004. *Painting a New World: Mexican Art and Life, 1521–1821* (Denver: Frederick and Jan Mayer Center for Pre-Columbian and Spanish Colonial Art at the Denver Art Museum)

PIERCE, FRANK. 1945. '*El Bernardo* of Balbuena: A Baroque Fantasy', *Hispanic Review*, 13: 1–23

PINEDA, VICTORIA. 2000. 'La invención de la écfrasis', in *Homenaje a la profesora Carmen Pérez Romero*, ed. by José Luis Sánchez Abal (Cáceres: Universidad de Extremadura), pp. 251–62

PINGREE, DAVID. 1980. 'Some of the Sources of the Ghāyat Al-Hakīm', *Journal of the Warburg and Courtauld Institutes*, 43: 1–15

—— (ed.). 1986. *Picatrix: the Latin version of the Ghāyat al-Ḥakīm* (London: Warburg Institute)

PLATNAUER, MAURICE (ed.). 2014. *Claudian*, 2 vols (Cambridge, Massachusetts: Harvard University Press)

PLATO. 2013. *Republic*, 2 vols, ed. by Chris Emlyn-Jones and William Preddy (Cambridge, Massachusetts: Harvard University Press)

POGGIOLI, RENATO. 1975. *The Oaten Flute: Essays on Pastoral Poetry and the Pastoral Ideal* (Cambridge, Massachusetts: Harvard University Press)

POLIZIANO, ANGELO. 2004. *Silvae*, ed. by Charles Fantazzi (Cambridge, Massachusetts: Harvard University Press)

PONCE CÁRDENAS, JESÚS (ed.). 2010. *Fábula de Polifemo y Galatea / Luis de Góngora* (Madrid: Cátedra)

——. 2012. '*San Ignacio. Poema heroico*: claves humorísticas en la imitación de las *Soledades* y el *Moretum*', *Criticón*, 115: 175–92

——. 2013. 'De nombres y deidades: Claves piscatorias en la *Soledad Segunda*', *Calíope*, 18: 85–125

——. 2014. 'Sobre el paisaje anticuario: Góngora y Filóstrato', in *La Edad del Genio. España e Italia en tiempos de Góngora*, ed. by Begoña Capllonch, Sara Pezzini, Giulia Poggi, and Jesús Ponce Cárdenas (Pisa: Edizioni ETS), pp. 369–89

——. 2016. *La imitación áurea: Cervantes, Quevedo, Góngora* (Paris: Éditions Hispaniques)

POUSSIN, NICOLAS. 1824. *Collection de lettres de Nicolas Poussin* (Paris: Imprimerie de Firmin Didot)

PRAZ, MARIO. 1970. *Mnemosyne: The Parallel between Literature and the Visual Arts* (London: Oxford University Press)

PRIEST, HAROLD MARTIN. 1967. 'Introduction', in *Adonis. Selections from l'Adone by Giambattista Marino* (Ithaca, New York: Cornell University Press), pp. xi–xlix

PROUST, MARCEL. 1981. *Remembrance of Things Past*, 3 vols, trans. by C. K. Scott Moncrieff and Terence Kilmartin (London: Chatto & Windus)

QUEVEDO, FRANCISCO DE. 1998. *Un Heráclito cristiano, Canta sola a Lisi, y otros poemas*, ed. by Lía Schwartz and Ignacio Arellano (Barcelona: Crítica)

QUINLAN-MCGRATH, MARY. 2013. *Influences: Art, Optics, and Astrology in the Italian Renaissance* (Chicago/London: The University of Chicago Press)

QUINT, DAVID. 1993. *Epic and Empire: Politics and Generic Form from Virgil to Milton* (Princeton: Princeton University Press)

RAMÍREZ, LEONARDO. 1982. 'El retablo del rapto de la iglesia de San Ignacio (Bogotá)', in *Simposio internazionale sul Barocco latino americano*, 2 vols, ed. by Vittorio Minardi (Roma: Istituto italo-latino americano), I, pp. 539–46

RAMOS, RAFAEL. 2013. 'Escultores y esculturas en la Antigua Capitanía General de Guatemala', in *La consolidación del Barroco en la escultura andaluza e hispanoamericana*, ed. by Lázaro Gila (Granada: Universidad de Granada), pp. 281–300

RAVASINI, INES. 2014. 'Éfire, Filódoces e i «prodigiosos moradores del líquido elemento». La caccia marina della *Soledad segunda*', in *La Edad del Genio. España e Italia en tiempos de Góngora*, ed. by Begoña Capllonch, Sara Pezzini, Giulia Poggi, and Jesús Ponce Cárdenas (Pisa: Edizioni ETS), pp. 397–414

READ, MALCOLM K. 1983. *The Birth and Death of Language: Spanish Literature and Linguistics, 1300–1700* (Madrid: Porrúa Turanzas)

REAL ACADEMIA ESPAÑOLA. 1734. *Diccionario de Autoridades. Tomo cuarto. Que contiene las letras G.H.I.J.K.L.M.*, 6 vols (Madrid: Imprenta de la Real Academia Española), IV

——. 1737. *Diccionario de Autoridades. Tomo quinto. Que contiene las letras O.P.Q.R.*, 6 vols (Madrid: Imprenta de la Real Academia Española), V

——. 2019. *Corpus diacrónico del español (CORDE)* <http://corpus.rae.es/cordenet.html> [accessed 5 October 2019]

REISS, TIMOTHY J. 2002. *Against Autonomy: Global Dialectics of Cultural Exchange* (Stanford: Stanford University Press)

RENSSELAER, W. LEE. 1940. '*Ut Pictura Poesis*: The Humanistic Theory of Painting', *The Art Bulletin*, 22: 197–269

REYNOLDS, WINSTON. 1980. 'Faro de navegantes, cristalina maravilla: de Alejandría a sor Juana', in *Actas del Sexto Congreso Internacional de Hispanistas, celebrado en Toronto del 22 al 26 agosto de 1977*, ed. by Alan M. Gordon and Evelyn Rugg (Toronto: University of Toronto), pp. 597–99

RIBADENEYRA, PEDRO DE. 1945. *Historias de la Contrarreforma*, ed. by Eusebio Rey (Madrid: Editorial Católica)

RICARD, ROBERT. 1964. *Estudios de literatura religiosa española* (Madrid: Gredos)

——. 1975. 'Reflexiones sobre *El sueño* de Sor Juana Inés de la Cruz', *Revista de la Universidad de México*, XXX: 25–32

RIPA, CESARE. 1618. *Nova iconologia* (Padova: Pietro Paolo Tozzi)

RITTER, HELLMUT, and MARTIN PLESSNER (eds.). 1962. *Picatrix. Das Ziel des Weisen* (London: Warburg Institute)

RITTER, JOACHIM. 1978. *Landschaft: zur Funktion des Ästhetischen in der modernen Gesellschaft* (Münster: Aschendorff)

ROBB, NESCA A. 1935. *Neoplatonism of the Italian Renaissance* (London: George Allen & Unwin)

ROBBINS, JEREMY. 2007. *Arts of Perception: The Epistemological Mentality of the Spanish Baroque, 1580–1720* (Abingdon: Routledge)

RODRÍGUEZ DE LA FLOR, FERNANDO. 1988. *Teatro de la memoria* (Valladolid: Junta de Castilla y León)

RODRÍGUEZ FREYLE, JUAN. 1979. *El carnero*, ed. by Darío Achury (Caracas: Ayacucho)

RODRÍGUEZ, MARIO. 1992. 'Estudio preliminar', in *El Ignacio de Cantabria / Pedro de Oña*, ed. by Mario Ferreccio, Gloria Muñoz, and Mario Rodríguez (Santiago de Chile: Universidad de Concepción), pp. 37–51

RODRÍGUEZ PADRÓN, JORGE. 2005. 'El cuerpo dormido', in *El cuerpo*, ed. by Eugenio Padorno and Germán Santana (Las Palmas de Gran Canaria: Servicio de Publicaciones de la Universidad de las Palmas de Gran Canaria), pp. 147–67

ROE, JEREMY. 2016. 'Carducho and *pintura de borrones*', in *On Art and Painting: Vicente Carducho and Baroque Spain*, ed. by Jean Andrews, Jeremy Roe, and Oliver Noble Wood (Cardiff: University of Wales Press), pp. 283–307

ROSES, JOAQUÍN. 1994. *Una poética de la oscuridad: recepción crítica de las Soledades en el siglo XVII* (Madrid/London: Tamesis)

ROSSHOLM, MARGARETHA. 1990. *Ideal Landscape: Annibale Carracci, Nicolas Poussin and Claude Lorrain* (New Haven/London: Yale University Press)

ROSSI, PAOLO. 1983. *Clavis universalis: arti della memoria e logica combinatoria da Lullo a Leibniz* (Bologna: Il Mulino)

ROTA, BERARDINO. 1990. *Egloghe pescatorie*, ed. by Domenico Chiodo (Torino: Edizioni RES)

ROVIRA, JOSÉ CARLOS. 2004. 'De cómo don Luis de Góngora viajó y se afincó definitivamente en América', in *Góngora hoy IV–V*, ed. by Joaquín Roses (Córdoba: Diputación de Córdoba, Delegación de Cultura), pp. 189–208

ROZAS, JUAN MANUEL. 1978. *Sobre Marino y España* (Madrid: Editora Nacional)

RUBENS, PETER PAUL, JEAN BAPTISTE BARBÉ, MIKOŁAJ ŁĘCZYCKI, and PÉTER PÁZMÁNY. 1622. *Vita Beati P. Ignatii Loiolae Societatis Iesu Fundatoris* (Rome: [publisher not identified])

RUIZ DE LEÓN, FRANCISCO. 1755. *Hernandía* (Madrid: Imprenta de la viuda de Manuel Fernández)

SAAVEDRA FAJARDO, DIEGO DE. 1640. *Idea de un príncipe político cristiano* (Monaco: Nicolao Enrico)

———. 1659. *Idea de un príncipe político cristiano* (Amsterdam: Apud Ioh. Ianssonium Iuniorem)

———. 1768. *República literaria* (Valencia: Salvador Faulí)

SABAT DE RIVERS, GEORGINA. 1976. *El 'Sueño' de Sor Juana Inés de la Cruz: tradiciones literarias y originalidad* (London: Tamesis)

———. 1992. *Estudios de literatura hispanoamericana: Sor Juana Inés de la Cruz y otros poetas barrocos de la colonia* (Barcelona: PPU)

———. 1997. 'Lírica culta de la colonia: Hernando Domínguez Camargo', *Calíope*, 3: 5–23

SABENA, JULIA, and TADEO P. STEIN. 2016. 'Gongorismo americano. Presentación', *Revista de crítica literaria latinoamericana*, 42: 9–16

SÁENZ OVECURI, DIEGO. 1667. *Thomasíada* (Guatemala: Joseph Pineda Ibarra)

SAID, EDWARD. 1985. 'Orientalism Reconsidered', *Cultural Critique*, 1: 89–107

———. 2003. *Orientalism* (London: Penguin)

SALCEDA, ALBERTO G. (ed.). 1994. *Obras completas de Sor Juana Inés de la Cruz. Comedias, sainetes y prosa*, 4 vols (México, D.F.: Fondo de Cultura Económica), IV

SALCEDO CORONEL, JOSÉ GARCÍA. 1636. *Soledades de don Luis de Góngora comentadas* (Madrid: Imprenta Real)

SALSTAD, M. LOUISE. 1979. 'Francisco de Aldana's Metamorphoses of the Circle', *Modern Language Review*, 74: 599–606

SAN JOSÉ, JERÓNIMO DE. 1651. *Genio de la Historia* (Zaragoza: Imprenta de Diego Dormer)

SÁNCHEZ DE LAS BROZAS, FRANCISCO (ed.). 1600. *Obras del excelente poeta Garcilaso de la Vega* (Madrid: Luis Sánchez)

SÁNCHEZ JIMÉNEZ, ANTONIO. 2011. *El pincel y el Fénix: pintura y literatura en la obra de Lope de Vega Carpio* (Pamplona/Madrid/Frankfurt am Main: Universidad de Navarra/ Iberoamericana/Vervuert)

——. 2015. 'Hipotiposis y defensa de la pintura: la silva "Si cuanto fue posible en lo imposible," de Lope de Vega (1633)', *Calíope*, 55: 151–70

SÁNCHEZ ROBAYNA, ANDRÉS. 1991. *Para leer 'Primero sueño' de sor Juana Inés de la Cruz* (México, D.F.: Fondo de Cultura Económica)

——. 2018. *Nuevas cuestiones gongorinas (Góngora y el gongorismo)* (Madrid: Biblioteca Nueva)

SANNAZARO, JACOPO. 1966. *Arcadia & Piscatorial Eclogues*, ed. by Ralph Nash (Detroit: Wayne State University Press)

SANTAYANA, GEORGE. 1947. *Three Philosophical Poets: Lucretius, Dante, and Goethe* (Cambridge, Massachusetts: Harvard University Press)

SCALIGER, JULES-CÉSAR. 1994. *La poétique. Livre V, Le critique*, ed. by Jacques Chomarat (Genève: Droz)

SCHONS, DOROTHY. 1939. 'The Influence of Góngora on Mexican Literature during the Seventeenth Century', *Hispanic Review*, 7: 22–34

SCOTT, NINA M. 1985. 'Sor Juana Inés de La Cruz: "Let Your Women Keep Silence in the Churches..." ', *Women's Studies International Forum*, 8: 511–19

SCOTT, WALTER (ed.). 1985a. *Hermetica: Introduction, Texts, and Translation*, 4 vols (Boston: Shambala), I

—— (ed.). 1985b. *Hermetica: Notes on the Latin Asclepius and the Hermetic Excerpts of Stobaeus*, 4 vols (Boston: Shambala), III

SEBASTIÁN, SANTIAGO. 1965. 'La importancia de los grabados en la cultura neogranadina', *Anuario Colombiano de Historia Social y de la Cultura*, 3: 119–33

SENECA. 1920. *Epistles*, 3 vols, trans. by Richard M. Gummere (Cambridge, Massachusetts/ London: Harvard University Press)

SERÉS, GUILLERMO. 1994. 'El concepto de "fantasía", desde la estética clásica a la dieciochesca', *Anales de literatura española*, 10: 207–36

SERRANO DE PAZ, MANUEL. 1673A. 'Comentarios a las *Soledades* del Grande Poeta don Luis de Góngora. Primera Parte a la *Soledad Primera*', Real Academia Española, ms. 114

——. 1673B. 'Comentarios a las *Soledades* del Grande Poeta don Luis de Góngora. Segunda parte contiene la *Soledad Segunda*', Real Academia Española, ms. 115

SEZNEC, JEAN. 1972. *The Survival of the Pagan Gods: The Mythological Tradition and its Place in Renaissance Humanism and Art*, trans. by Barbara F. Sessions (New York: Pantheon Books)

SIGÜENZA Y GÓNGORA, CARLOS DE. 1928. *Obras*, ed. by Francisco Pérez Salazar (México, D.F.: Sociedad de Bibliófilos Mexicanos)

——. 1959. *Libra astronómica y filosófica*, ed. by Bernabé Navarro (México, D.F.: Universidad Nacional Autónoma de México)

——. 1984. *Seis obras*, ed. by William G. Bryant (Caracas: Biblioteca Ayacucho)

SMITH, COLIN C. 1965. 'An Approach to Góngora's *Polifemo*', *Bulletin of Hispanic Studies*, 42: 217–38

SOLERVICENS, JOSEP (ed.). 2012. *La poètica del Barroc. Textos teòrics catalans* (Barcelona: Punctum)

SOLÍS, ANTONIO DE. 1684. *Historia de la conquista de México* (Madrid: Imprenta de Bernardo de Villa Diego)

SORIANO, ALEJANDRO. 1996. 'La invertida escala de Jacob: filosofía y teología en *El sueño* de sor Juana Inés de la Cruz', in *Premio nacional de ensayo Sor Juana Inés de la Cruz (1995)* (Toluca: Instituto Mexiquense de Cultura), pp. 19–100

——. 2000. *El Primero sueño de Sor Juana Inés de la Cruz. Bases tomistas* (México, D.F.: Universidad Nacional Autónoma de México)

—— (ed.). 2014. *Sor Filotea y Sor Juana. Cartas del obispo de Puebla a Sor Juana Inés de la Cruz* (México, D.F.: Fondo Editorial Estado de México)

SPITZER, LEO. 1955. 'The "Ode on a Grecian Urn", or Content vs. Metagrammar', *Comparative Literature*, 7: 203–25

STOLZENBERG, DANIEL. 2004. 'Four Trees, Some Amulets, and the Seventy-Two Names of God. Kircher Reveals the Kabbalah', in *Athanasius Kircher: The Last Man Who Knew Everything*, ed. by Paula Findlen (New York: Routledge), pp. 149–69

——. 2013. *Egyptian Oedipus: Athanasius Kircher and the Secrets of Antiquity* (Chicago/London: The University of Chicago Press)

SUÁREZ, JUAN LUIS. 2007. 'Hispanic Baroque: A Model for the Study of Cultural Complexity in the Atlantic World', *South Atlantic Review*, 72: 31–47

SUTTON, PETER C. 1987. 'Introduction', in *Masters of 17th-Century Dutch Landscape Painting*, ed. by Peter C. Sutton (Philadelphia: University of Pennsylvania Press), pp. 1–63

SYDOR, MALGORZATA ANNA. 2006. 'La *concordia discors* en Sarbiewski y Gracián', in *Edad de oro cantabrigense: Actas del VII Congreso de la AISO*, ed. by Anthony J. Close and Sandra María Fernández Vales (Madrid: Iberoamericana/Vervuert), pp. 585–90

TAMAYO, AUGUSTO (ed.). 1982. *Apologético / Juan de Espinosa Medrano* (Caracas: Ayacucho)

TANSILLO, LUIGI. 1996. *Il canzoniere*, 2 vols, ed. by Tobia R. Toscano (Napoli: Liguori)

TASSO, TORQUATO. 1607. *Le sette giornate del mondo creato* (Viterbo: Girolamo Discepolo)

TÉLLEZ, JORGE. 2012. *Poéticas del Nuevo Mundo. Articulación del pensamiento poético en América colonial: siglos XVI, XVII y XVIII* (México, D.F.: Siglo XXI)

TENORIO, MARTHA LILIA. 2013. *El gongorismo en Nueva España. Ensayo de restitución* (México, D.F.: El Colegio de México)

TERESA DE ÁVILA. 2011. *Libro de la vida*, ed. by Dámaso Chicharro (Madrid: Cátedra)

TERRY, ARTHUR. 1993. *Seventeenth-Century Spanish Poetry: The Power of Artifice* (Cambridge/New York: Cambridge University Press)

TESAURO, EMANUELE. 1664. *Il cannocchiale aristotelico* (Roma: Guglielmo Hallé Libraro)

THOMAS, GEORGE ANTONY. 2012. *The Politics and Poetics of Sor Juana Inés de La Cruz* (Surrey/Burlington: Ashgate)

TORD, LUIS ENRIQUE. 1989. 'La pintura virreinal en el Cusco', in *Pintura en el Virreinato del Perú*, ed. by Luis Nieri Galindo (Lima: Banco de Crédito del Perú), pp. 167–211

TORQUEMADA, JUAN DE. 1975. *Monarquía indiana*, 7 vols (México, D.F.: Universidad Nacional Autónoma de México), I

TORRES, DANIEL. 1993. *El palimpsesto del calco aparente: una poética del Barroco de Indias* (New York: Peter Lang)

——. 1995. 'Imágenes americanistas en el *San Ignacio de Loyola, Fundador de la Compañía de Jesús, Poema heroico* (1666) de Hernando Domínguez Camargo', *Verba Hispánica*, 5: 27–33

TORRES QUINTERO, RAFAEL (ed.). 1960. *Obras / Hernando Domínguez Camargo* (Bogotá: Instituto Caro y Cuervo)

TRIVIÑOS, GILBERTO. 1980. 'Bernardo del Carpio desencantado por Bernardo de Balbuena', *Revista Chilena de Literatura*, 16/17: 315–38

VALDIVIELSO, JOSÉ DE. 1984. *Romancero espiritual*, ed. by J. M. Aguire (Madrid: Espasa-Calpe)

VALERIANO, PIERIO. 1604. *Hieroglyphica* (Venice: Apud Io. Antonium, & Iacobum de Franciscis)

VAN HORNE, JOHN. 1927. *El Bernardo of Bernardo de Balbuena* (Urbana: The University of Illinois)

VEGA, LOPE DE. 1941. *Romancero espiritual*, ed. by Luis Guarner (Valencia: Jesús Bernés)

——. 2003. *Sonetos*, ed. by Ramón García González (Alicante: Biblioteca Virtual Miguel de Cervantes) <http://www.cervantesvirtual.com/obra/sonetos--34/> [accessed 5 October 2019]

———. 2006. *Arte nuevo de hacer comedias*, ed. by Enrique García Santo-Tomás (Madrid: Cátedra)

———. 2015. *Epístolas de La Filomena*, ed. by Pedro Conde (OBVIL) <http://obvil.paris-sorbonne.fr/corpus/gongora/1621_censura-lope/> [accessed 5 October 2019]

VELÁZQUEZ DE AZEVEDO, JUAN. 1626. *El Fénix de Minerva y arte de memoria* (Madrid: Juan González)

VIDA, MARCO GIROLAMO. 2009. *Christiad*, ed. by James Gardner (Cambridge, Massachusetts/London: Harvard University Press)

VILÀ, LARA. 2014. '"Han escrito cosas prodigiosas fuera de toda verdad". Magia y maravilla en la épica española del Renacimiento', in *Señales, portentos y demonios: la magia en la literatura y la cultura españolas del Renacimiento*, ed. by Eva Lara and Alberto Montaner (Salamanca: Semyr), pp. 465–88

VILLALOBOS, MARÍA CONSTANZA. 2012. *Artificios en un palacio celestial: retablos y cuerpos sociales en la iglesia de San Ignacio* (Bogotá: Instituto Colombiano de Antropología e Historia)

VILLAR, FRANCISCO DEL. 2016. *Fragmentos del Compendio poético*, ed. by Jesús Ponce Cárdenas (OBVIL) <http://obvil.paris-sorbonne.fr/corpus/gongora/1636_compendio-poetico/> [accessed 5 October 2019]

VILLASEÑOR, CHARLENE. 2016. 'Portraits of Sor Juana Inés de la Cruz and the Dangers of Intellectual Desire', in *Sor Juana Inés de la Cruz: Selected Works*, ed. by Anna More (New York/London: W. W. Norton & Company), pp. 213–30

VILLEGAS, MARCELINO (ed.). 1982. *Picatrix: el fin del sabio y el mejor de los dos medios para avanzar* (Madrid: Editora Nacional)

VITAGLIANO, MARIA A. 2013. 'Painting and Poetry in Early Modern Spain: The Primacy of Venetian *Colore* in Góngora's *Polyphemus* and *The Solitudes*', *Renaissance Quarterly*, 66: 904–36

VITULLI, JUAN. 2012. '*Blanco pequeño de ambos mundos*: una lectura del "Agasajo" de Hernando Domínguez Camargo', *Calíope*, 18: 139–60

VOLEK, EMIL (ed.). 2019. *El sueño (1690) / Sor Juana Inés de la Cruz* (Madrid: Visor Libros)

VOLLENDORF, LISA, and GRADY WRAY. 2013. 'Gender in the Atlantic World: Women's Writing in Iberia and Latin America', in *Theorising the Ibero-American Atlantic*, ed. by Harald Braun and Lisa Vollendorf (Leiden/Boston: Brill), pp. 99–116

VOSSLER, KARL. 1946. *Die Welt im Traum: eine Dichtung der 'Zehnten Muse von Mexiko', Sor Juana Inés de la Cruz* (Karlsruhe: Stahlberg)

VOUILLOUX, BERNARD. 2002. *Le tableau vivant: Phryné, l'orateur et le peintre* (Paris: Flammarion)

WARDROPPER, BRUCE W. 1970. 'La imaginación en el metateatro calderoniano', in *Actas del Tercer Congreso Internacional de Hispanistas, celebrado en México, D.F., del 26 al 31 de agosto de 1968*, ed. by Carlos Horacio Magis (México, D.F: Asociación Internacional de Hispanistas / El Colegio de México)

WARNOCK, CHRISTOPHER, and JOHN MICHAEL GREER (eds.). 2011. *The Picatrix: The Occult Classic of Astrological Magic in One Volume* ([Place of publication not identified]: Adocentyn Press)

WATERWORTH, J. (ed.). 1848. *Canons and Decrees of the Sacred and Oecumenical Council of Trent* (London: Dolman)

WEBB, RUTH. 1999. 'Ekphrasis Ancient and Modern: The Invention of a Genre', *Word & Image*, 15: 7–18

———. 2000. 'Ekphrasis, Amplification and Persuasion in Procopius' *Buildings*', *Antiquité Tardive*, 8: 67–71

———. 2009. *Ekphrasis, Imagination and Persuasion in Ancient Rhetorical Theory and Practice* (Aldershot: Ashgate)

WITTGENSTEIN, LUDWIG. 2001. *Tractatus Logico-Philosophicus*, trans. by David Francis Pears and Brian McGuinness (London/New York: Routledge)

WÖLFFLIN, HEINRICH. 1950. *Principles of Art History: The Problem of the Development of Style in Later Art*, trans. by Mary Hottinger (New York: Dover Publications)

——. 1964. *Renaissance and Baroque*, trans. by Kathrin Simon (London: Collins)

WOODS, MICHAEL J. 1978. *The Poet and the Natural World in the Age of Góngora* (Oxford: Oxford University Press)

——. 1995. *Gracián Meets Góngora. The Theory and Practice of Wit* (Warminster: Aris & Phillips)

WRIGHT, N. T. 1996. *Jesus and the Victory of God* (London: SPCK)

YATES, FRANCES. 1999A. *Giordano Bruno and the Hermetic Tradition* (London/New York: Routledge)

——. 1999B. *The Art of Memory* (London/New York: Routledge)

ZAMORA, MARGARITA. 1995. 'América y el arte de la memoria', *Revista de Crítica Literaria Latinoamericana*, 21: 135–48

ZUCCARO, FEDERICO. 1768. *L'idea de' pittori, scultori ed architetti* (Roma: Pagliarini)

ZULAICA, MARTÍN. 2016. '"Obra toda tejida de una admirable variedad de cosas": la écfrasis en *El Bernardo* de Balbuena', *Hipogrifo: Revista de Literatura y Cultura del Siglo de Oro*, 4: 171–81

INDEX

Lightning Source UK Ltd.
Milton Keynes UK
UKHW051014190220
358946UK00001B/3